THEY BEHELD HIS GLORY

THEY BEHELD HIS GLORY

HIS GLORY

Stories of the Men and Women
Who Knew Jesus

ALICE PARMELEE

Keats Publishing, Inc.
New Canaan, Connecticut

THEY BEHELD HIS GLORY

Copyright © 1967 by Alice Parmelee

Published by arrangement with
Harper & Row, Publishers. Pivot edition published 1977.

ISBN: 0-87983-162-6
Library of Congress Catalog Card Number: 67-11504

Printed in the United States of America

Keats Publishing, Inc.
36 Grove Street, New Canaan, Connecticut

TO THE MANY PEOPLE I KNOW
WHOSE LIVES REFLECT
HIS GLORY

Foreword

THIS BOOK is an attempt to see Jesus through the eyes of the men and women who knew him face to face, the people who became his friends. The Gospel stories of their encounters with the man of Nazareth help us to understand him and to find answers to our questions: Who was Jesus? What was his message? Is it relevant today?

At a time like ours when faith is in crisis, we ask such questions urgently, knowing that, though we succeed in standing upon the moon and reaching toward the stars, the real issues of life are determined in the depths of our being. Jesus' life and teachings and his effect upon the people he met illuminate these depths where man meets God.

So we turn to the stories of Jesus' friends, stories that range from eyewitness records to accounts that are colored by later beliefs. In these narratives we meet many who tramped along the stony roads of Palestine in the Master's company, or came to him in their need and were transformed by him. They heard the sound of his voice, saw the shape of his gestures and the grace of his person, felt the touch of his hand. They watched while he banished evil and renewed life in all its abundance and joy. In his presence they felt the meaninglessness and anguish of existence overcome by the love of God. Because they beheld in him the very glory of the Lord, one of their spokesmen declared, "And the Word became flesh and dwelt among us, full of grace and truth; we have beheld his glory, glory as of the only son from the Father" (John 1.14).

These are the men and women whose stories we shall examine for firsthand news of Jesus Christ. Who can lead us more directly to him than the people who knew him, believed in him, and were witnesses of his glory?

They are as varied and representative a group of human beings as can be met anywhere, including the old and the young, beggars and wealthy men, righteous Pharisees and social outcasts. Most of them were Jews of Galilee and Judea, descendants of Abraham, taught by Moses and the prophets to worship Israel's God. These people who followed Jesus can hardly be understood apart from their extraordinary spiritual heritage, for from this rich soil their new life in Christ grew.

Searching the Gospels for records of the men and women who knew the Master, and reading their brief stories with our imaginations alert, we find ourselves in first-century Palestine and hear, above its lively bustle and tumult, scores of voices exclaiming, questioning, entreating, and crying out to Jesus. He answers them incisively and with telling effect, all the while moving among his countrymen, not as some exalted being remote from human concerns, but as a man among men. It was thus that he set his mark upon the world.

In trying to present the people around Jesus so that they will live for us today, I introduce background material and permit them to speak a few words not found in the Scriptures. With Jesus himself no such liberties are taken. No ideas of my devising are assigned to him, nor do I venture into the unknowable realm of his mind. Whenever I spread the sail of imagination to catch some of the interlinear winds of the Gospels, I keep it close-reefed. My aim is not to invent, but to interpret.

I want to express my gratitude to many, from archaeologists to theologians, from textual critics to translators who, during the past century, have provided new clues to a better understanding of the Bible. On the labors of these scholars my own work greatly depends. I have studied many books and articles on various aspects of the subject and have consulted commentaries, Bible dictionaries, and concordances. Seven English versions of the Gospels were constantly used, though I depended chiefly upon the Revised Standard Version of the Bible.

Below each chapter title, references are given to the primary sources of each story. These references are arranged to give prominence to Mark, generally believed to be the oldest Gospel and the one on which Matthew, Luke, and, to some degree, John are based. Whenever these three later Gospels contain passages parallel to those in Mark, the references to Matthew, Luke, and John are enclosed in parentheses.

The interpretations and explanatory material woven into my text will, I hope, illuminate the Bible record. No retelling such as mine, however, can convey the splendor and authority of the Scriptures themselves, to which, if I have achieved my purpose, the reader will eagerly turn.

ALICE PARMELEE

New York City
October 3, 1966

Contents

I

DURING HIS EARLY YEARS

I

Shepherds of Bethlehem

LK 2.8-20

"I bring you good news of a great joy which will come to all the people; for to you is born this day in the city of David a Savior, who is Christ the Lord."

LUKE 2.10-11

NOT TO Caesar Augustus ruling the world from his imperial palace in Rome; nor to Herod the Great, the feared and hated king of Judea; nor even to Israel's high priest presiding over Jerusalem's splendid temple—not to these rulers came the first tidings of the dawn of the new age of God. These powerful men wrestled with their problems or slept through the night of Jesus' birth, unaware that the light of God's glory shone in the dark sky over Bethlehem while a voice from heaven proclaimed news of great joy. As often before in Israel's long history, the divine message came, not to the mighty on their thrones, but to men of low degree waiting in expectation for their Lord. These men were shepherds, so the well-loved story goes, who, while guarding their flocks in Bethlehem's pastures, beheld the heavenly splendor and heard the good news of a great joy.

The life these men led was far from a pastoral idyl. Day and night, during the burning midday heat or the fury of storms, they guarded their sheep from prowling jackals and wolves as well as from thieving men. Centuries earlier the patriarch Jacob complained of his sheepherding years, "By day the heat consumed me, and the cold by night, and my sleep fled from my eyes" (Genesis 31.40). Always in the semibarren uplands of Judea a shepherd must search for flowing streams and plod weary miles to find good grazing. Years of hardship and poverty had made the Bethlehem shepherds uncouth and rough in their ways.

Difficult as it was to wrest an uncertain living from Judea's gray limestone hills, these men of the pastures might have walked in dignity and honor, as had Israel's shepherds in earlier years, but today their fellow Israelites despised them for failing to obey the holy Law. It was true that they seldom attended such great religious celebrations as the Passover and the Feast of Tabernacles. But how, they asked, could they keep the feasts without abandoning their sheep on remote and dangerous hillsides? The rabbis had imposed a ban on shepherds because of their religious laxity and the Pharisees regarded them with scorn.

Out in the sunlit pastures on spring days when soft clouds flecked the sky and nature seemed to smile, a shepherd could forget his troubles while he played his flute or watched his young lambs frolicking in the fresh green grass. On such days his bitterness melted and life seemed good. But during cold night watches when he could hear the far-off howling of wolves or when a piercing wind tore savagely at his tattered cloak, chilling his very bones, a shepherd's lot seemed harsh. At such times he warmed his heart with a great hope, which was to him as "a lamp shining in a dark place, until the day dawns and the morning star rises in your hearts" (2 Peter 1.19).

This "lamp" shining in dark places was the shepherd's hope that the Savior, long promised to Israel, would soon arrive. When he came he would, in his great power, deliver them from all the snares of their existence, from insecurity, pain, and sorrow, from guilt and anxiety, and from a tormenting sense of life's futility. He would invest their lives with meaning and cause them to dwell secure in the providence of God.

The shepherds of Bethlehem treasured one of Micah's prophecies in which, speaking for the Lord, the eighth-century prophet described the coming Savior as a shepherd from these very pastures.

But you, O Bethlehem Ephrathah . . .
from you shall come forth for me

one who is to be ruler in Israel. . . .
And he shall stand and feed his flock in the strength of the Lord. . . .
And they shall dwell secure, for now he shall be great
to the ends of the earth.

MICAH 5.2,4

In the days of the great prophets like Micah, when flocks and herds comprised the chief source of Israel's wealth, shepherds were highly esteemed and people saw in their care of the sheep a reflection of the Lord's loving-kindness to his people. The beloved verses of the Twenty-third Psalm sang of a shepherd who made his flock lie down in green pastures and who led them beside still waters. The good shepherd, according to the prophet Ezekiel (34.16), sought out the lost, brought back the strayed, bound up the crippled, strengthened the weak, and watched over the strong. Isaiah 40.11 pictured the tenderness of one who gathered his lambs in his arms or carried them in his bosom, while he gently led those that were with young.

Would the coming Savior be such a shepherd? The men shivering in Bethlehem's pastures on a certain dark night could only wonder. Little did they imagine an even loftier role for him—a role in which he would take upon himself the griefs and sorrows of men and finally give his life for them. This sacrifice, prefigured in one of the Servant Songs (Isaiah 53.1-12), would finally be expressed in the Gospel of John. "I am the good shepherd. The good shepherd lays down his life for the sheep" (John 10.11).

If such an idea still lay beyond their comprehension, the shepherds were familiar with old stories from the Scriptures that revealed God's ways with men. To while away monotonous hours these men of Bethlehem sometimes indulged in daydreams about young David keeping the flocks of his father Jesse in these same pastures centuries ago. They recalled the story of Samuel the prophet with his horn of anointing oil coming secretly to Bethlehem. He came in search of a man for the Lord, a new king of Israel to replace King Saul. Hearing of Samuel's mission, Jesse of Bethlehem called his seven sons, one by one, before the prophet. Each in turn appeared, tall, splendid, fit, yet Samuel chose none of them, for "the Lord sees not as man sees; man

looks on the outward appearance, but the Lord looks on the heart"
(1 Samuel 16.7).

Jesse had another son, his youngest, not as strong or as experienced
as his brothers, a mere shepherd lad, though handsome with his ruddy
countenance and beautiful eyes. When young David was summoned
from the pastures to stand before Samuel, the old prophet heard the
Lord command him, "Arise, anoint him; for this is he" (1 Samuel
16.12). Thus by the Lord's own choosing, a shepherd boy of Bethlehem was anointed by the prophet to be Israel's king.

Tonight the stars shone brightly over David's dark and silent pastures. The long night grew colder. Both Samuel with his horn of
anointing oil and beloved King David slept among the ancient dead.
When would Micah's prophecy be fulfilled? Would God again reveal
himself in mighty acts like those once recorded in the Scriptures?
Could life ever shine for these toil-worn men huddled in their thread-
bare cloaks? Far off a dog barked in the darkness. Sure that their
animals were safe within the sheepfold, the shepherds dozed and
finally drifted off to sleep.

One man, as was their custom, remained awake and on guard. He
was the first to behold the radiance and in its light the likeness of an
angel. In a moment all the shepherds were awake and on their feet,
scanning the brilliance overhead. Dawn had not arrived prematurely
as they first thought, or at least, it was not an ordinary dawn, for
night still shrouded the remote Judean hills. But the sky overhead
blazed with that heavenly splendor which signified to these men, as
it had of old to the people of Israel, that their Lord was near. He had
spoken to Moses from a burning bush and guided the wandering
tribes by a pillar of fire. Ezekiel had seen the Lord sitting in the midst
of brightness all around him. Sons of Israel as they were, the men in
Bethlehem's pastures understood the meaning of the shining marvel
and fell silent, trembling with holy awe, for they knew that they were
in the divine presence. "Be not afraid," they heard the angel say to
them, calming their fear.

Reassured, the men could now listen to the angel's message, the
good news of a great joy proclaimed to them and through them to

all people. "To you is born today in David's city a Savior who is Christ the Lord." Over the hill yonder in the little town of Bethlehem the long-expected Savior had come at last.

"How shall we find him?" whispered the shepherds to one another. In the angel's message there had been an exact description, "a baby wrapped in swaddling cloths and lying in a manger." Could a manger where animals feed be the Savior's cradle?

Mute with wonder, the men watched and listened as the herald angel was joined by "a multitude of the heavenly host praising God and saying,

> "Glory to God in the highest,
> and on earth peace among men with whom he is pleased!"
> LUKE 2.14

Glory and peace, God and man—the song formed a celestial preface to the mission and message of Jesus who, in establishing a new relationship between man and God, would bring peace to men's hearts.

The angelic news answered the ultimate question of every man, "Where is God?" At last these shepherds had found him, or rather, God, who is ever in search of his own, had found them. He came to them in all their unworthiness and henceforth the reality of his love would possess their hearts.

Leaving one of their company to guard the sheep, the men, after fastening their cloaks about them and taking their staffs, set forth upon their quest. "Let us go and see," they said to one another, for the angel's message implied a command, "You will find a baby. . . ." To them, as to others in the Bible, divine revelation came, not as a beautiful dream for idle enjoyment, but as a call to action.

"Go from your country and your kindred and your father's house to the land that I will show you. And I will make of you a great nation" (Genesis 12.1-2). Such was Abraham's call. Moses was summoned to "bring forth my people, the sons of Israel, out of Egypt" (Exodus 3.10). The voice Isaiah heard shook the very temple when it asked, "Whom shall I send, and who will go for us?" The prophet replied, "Here am I! Send me" (Isaiah 6.8).

At these former turning points in God's dealings with men, Abraham, Moses, and Isaiah were obedient to their heavenly visions as were the shepherds who, on the night of Jesus' birth, set out along the rough and stony paths leading over the Judean hills to Bethlehem.

The scene of their arrival at the stable needs no describing, for who cannot summon up the lovely image of Mary, the young mother, and Joseph standing guard while the rough shepherds adored the baby in the manger? He lay there as frail and helpless as any infant, yet mighty in power as the Son of God. Only faith can comprehend the mystery of this scene in which strength is concealed in weakness, splendor in lowliness, eternity in time, and where divine glory, lest it blind human eyes, veils itself in humanity.

The story ends, not in an anticlimax after transcendent glory, but on a sustained note of triumph as the shepherds continued to praise and glorify God for all they had seen and heard. Though the sky no longer blazed and angel voices were silent, the reality of the heavenly message possessed these rugged men, transforming their lives. During the days that followed they felt constrained to spread abroad their news concerning the child. Everyone who heard of him marveled.

Remote, even legendary though these men are, their story provides a fitting prologue to the unfolding drama of Christ's mission. Not only is the shepherds' narrative one with the coming of Christ, but it demonstrates the central fact of Christian experience—the new life given to those who behold Christ's glory.

2

Mary

LK 1.26-56; 2.1-52; MT 1.18-
25; JN 2.1-12; MK 3.31-35
(MT 12.46-50; LK 8.19-21);
JN 19.25-27; ACTS 1.14

*"My soul magnifies the Lord,
and my spirit rejoices in God my
Savior."*

LUKE 1:46-47

WITHIN THE DARK stable where the shepherds found Jesus lying in a manger on the night of his birth, they saw his mother, her face shining with a reflection of her son's radiance. This seems to enfold her in the first two chapters of Luke's and of Matthew's Gospels, chapters which are among the best known and most beloved of the Bible. Mary presides over them in the wonder and mystery of her motherhood, sharing the divine glory of her son.

Her story begins among the hills of Galilee in the little village of Nazareth. It was an insignificant place off the main highways. Nazareth had no history and was not even mentioned in the Scriptures. In this village, we are told, Mary awaited her marriage to her betrothed husband Joseph, the carpenter. One day, startled by the sight of the angel Gabriel standing before her, she began to tremble, not knowing the meaning of his heavenly greeting, "Hail, O favored one, the Lord is with you!"

"Do not be afraid, Mary," she heard the angel say, "for you have found favor with God."

Gabriel's message concerned the son Mary would bear, the son to be named Jesus. He would be no ordinary child, for, in the angel's song, Mary heard him described in terms that could apply only to the Messiah.

9

> "He will be great, and will be called the Son of the Most High;
> and the Lord God will give him the throne of his father David,
> and he will reign over the house of Jacob forever;
> and of his kingdom there will be no end."
>
> LUKE 1.32-33

Faced with her overwhelming role as mother of the coming Messiah, Mary hesitated, as had others of her race when the Lord called them to high undertakings. Centuries earlier Moses had cried, "Who am I that I should go to Pharaoh, and bring the sons of Israel out of Egypt? . . . Behold, they will not believe me or listen to my voice" (Exodus 3.11;4.1). In similar fashion Jeremiah had tried to excuse himself from his call to prophesy, saying, "Ah, Lord God! Behold, I do not know how to speak, for I am only a youth" (Jeremiah 1.6). Mary's momentary hesitation, like that of Moses and of Jeremiah, sprang from the human impossibility of her role. It was, perhaps, in an effort to escape from the situation that she asked, "How can I bear a son, since I am not married?"

The angel's reply was a song, one of the glorious anthems of Luke's Gospel.

> "The Holy Spirit will come upon you,
> and the power of the Most High will overshadow you;
> therefore the child to be born will be called holy,
> the Son of God."
>
> LUKE 1.35

Then Mary heard a truth she had always known—with God nothing is too difficult. Under the Lord, the people of Israel had often accomplished that which seemed hopeless. They had crossed the impassable sea, captured the impregnable city of Jericho, won the unconquerable Promised Land. Such apparently impossible undertakings were accomplished when men obeyed divine commands. The Lord sought willing agents to carry out his design; he now sought Mary.

By training and in her devotions she was a spiritual daughter of Israel's prophets and psalmists. Possibly she was a lineal descendant of King David and of the priestly house of Aaron as well. All that was finest in Jewish womanhood was embodied in her in whom the centuries of Israel's faith flourished. Love of God was basic in her nature. Gratitude to him welled up in her heart as she swept the house, talked with her neighbors, or carried her dripping pitcher from Nazareth's single well. Praise of the Most High was ever on her lips, whether she was alone or sitting among the women in the synagogue. Worship kept alive within her heart life's great realities. For such a woman it was not hard to accept God's will. She bowed her head and expressed her consent in simple words.

In her willing obedience to divine command, Mary was the opposite of Eve, the legendary first mother of humanity. Eve's disobedience in eating the forbidden fruit symbolizes man's rebellion against the Lord. Proud, self-sufficient Eve, ambitious to "be like God" (Genesis 3.5), contrasts sharply with Mary who in lowliness of heart desired only to be God's handmaid. Later Paul compared Adam with Christ, saying, "For as in Adam all die, so also in Christ shall all be made alive. . . . The first man was from the earth, a man of dust; the second man is from heaven" (1 Corinthians 15.22, 47). If Christ is regarded as the new and second Adam, may we not see his mother as a new and holy Eve whose humble acceptance of God's will prepared the way for a new life for humanity?

We also see in Mary's willingness to undertake the role to which the Lord called her a prelude to her son's complete harmony with God's will. Her simple reply to the angel on the sunlit day in Nazareth, "Behold, I am the handmaid of the Lord. Let all that you have spoken of be done through me," was to be echoed years later by Mary's son in the darkness of Gethsemane. Faced with the bitter cup of death, Jesus would pray his great prayer of obedience, saying, "Abba, Father, all things are possible to thee; remove this cup from me; yet not what I will, but what thou wilt" (Mark 14.36).

Before Jesus' birth, Mary left Nazareth and hastened south into Judea to visit her cousin Elizabeth, wife of the priest Zechariah. The song attributed to Mary and known as the Magnificat from its initial word in Latin is assigned to the happy period when Mary lived in the warm and understanding atmosphere of her cousin's home. Her song begins,

> "My soul magnifies the Lord,
> and my spirit rejoices in God my Savior,
> for he has regarded the low estate of his handmaiden.
> For behold, henceforth all generations will call me blessed."
>
> LUKE 1.46-48

The entire song expressing Mary's faith and joy is alive with the revolutionary spirit of the prophets and the hope of deliverance that pervades the Old Testament. Such a psalm, modeled on Hannah's song in the second chapter of 1 Samuel, but filled with its own spiritual insight, could have come only from one well versed in the Scriptures, one who lived close to the Lord. Was this not true of Mary as, later, it was of her son?

In praising the Lord who "exalted those of low degree" and "filled the hungry with good things," she raised, as it were, a banner of hope for the lowly, the hungry, the poor, and the oppressed, in short the great mass of common people of the land who later were to flock to Jesus. Thus Mary's song anticipated important aspects of her son's ministry and was an overture to the Beatitudes.

The opening chapters of Luke continue to portray Mary as a loyal daughter of Israel, obedient to its holy Law. Eight days after her son's birth she had him duly circumcised and given a name, the name proclaimed for him by the angel. At the appointed time, forty days after his birth, she and Joseph traveled from Bethlehem up to Jerusalem to present him in the temple. She herself offered two turtledoves in the required sacrifice of her purification. Each year thereafter, in company with crowds of faithful Jews, she journeyed from her home in Nazareth to the Holy City for the Passover. The Gospels show that Jesus, like his mother, availed himself of his religious heritage, customarily attending the synagogue on the Sabbath, going to Jerusalem for the great feasts, and loyally paying his annual half-shekel temple tax. Scriptural references abound in his teachings as they do in Mary's words. Son of a devoted mother in Israel, Jesus lived and died a faithful Jew as his declaration shows: "Think not that I have come to abolish the law and the prophets; I have not come to abolish them but to fulfil them" (Matthew 5.17).

When Jesus was twelve years old, his mother and father took him on their annual Passover pilgrimage to Jerusalem. It was on the homeward journey that Mary first missed her son.

"He must be running ahead of our slow-moving caravan," she remarked to her husband. She imagined the high-spirited lad leading a group of boys on an exploration of sights along the road. "By nightfall he will be hungry enough to join us for our evening meal," Mary concluded.

But when the company of friends and relatives with whom Mary and Joseph were traveling pitched camp for the night and each family gathered around its own campfire, Jesus was still missing. Mary was worried. Despite its holy name, Jerusalem was not safe for a friendly, trusting boy from a country village. Though now at the age of twelve he had attained the status of a son of the Law and would henceforth be responsible for performing his own religious duties, his mother still watched lovingly over his welfare.

Promptly she and Joseph retraced their steps and spent three days in the Holy City frantically searching for their missing boy. At last they found him in the temple, sitting among the most learned men of Israel, the teachers of the Law, listening to them and asking them questions.

When Mary reproved her son for what seemed to her to be a boyish escapade, he answered her gravely, characteristically replying with questions. They are his first recorded words. "How is it that you sought me? Did you not know that I must be in my Father's house?" (Luke 2.49)

"My Father's house," Mary repeated to herself as she stood in one of the temple's imposing courtyards, gazing with new eyes at her son. His simple, direct words revealed a depth of personal communion, a nearness to God, that was beyond her own experience. She knew, of course, that his three words referred to this holy place long acknowledged as the Lord's dwelling. It was the expression, "my Father," that amazed her. Jesus could hardly have learned it at home or in the synagogue school in Nazareth. It encompassed an idea that seemed to stem from deeper reaches of his being than even his mother could fathom.

Mary knew that God was the Father of Israel. This belief, implicit from the earliest days, was clearly expressed by the prophets. In dramatically personal words Hosea revealed God's love for his people: "When Israel was a child, I loved him" (Hosea 11.1). By the "child" Israel, Hosea meant not a particular individual but the entire people of God. The same was true of the great prayer,

> Yet, O Lord, thou art our Father;
> we are the clay, and thou art our potter;
> we are all the work of thy hand.
> ISAIAH 64.8

These words are the cry, not of a single man, but of a whole people who, despite many failures, aspired, as loyal children, to obey the Lord. When Jesus spoke of God as his own Father, he sounded a new note in man's relationship to God.

As Mary journeyed home with her husband and son over the rough roads of Judea and through Galilee's fertile valleys, she pondered the meaning of her son's words. Did they indicate the future course of his life? Because of his unique sense of being God's son, would Jesus lead others closer to the Lord? Would he endow others with sonship to God? Paul would one day declare: "God sent forth his Son, born of woman, born under the law, to redeem those who were under the law, so that we might receive adoption as sons. And because you are sons, God has sent the Spirit of his Son into your hearts, crying, 'Abba! Father!'" (Galatians 4.4-6). Paul's insight was based on his own experiences, but these lay far in the future and so Mary, on her return journey to Nazareth, could only wonder at her son's momentous words and wait for their meaning to be disclosed.

Matthew's and Luke's two familiar cycles of stories about Jesus' birth and childhood depict Mary as indeed worthy of being the mother of the Lord. These chapters reflect their authors' mature understanding of Christ and their well-developed theology. Happily this is not conveyed in impenetrably difficult prose, but in exquisite tales and songs that sing themselves into our hearts. Even children can understand the coming of Christ, while learned scholars find rich meaning in the ancient stories.

A key to Mary's later story appears near the end of the shepherds' narrative. "But Mary kept all these things, pondering them in her heart" (Luke 2.19). A pondering, an uncertainty, a wonder, seems to accompany Mary through much of the New Testament record. During the eighteen silent years between Jesus' boyhood visit to Jerusalem and the beginning of his ministry, she must have learned, little by little, in close and loving association with her son, of his unusual powers. But as John's story of the wedding at Cana and Mark's of her seeking her son in the midst of a crowd—as these stories seem to indicate, Mary long remained unaware of the full range of her son's glory. In view of these two incidents, we must interpret the angel's first announcement to her, that Jesus would be called the Son of the Most High, as a reading back into an earlier day of a truth that she fully realized only after the resurrection.

During the wedding feast at Cana Mary noticed that all the wine had been consumed. For this to happen in the midst of a feast was a social disgrace. Jesus, now a man of thirty, was attending the party with his mother, his brothers, and his first disciples. Had the unexpected arrival of these latter guests upset the host's calculations as to the amount of wine that would be needed? For some reason Mary wanted to help at this embarrassing moment. She may have been a relative of the bridegroom or merely a kind and sympathetic friend.

Hastening to Jesus, she whispered, "They have no wine." It was a simple statement of fact. Though she did not urge him to act, she doubtless expected him to do something to remedy the situation. Few words were needed between mother and son. Through the years, the difficulties they had met and overcome had bound them closely together in mutual confidence and affection.

Often in household emergencies Mary must have turned to Jesus. He always knew what to do. He was ever ready to help. With his skillful carpenter's hands he could mend or do almost anything. He was wise, too. She was proud of him. Perhaps, in her mother's heart, she believed him capable of performing truly marvelous deeds. She saw the lack of wine as an opportunity for him to display his unusual powers to the entire wedding party.

Understanding her thoughts, Jesus answered her kindly. His seemingly harsh reply, rendered in English by, "O woman, what have you to do with me? My hour has not yet come" (John 2.4), fails to convey his undoubted tenderness. His tone and meaning are perhaps better expressed by, "Mother, do not worry about this problem. I will take care of it. But the hour to show forth my glory has not yet come." The power he possessed from God was not to be commanded by others, even his mother, nor would he ever use it for himself or his own glorification.

Mary wisely kept silent, realizing that Jesus was no longer a child to be directed, but an adult who was master of his own life. She left him free to act in his own way, at his own time. Apparently she did not take his reply as a refusal to do anything about the wine. She knew his kindness and his ready sympathy for others, so she quietly bade the servants to do whatever he might ask them. The story of what happened belongs to a later chapter.

After the miracle of the water turned into wine, Jesus' relationship with his mother remained close. Now that he was surrounded by a group of disciples and had manifested his power, he did not go his own way, leaving his mother, as another son might have done. Instead, we read that "After this he went down to Capernaum, with his mother and his brothers and his disciples" (John 2.12). Family ties were still strong and the bond between mother and son remained unbroken.

Yet at some point during Jesus' ministry in Galilee, Mary's relationship with her son became strained. The reason for this is not entirely clear. Did the violent hostility against him on the part of her friends and neighbors in Nazareth cause Mary to have misgivings about her son? Perhaps she expected his ministry to become a triumphant messianic progress. When this did not happen and the religious authorities became critical of him, possibly her confidence in him wavered. When his enemies began to circulate a dark rumor that he was beside himself, she became concerned for his welfare. She wondered if the strain of his being constantly surrounded by importuning crowds was undermining his health and sanity. Fearing this might be true, she and other members of the family went to the house where he was staying to urge him to go home with them so that they could take care of him.

When the dense crowd around the house prevented Mary from reaching her son, she sent him a message to be passed from person to person through the crush. "Your mother and your brothers have arrived and are standing outside asking for you," ran the message.

Hearing these words, Jesus seized the opportunity to teach his followers that family claims are second to the claims of God. Turning to the people surrounding him, he asked, "Who are my mother and my brothers?"

His characteristic way of gaining attention by asking a question produced a murmur in the crowd. Everyone knew that instead of giving a dull and obvious answer to his own question he would spring a surprise on them, as indeed he did.

"Here are my mother and brothers!" he exclaimed, raising both arms as if to embrace the multitude. When the happy murmurs subsided, he drove his lesson home. "Anyone who obeys the will of my Father in heaven is my brother or my sister or my mother."

Listening to him from the edge of the crowd, Mary knew that her son was both well and sane. For this she was thankful. She understood his statement for what it was, a dramatic method of teaching, not a repudiation of his human family. She knew that, despite occasional strains, the bonds uniting him to his mother, his brothers, and his sisters remained strong and true. But she also saw that his first and highest loyalty was not to his family but to his heavenly Father. With a sense of pride she realized that Jesus would never retreat from the difficulties and dangers of a prophet of the Lord

into the safe obscurity of his home. Nor could he allow family inter-
ference to impede his mission.

The last time Mary figures in the Gospel story is on Golgotha.
She stood at the foot of the cross with the beloved disciple, unable
to do anything for her son during his hours of agony except steady
him by her loving presence. As she watched him die, she may have
believed that God had failed her. Where now was the Messiah of
whose kingdom there would be no end? Why did God allow Jesus
to die thus?

In the midst of her grief she heard Jesus speak to her and she
experienced a fierce joy. She was assured that his lifelong love for her
survived the torments of crucifixion and that he still enfolded her in
his care. In that hour she also gained the devotion of a new "son"
in God.

When Jesus saw his mother, and the disciple whom he loved, standing
near, he said to his mother, "Woman, behold, your son!" Then he said to
the disciple, "Behold, your mother!" And from that hour the disciple took
her to his own home.

JOHN 19.26-27

Mary's biblical story ends in the Book of Acts, as it began in
Luke's Gospel, with a divine manifestation. After the resurrection
she remained with Jesus' larger family, including his disciples,
the women who had followed him from Galilee, and his brothers.
These witnesses of Christ's resurrection gathered in an upper room
in Jerusalem, devoting themselves to prayer while they waited for
the promised coming of the Holy Spirit. When a rushing sound like
that of a mighty wind filled the house, these devoted men and
women saw tongues of fire resting upon every head and they became filled with the Holy Spirit. They felt the ineffable presence
and power of God within themselves enabling them to be effective
witnesses of Christ's glory. Mary herself became one of these witnesses and uniquely so, for she alone of the little company in the
upper room was privileged to know her son from birth to death.

3

Simeon and Anna

LK 2.25-38

Your eyes will see the king in his beauty.

ISAIAH 33.17

FORTY DAYS AFTER Jesus' birth, an aged man of Jerusalem slowly made his way through the crowded temple courtyards, walking unsteadily on his feeble legs. His name was Simeon. Though bent in body, he carried the burdens of old age gallantly. Like Mary of Nazareth, he embodied all that was best in Israel's past—its faith and righteousness, its piety and its enduring hope in the coming of a Messiah. This hope lit the old man's wrinkled face with unusual beauty. He believed, indeed it had been revealed to him, that before he died he would see the promised Messiah. Simeon, therefore, greeted each morning with happy anticipation, saying to himself at each sunrise, "Perhaps this is the day!" Animated by such an expectation, yet not knowing the precise hour when the Savior would appear, Simeon spent his days in the temple, waiting, watching, praying.

Unknown to him, Jesus had already been born only six miles south of Jerusalem in David's city of Bethlehem. It was now the day when the child's parents were to bring him over the Judean hills to the Holy City to present him to the Lord.

On this same day the widow Anna also entered one of the temple's spacious courts. She may have been even older than Simeon, being all of eighty-four years. To have lived to such an age in a period when most people died young was in itself a distinction, but Anna was outstanding for more than her age. Daughter of a certain Phanuel, she could trace her lineage to the tribe of Asher, one of the twelve tribes noted for its handsome, gifted women. Anna was well known in Jerusalem where day and night she was seen worshiping in the temple. Esteemed both for her fasting and her praying, she was regarded as a prophetess because, like Deborah and Huldah of old, she announced God's will for his people.

Despite her many years, Anna expected that she would live to see the Lord's salvation, the coming spiritual rebirth of Israel. The divine promise once made to an ancient man of faith might well have been made to Anna:

> Because he cleaves to me in love, I will deliver him;
>   I will protect him, because he knows my name. . . .
> With long life I will satisfy him,
>   and show him my salvation.
>
>   PSALM 91.14,16

Pious though this aged prophetess was, she did not live a solitary life, for she moved serenely in a small circle of like-minded people, devout men and women who looked forward to the coming of the Savior and sustained one another's hope during a period of spiritual barrenness.

The world Simeon and Anna knew was largely uncongenial to them, for the lofty religion of their ancestors had become rigid and well-nigh empty. Outward forms assumed more importance among the religious leaders of the time than inward reality. Men argued heatedly about trivial details, all the while neglecting the fundamentals of love and justice. Here and there, however, in people like Mary and Joseph, Elizabeth and Zechariah, Simeon, Anna and her circle, genuine holiness survived and faith kept the flame of hope glowing in the world's darkness.

On the day when Mary and Joseph presented Jesus to the Lord in accordance with the Law's age-old ritual, the temple was crowded. Hurrying people brushed past Joseph with his basket of sacrificial turtledoves, hardly noticing that beside the toil-worn man walked a young mother proudly carrying her baby. If some individuals glanced briefly at Mary's infant—for who can resist looking into the face of a newborn child?—one look was enough, the mystery of new life having become for them a mere commonplace. "A first-born son being presented to the Lord," they remarked as they turned away from just another child.

Impelled by the Holy Spirit to enter the temple at that very hour, Simeon encountered the little family from Bethlehem and saw something more than had the heedless throngs. When he gazed into the tiny face, he was both startled and puzzled, for his old eyes, made acute by prayer and hope, recognized the baby as the promised Savior of men. Could this infant be he for whom Israel waited? Somehow the old man had expected the Messiah to arrive as a hero, or at least as a mature and powerful man. But Simeon knew that God enters into the affairs of men in surprising ways. Seldom in Israel's history had outward appearance indicated inward reality. Could not the Savior first come as a child, even as this infant? Yes, thought Simeon as he tenderly took Jesus in his arms. While his old heart fairly stood still in rapture, he sang,

> "Lord, now lettest thou thy servant depart in peace,
> according to thy word;
> for mine eyes have seen thy salvation
> which thou hast prepared in the presence of all peoples,
> a light for revelation to the Gentiles,
> and for glory to thy people Israel."
>
> LUKE 2.29-32

At the end of his song, Simeon graciously blessed the poor couple standing before him. He noticed the young mother's happiness, but foresaw sorrow for her in the future when men became hostile to Jesus. Then it would be as though a sword pierced her soul.

In the temple that day, Mary's joy was too full to be clouded by Simeon's prophecy concerning a sword. His words about the Gentiles, however, foreign peoples regarded with disfavor by the Jews, surprised both Mary and her husband. The angel who had told them that Jesus would "save his people from their sins" (Matthew 1.21) and "reign over the house of Jacob for ever" (Luke 1.33), had not mentioned the Gentiles. Simeon's song now awakened in Mary and Joseph half-understood words of the prophets.

> "I will give you as a light to the nations,
>   that my salvation may reach to the end of the earth."
>   ISAIAH 49.6

While Joseph and Mary still stood in the courtyard, Anna joined them. Despite the dimness of her eyes, she, like Simeon, saw that the infant Jesus was the Savior. Immediately she gave thanks to God, her first impulse being to pray. But her reaction to the astonishing event did not end there. The aged widow was a woman of action, outgoing and practical. With renewed strength animating her tired body, she hurried away to announce to those who awaited him that the Savior had at last arrived. Thus Anna became the first recorded witness in Jerusalem of the coming of Christ.

Weakness, defeat, suffering, guilt, sin, and death still held men in bondage but, as Simeon and Anna knew, the power of evil was overcome by the arrival of the holy child. These two people were given eyes to see and recognize him and they rejoiced.

These two who recognized the infant Jesus as the Savior stand symbolically between the old Israel and the new—between historic Israel and the new people of God, incarnating all that was best in the old covenant and bestowing their blessing upon the new covenant established by Christ.

4

Wise Men from the East

MT 2.1-12

*And nations shall come to your light,
and kings to the brightness of your
rising.*

ISAIAH 60.3

SIMEON'S STRANGE PROPHECY concerning Jesus continued to haunt
Mary as she departed from the Holy City. "A light for revelation to
the Gentiles," she repeated to herself, puzzled by his words. With
her baby in her arms she rode upon a donkey which Joseph led over
the stony upland track. Though Luke's Gospel states that at this time
Joseph and Mary journeyed north to their own city of Nazareth,
it is possible that they returned briefly to Bethlehem where the
events narrated in the second chapter of Matthew took place.

"Is it not enough for my son to become the glory of the people
of Israel?" Mary asked herself. Israel was the people of God and the
temple his dwelling place. She recalled how impressive its vast, stone
courtyards had appeared, crowded with worshipers and filled with
smoke rising from the sacrifices. The blare of trumpets, the fragrance
of incense, and the solemn chanting of temple choirs had stirred her
deeply. Her greatest wish was for her son to bring the light of God's
truth to his own people. The thought of unenlightened Gentiles
joining the Lord's own people made her shudder. "Why a mission to
the Gentiles?" she asked herself. "Why should alien peoples be
brought within the circle of God's love?"

Then she remembered the words of God's covenant with his

23

people, "Now therefore, if you will obey my voice and keep my
covenant, you shall be my own possession among all peoples; for
all the earth is mine, and you shall be to me a kingdom of priests
and a holy nation" (Exodus 19.5-6).

Here was the clue—"a kingdom of priests." Israel's function was a
priestly one, to bring all peoples to God. Would Mary's son transform Israel into a kingdom of priests set apart to bring the light of
truth to the Gentiles? Her answer lay in the future. One day it would
be written of Christ's followers, who called themselves the new
Israel of God, "But you are a chosen race, a royal priesthood, a holy
nation, God's own people, that you may declare the wonderful deeds
of him who called you out of darkness into his marvellous light"
(1 Peter 2.9).

Back in Bethlehem, Mary stood one evening in the doorway of
her dwelling. Perhaps she and Joseph had by this time found there
a more suitable lodging than the stable where Jesus had been born.
The town was hushed, its streets empty of children calling shrilly
to one another as they played. Faint lights glowed from each house
while, high above, the stars shone in remote, mysterious grandeur.
Ancient verses that Mary remembered from her childhood now came
to her mind.

> Arise, shine; for your light has come,
>   and the glory of the Lord has risen upon you. . . .
> And nations shall come to your light,
>   and kings to the brightness of your rising.
>   ISAIAH 60.1-3

Mary's reverie was interrupted by the distant tinkle of camel
bells. As the musical sound came nearer, it was all but lost in the
harsh cries of camel drivers urging on their beasts. A caravan must
be approaching town, thought Mary. Pack trains of ungainly, swaying animals piled high with bales of goods were familiar to her,
Bethlehem being the first halting-place of merchants traveling south
from Jerusalem to Egypt.

The caravan now approaching Bethlehem did not remain outside the gate where strangers were supposed to spend the night, but threaded its way through the town's narrow streets until it stopped at Mary's door. A group of travelers wearing curious, foreign garments glanced overhead at a brilliant star before they dismounted. Thus the wise men of Matthew's Gospel, the vanguard of all the Gentiles, reached their goal.

The story of the wise men is made up of diverse elements—legend, symbolism, and history all fused into one of the Bible's most poetic tales. It features mysterious travelers from the East, a guiding star, a vicious king, suspicions and strategems, fabulous gifts, besides certain historical facts concerning the ancient world.

During the first century A.D. wise men from Arabia, Mesopotamia, and Persia traveled through many countries bordering the Mediterranean. These wise men or Magi, as they were often called, claimed that they could predict the future from the stars, interpret dreams, and communicate with the spirits of the dead. Often the Magi astonished people by performing acts of magic. The wise men of Matthew's story may have been Persian astrologers who, from their observation of the stars, believed that a bright new one seen in the sky heralded the birth of a great personage. At this time such beliefs were common.

The wise men of our story, having journeyed to Judea, first went to its capital city of Jerusalem. As distinguished visitors they must pay their respects to the king and perhaps learn from him the whereabouts of the child whose star proclaimed him to be a future king.

The reigning king at this time was Herod the Great, infamous in history as the murderer of his wife, his son, and many of his relatives. Whoever threatened his throne risked death at the command of this insanely jealous ruler. When the wise men brought him news of a child born to be a king, Herod was furious. He demanded that the religious authorities tell him where such a child could be found. Herod was an absolute ruler whose rage caused everyone in Jerusalem to tremble and sent the scribes in a frantic search through dusty scrolls. At last a prophecy was found naming Bethlehem as the appointed birthplace of the future king.

After informing Herod about Bethlehem, the religious leaders of Israel withdrew from the kingly presence to return to their ancient scrolls and continual quarrels, careless of what Herod might do about Israel's coming Savior. Did their feeling of superiority as descendants of Abraham cause them to disdain any divine news brought them by Gentiles?

Herod, on the other hand, showed keen interest in the wise men's news. To further his own nefarious purpose he summoned the travelers to a secret conference in which he urged them to search diligently in the city of David for the coming king. "When you find the child, bring me word of him," Herod commanded, smiling slyly, "so that I, too, may go to worship him."

The Magi continued their journey southward from Jerusalem until the star that had moved before them on their journey from the East came to rest at Bethlehem, as we have seen, over the house where Jesus lay. Filled with joy, the wise men fell on their knees in worship before the child in his mother's arms. They offered him the exotic treasures they had brought from the East: gold, frankincense, and myrrh.

Gold from mysterious Ophir symbolized the tribute due a king. Frankincense, a fragrant resin produced from trees growing in remote Arabia, was, according to the formula in Exodus 30.34-38, an ingredient of the holy incense burned in the temple as an offering to God. The third gift, myrrh, a fragrant gum also from Arabia, was compounded with spices and olive oil, as Exodus 30.23 specifies, to make the sacred anointing oil. Later myrrh would be the anodyne offered to Jesus on the cross, and one of the spices bought for his burial. Thus the three gifts of the wise men speak a symbolic language—myrrh signifies Jesus' death, gold his kingship, and frankincense his deity.

After offering their gifts, the Magi prepared for their return journey. Having astutely taken Herod's measure and having also been warned about him in a dream, they avoided the main road back to Jerusalem where Herod awaited their report, and traveled home secretly by another road.

Though the Gospel account nowhere states how many wise men came to Bethlehem, their three gifts may indicate three men. Christian imagination has endowed these mysterious travelers with kingship, an idea suggested both by the costliness of their gifts and by Isaiah's prophecy that "kings [shall come] to the brightness of your rising." In later legends they are assigned names and even given kingdoms— Gaspar, king of India; Melchior, king of Persia; and Balthasar, king of Arabia. Renaissance painters sometimes heightened the symbolism of this story by portraying the three kings as representatives of three races.

The coming of these Gentiles to Jesus Christ sounds the first note of a swelling chorus. In the early days of his ministry, crowds of non-Jews from "Idumea and from beyond Jordan and from about Tyre and Sidon a great multitude, hearing all that he did, came to him" (Mark 3.8). They were followed by such individual foreigners as the Greek or Syrophoenician mother (Mark 7.26), a Roman centurion (Matthew 8.5), and a group of Greeks (John 12.20-21). With people such as these among his followers, his disciples were prepared for the astonishingly wide scope of their mission. "Go," he charged them, "and make disciples of all nations" (Matthew 28.19).

According to the inspired song in Revelation, Christ, at whose cradle the wise men worshiped,

> . . . didst ransom men for God
> from every tribe and tongue and people and nation,
> and hast made them a kingdom and priests to our God,
> and they shall reign on earth.
>
> REVELATION 5.9-10

5

Joseph

MT 1.18-25; 2.13-23;
LK 2.1-52; MT 13.55 (LK
4.22)

*And what does the Lord require of
you
but to do justice, and to love kindness,
and to walk humbly with your
God?*

MICAH 6.8

THE AURA SURROUNDING Mary in the opening chapters of Matthew
and Luke seems to encompass her husband, Joseph, also. He remains largely in the background of the nativity and childhood stories,
none of his words being recorded. But the quality of this silent man
is eloquently conveyed in his acts—a quality befitting one who guarded
the child Jesus. Joseph is portrayed as a competent person who provided his family with their necessities and protected them on their
frequent journeys. He appears to have been kind and loyal in his
relationships and deeply committed to Israel's God whom he devoutly
worshiped.

According to Matthew 13.55, Joseph was a carpenter. Undoubtedly
he taught Jesus his trade, for in Mark 6.3 Jesus is described as a
carpenter also. In the ancient world carpenters were generally poor
and obliged to work long hours for their livelihood. The stable in
Bethlehem and the turtledoves Joseph and Mary sacrificed in the
temple are proofs of their poverty. In a similar situation a rich man
would have afforded a better shelter for his wife and offered a lamb
as a sacrifice. Poverty being the common lot in Jesus' day, Joseph
labored uncomplainingly, finding compensation for his hard life

28

in the skill of his hands and in the useful work he accomplished. He fashioned plows, yokes, and threshing floors for farmers. For young couples he made such household necessities as benches, tables, lampstands, beds, and cradles. Doubtless he also mended broken furniture for those too poor to buy new.

Carpenters in Joseph's day often performed the work of builders. Not only did they make door and window frames for mud or stone houses, but they also added to them a wooden upper floor. Many a devout Jewish carpenter, conscious of the hand of God in human affairs, agreed with the Psalmist who wrote,

> Unless the Lord builds the house,
> those who build it labor in vain.
> PSALM 127.1

When work was scarce in their own locality, carpenters traveled wherever they could find employment. The frequent journeys of Joseph recorded in the Gospels suggest that he may have been an itinerant craftsman. Be that as it may, on his annual visits to Jerusalem for the Passover, he surely watched with professional interest while masons and carpenters rebuilt and enlarged the temple. This undertaking, begun by Herod the Great about 20 B.C., was continued throughout the lifetime of Jesus and did not cease until the temple was destroyed in A.D. 70.

The tools and materials with which ancient carpenters worked are mentioned in the Bible. Joseph must have taught Jesus the use of the saw, hammer, ax, chisel, file, and adz. Like the craftsman described in Isaiah 44.13-14, Joseph also used pencil, compass, plumb line, and plane. He learned the qualities and uses of various kinds of lumber—the fragrance and permanence of cedar, the strength of oak, the close-graining of cypress, the extreme hardness of olive, and the durability of acacia and fir.

This Nazareth carpenter was proud of the quality of the articles he made. Though certain people doubtless disdained him as a lowly artisan performing the kind of manual labor that was often assigned to slaves, Joseph himself respected his own carpentry as work be-

fitting a descendant of King David and a member of the chosen
people of God. Patronizing words had been written about craftsmen in the apocryphal book of *Ecclesiasticus*, sometimes called
Sirach. Yet even the learned writer of these verses acknowledged
the essential role of a man who worked with his hands.

> All these rely upon their hands,
>   and each is skilful in his own work.
> Without them a city cannot be established,
>   and men can neither sojourn nor live there.
> Yet they are not sought out for the council of the people,
>   nor do they attain eminence in the public assembly. . . .
> But they keep stable the fabric of the world,
>   and their prayer is in the practice of their trade.
>   SIRACH 38.31-32,34

These verses may well describe Joseph who, though he doubtless
did not "attain eminence in the public assembly," surely labored to
make many of Nazareth's homes pleasanter and more livable. But he
presented more than his craftsmanship to God, for, as the Gospel
stories show, he devoted himself wholeheartedly to the Lord.

According to the first story told of him, Joseph discovered that his
betrothed wife Mary was with child before their wedding. A woman
found guilty of infidelity to the man she had promised to marry was
condemned by the Law to death by stoning. Joseph, a faithful up-
holder of the Law, abhorred cruelty. His compassion and his love
for Mary struggled with his lifelong habit of obedience to the sacred
ordinances enshrined in the Law. Finally he decided to have his
marriage contract privately revoked so that Mary would escape disgrace and punishment.

Much more than this compassionate legal arrangement was to be
required of him. Soon he learned the truth of the situation through
a divine revelation. An angel of the Lord appeared in a dream to
this spiritually sensitive carpenter. "Joseph, son of David," said
the angel, "do not fear to take Mary as your wife, for what she has
conceived is through the Holy Spirit. She will bear a son and you

will name him Jesus, which means the Savior, for he will save his people from their sins."

Awaking from his dream, Joseph took Mary into his home in Nazareth, thus giving her protection as his legal wife. Later, on their journey south to Bethlehem, he guarded her and found shelter for her on the night of Jesus' birth. The shepherds saw him in the stable, a lowly man of quiet dignity who had been appointed protector of the holy child. As the angel had commanded him, Joseph gave the child the name of Jesus and by this act acknowledged him as his legal son.

Thereafter Joseph fulfilled his role of father, raising his son in accordance with the Law, guarding him from danger, and training him to be a man. All this is reflected in such stories as the presentation of the infant Jesus in the temple, the flight to Egypt and return to Nazareth, and the Passover journey to Jerusalem. Clear evidence that Joseph was not an indifferent father but exercised loving care of his young son is found in Mary's words to Jesus after they found him among the learned men in the temple. "Son, why have you treated us like this?" she asked. "Your father and I were worried and looked everywhere for you."

Returning with his parents to Nazareth, Jesus continued to be subject to their authority. His new-found understanding of his heavenly Father did not cancel his human obligation to the father who raised him. Under Joseph's tutelage he learned to meet life's conflicts and uncertainties, its hardships and suffering. The Gospel record states that he grew "in wisdom and in stature, and in favor with God and man" (Luke 2.51). Secure in the comradeship of a well-knit family, he became strong by accepting its strains and responsibilities, its sorrows and joys. Such was the attractiveness of his personality that, even in his youth, people knew that God's blessing rested upon him.

Before the beginning of Jesus' ministry Joseph may have died for he disappears from the Gospels after the family's return to Nazareth from their Passover journey. The support of Joseph's widow, together with the four sons and at least two daughters mentioned in Mark 6.3, would have to be undertaken by some responsible member of the family. Was it Jesus? If so, this might account for the fact that Jesus apparently did not begin his public ministry until his thirtieth year.

Jesus' relationship with the man whom the world regarded as his father remains a mystery, but it is clear that Joseph, God's faithful servant, was the man from whom the boy of Nazareth first learned the meaning of the word "father."

II

AT THE BEGINNING

OF JESUS' MINISTRY

6

John the Baptist

LK 1.5-25, 39-45, 57-80;
MK 1.2-11 (MT 3.1-17;
LK 3.1-22; JN 1.6-8, 19-36);
MT 11.2-19 (LK 7.18-35);
MK 6.14-29 (MT 14.1-12;
LK 9.7-9)

There was a man sent from God, whose name was John. He came for testimony, to bear witness to the light, that all might believe through him. He was not the light, but came to bear witness to the light.

JOHN 1.6-8

"WHO IS HE?" many people asked as they flocked to the Jordan River to hear John the Baptist preach.

He was the son of the priest Zechariah and his wife, Elizabeth, and had been born some thirty years earlier in a village among the Judean hills. This simple truth seemed inadequate to many who came under the spell of John's electrifying personality and his compelling message, so they tried to find a more colorful explanation of his origin. A rumor began to circulate that he might be the prophet long ago promised by Moses.

Another conjecture as to his identity connected him with the fiery prophet Elijah. Because John announced that the day of the Lord was at hand, people asked, "Is he Elijah come again to warn Israel and to prepare her for divine judgment?" There were scriptural grounds for this question. The last book of prophecy said, "Behold, I will send you Elijah the prophet before the great and terrible day of the Lord comes" (Malachi 4.5). John preached that the day of the Lord was at hand and his fiery exhortations reminded people of Elijah, who

35

had last been seen, eight hundred years before, riding up to heaven in a chariot of fire.

After John's lonely, self-disciplined years of prayer and meditation in the wilderness, he had begun to look like an ancient prophet. He was gaunt and uncouth and his eyes glowed with an inner fire. Even his clothing, a rough, camel's hair garment belted with a leather girdle, was the garb of the prophets of old. He ate locusts and wild honey, food approved by the Law as ceremonially "clean."

According to Luke's story, John was growing to manhood in the hill country of Judea at the time that Jesus was helping Joseph in the carpenter's shop far away in Nazareth of Galilee. Luke says Elizabeth was a kinswoman of Mary of Nazareth. If this was so, Jesus and John would have been relatives, but, when they met as grown men at the Jordan, John did not know Jesus.

John began to preach during a time of great religious ferment. Many religious parties and groups, each offering its own program of salvation, clamored for men's allegiance. Among the best-known were the scribes, Pharisees, Sadducees, Herodians, Zealots, Samaritans, and Essenes. The religious leaders in Jerusalem became uneasy when they heard of still another sect springing up, this one in response to the Baptist's message. "Is this new sect an offshoot of one of the Essene monastic communities near the Dead Sea?" they asked. "Will these people rebel against our established religious authority?" John's movement became so powerful that at last the temple hierarchy in Jerusalem decided to investigate it.

Crowds from Judea and Galilee had assembled at one of the fords of the swift-flowing Jordan to hear John. He announced that the Messiah would soon arrive to usher in the kingdom of God. To prepare for this divine event, Israel, he said, must be purified. He exhorted people to repent of their wrongdoing and live henceforth in goodness and integrity as befitted members of the heavenly kingdom. Though his requirements were uncompromising, his message offered new hope to many who were burdened by the evils of the time. Scores of people accepted his summons and, to show their change of heart and their desire to be worthy of the coming kingdom, they waded into the turbid waters of the Jordan to be baptized by him. This baptism, according to the contemporary historian Josephus, was a ritual cleansing "to purify the body when the soul had already been cleansed by righteous conduct."

It was August, the season of repentance preceding the Jewish New Year, when the Jerusalem authorities sent an investigating committee of priests and Levites to interview the Baptist. On their way down to the Jordan, they passed fields where the grain had been harvested and fires kindled to burn off the stubble. In fascination the officials watched snakes slithering away from the advancing flames. John's words abounded with allusions to autumnal sights like these.

"You brood of vipers!" he cried, "who warned you to escape from the coming punishment? You must prove that your hearts are really changed by performing acts of repentance."

"Brood of vipers, indeed!" exclaimed the disdainful emissaries, angered because John's words struck home. The priests and Levites winced under the uncouth prophet's denunciations, knowing only too well that many of the Jerusalem hierarchy had compromised Israel's holiness by selfishly disregarding the Law to make common cause with Gentile rulers.

When John spoke about a purifying fire to destroy Israel's corruption, the investigating committee became alarmed. "Is this a threat of an uprising?" they asked.

To the common people the idea of a destroying fire was terrifying. What could men do to escape it? According to John, no Jew would avoid punishment merely because he was a son of Abraham, one of the chosen people. Only by sincerely repenting and by performing deeds that sprang from a changed heart could men escape "the wrath to come."

Autumn was the season when men sharpened their axes for the yearly task of chopping down unproductive trees. John sounded his dire warning, "The axes are ready at the tree roots, and every tree that fails to produce good fruit is cut down and thrown on the fire."

John spoke again of God's judgment, this time in terms of a farmer threshing grain, tossing it with a winnowing fork to separate good kernels from the light, worthless chaff. The wheat would be gathered into his barn, but the chaff burned in an unquenchable fire.

"What shall we do?" cried the frightened multitudes, already beginning to feel the heat of a fire that could not be put out.

John's program was specific and practical. It came to grips with the evils of a time when the selfishness and inhumanity of those in power burdened the great mass of common people. John admonished tax collectors who levied cruelly unjust and often ruinous taxes to exact no more than the legal amount. He ordered soldiers to cease robbing and blackmailing unarmed citizens and to be satisfied with their honest, military wages. He urged prosperous people to share their extra food and clothing with the ragged and the hungry. Everyone, John said, must live uprightly to prepare for the Messiah's coming.

News of this powerful message reached Jesus in Nazareth. Alone and unknown he journeyed down from Galilee to join the enthusiastic people clamoring to hear the Baptist. Jesus perceived that John's words bore the stamp of divine tidings and that here on the banks of the Jordan men were experiencing an authentic outpouring of the Spirit.

As for the investigating committee from Jerusalem, though they listened critically, they could find no fault in the Baptist's ethical teachings. For nearly a millennium Israel's prophets had preached in a vein similar to his. Nor did the officials object to the fact that this popular preacher had enlisted a band of followers, for religious leaders were usually accompanied by disciples. But the priests and Levites found John's messianic preaching suspicious. Did this wilderness prophet claim to be the Messiah? In lordly self-importance the members of the committee gathered their robes around them and pushed through the crowd to confront the gaunt figure clothed in camel's hair. People shrank from them. Jesus watched the drama unfold.

John answered the emissaries' first question directly, declaring explicitly, "I am not the Christ."

"Who are you then?" they persisted. "Are you Elijah who will prepare the world for the Messiah?"

"I am not," John stated emphatically.

"Are you the prophet foretold by Moses?" they asked, referring to the leader promised long ago (Deuteronomy 18.15).

With growing irritation the Baptist answered curtly, "No!"

Who he was did not matter; only his mission counted. He was sent to prepare men's hearts for the Messiah, to open their eyes so that they might behold his glory.

"Who are you then?" demanded the committee, exasperated by their fruitless investigation. "We must make some report to the high priest. What do you call yourself?"

The crowd edged closer to hear what this immensely popular preacher would reply. His answer revealed his true greatness. He acknowledged that he himself was nothing but a voice. His, however, was the voice of a prophet, the voice of God.

"I am a voice crying in the wilderness in the words of the prophet Isaiah, 'Make straight the way of the Lord!' "

"After me," he continued, "will come One who is so much greater than I, that I am not even worthy to stoop down and untie the thongs of his sandals. I have baptized you with water, but he will baptize you with the Holy Spirit."

Baffled by their interview, the priests and Levites withdrew, realizing that further questioning would be in vain.

All this time Jesus stood unnoticed in the crowd, his hour of dedication at hand. He would now identify himself with the people whom God had sent him to liberate from despair and from all the futility of existence. In becoming one with these people he would take upon himself the burden of their sin and all their estrangement from God and lead them into fullness of life. As one of the New Testament letters declares, "he had to be made like his brethren in every respect, so that he might become a merciful and faithful high priest in the service of God. . . . For we have not a high priest who is unable to sympathize with our weaknesses, but one who in every respect has been tempted as we are, yet without sinning" (Hebrews 2.17;4.15). Sinless himself, being in complete harmony with his heavenly Father, Jesus was free of those offenses from which the people around him sought cleansing. Yet as the representative of the people, Jesus came forward to the Jordan's edge to ask for baptism from John.

Seeing Jesus standing there, the Baptist perceived that here was no ordinary man, but, as he later testified, "I myself did not recognize him." Though he did not recognize Jesus as the coming One whose sandal he was unworthy to untie, John saw something unique in him —a man utterly at peace with himself and the world.

The wonders at Jesus' baptism—the open heavens, God's Spirit descending as a dove, and the divine voice saying, "You are my beloved Son in whom I am well pleased"—all these signs of Jesus' consecration were, according to Mark's early record, seen and heard only by Jesus. The three later Gospels, possibly in their effort to enhance the story, interpret his subjective experience as a miracle that was both seen and heard by the bystanders. Without probing too deeply into the mysterious realm of Jesus' mind, we may perhaps understand his experience at the Jordan as one of self-dedication and ordination. Standing beside John in the shallow water, Jesus received assurance of his unique Sonship and heard his intimacy with the heavenly Father, of which he had been conscious since boyhood, acknowledged by the divine Voice.

The sublime certainties of later theology find expression in the Fourth Gospel in words assigned to John the Baptist at this time, "Behold, the Lamb of God, who takes away the sin of the world! . . . And I have seen and have borne witness that this is the Son of God" (John 1.29,34).

When Jesus withdrew to the wilderness for forty days, John the Baptist continued to preach, daring to attack even Herod Antipas, Tetrarch of Galilee and Perea. John denounced Herod's evil rule and his shameful marriage to his sister-in-law Herodias, who was his brother Philip's wife. She was furious and demanded John's death. But Herod, fearing a popular outcry from the multitudes who revered John as a prophet, merely imprisoned the intrepid reformer in the lofty fortress of Machaerus overlooking the Dead Sea.

There the days passed relentlessly for the rugged Baptist locked in his dungeon. His youth so bright with promise, when the Lord's hand had seemed to be upon him, his years of austerity in the wilderness, the period of his successful preaching and baptizing—those free and active years seemed to mock his wretchedness as a prisoner chained to a dank stone wall.

While fetters chafed his feet, despair darkened his mind. He wondered why Jesus, if he were indeed the Messiah, did not bring devastating power against Herod and utterly destroy evil from the earth. John, like many of his fellow countrymen, thought of the coming Messiah as a figure of irresistible might who would be able quickly to subdue the Gentiles and rule a restored Israel. But from reports that reached him in prison, John knew that his triumphant dream was entirely different from the facts of Jesus' ministry. Jesus was not marching at the head of an invincible army fighting the world's evil nor did he bear any likeness to the longed-for Davidic king trampling upon prostrate enemies and reigning in majesty over a reborn Israel.

Puzzled by the news his disciples smuggled in to his prison, and sick at heart, John sent two emissaries to Jesus with the question, "Are you the coming Messiah, or must we continue to look for him?"

Jesus perceived that John's question arose from a misconception of the Messiah's role. Jesus had come, not to punish a sinful world, but to offer men the healing grace of God; not to condemn, but to save. In his merciful deeds, in the whole life-giving sweep of his ministry, the character of his mission was already apparent.

"Go and tell John what you see and hear," Jesus replied to the Baptist's disciples. "The blind are recovering their sight, the lame are walking, lepers are being healed, the deaf can hear, the dead are being restored to life, and despairing people are listening to the good news of God's love that is preached to them."

To all who remembered the ancient prophecies, Jesus' statement meant that the reign of God, the new age for whose coming John had prepared the way, was now present in those who accepted Jesus. Their sorrow and sighing had already fled away. Long ago it had been written that when God came in all his glory

> Then the eyes of the blind shall be opened,
>   and the ears of the deaf unstopped;
> then shall the lame man leap like a hart,
>   and the tongue of the dumb sing for joy. . . .
> And the ransomed of the Lord shall return,
>   and come to Zion with singing;
> everlasting joy shall be upon their heads;
>   they shall obtain joy and gladness,
>   and sorrow and sighing shall flee away.
>   ISAIAH 35.5-6,10

Did John the Baptist understand Jesus' reply? Did Herod's prisoner glimpse the radiance of the new dawn and experience the joy of abundant life which Jesus was already bringing to many? The records do not answer these questions, but proceed to John's tragic end.

It came swiftly on the night of Herod's birthday celebration. Herodias had a beautiful daughter named Salome. At the banquet Salome danced before the Tetrarch and his guests in a manner considered shocking for a royal princess. But Herod was so pleased with her that, with a binding oath, he offered the girl anything up to half his kingdom.

"What shall I ask?" Salome inquired of her mother.

"The head of John the Baptist on a platter," shot back Herod's vengeful wife.

To Herod the sanctity of his oath outweighed that of a human life, so that night John was beheaded in his dungeon.

Thus died the last of the prophets, a man of such towering moral and spiritual stature that Jesus said of him,

> "What then did you go out to see? A prophet? Yes, I tell you, and more than a prophet. This is he of whom it is written,
>   'Behold, I send my messenger before thy face,
>   who shall prepare thy way before thee.'
> I tell you, among those born of women none is greater than John. . . ."
>   LUKE 7.26-28

John had indeed, in the words of his father, Zechariah, turned the hearts of the disobedient to the wisdom of just men. He had prepared a people for the Lord. The Baptist saw from afar the kingdom of God, but, like Moses and the Promised Land, he never entered it. Even the least in God's coming kingdom would be greater than John. He preached, as had Elijah of old, the fiery judgment of the Lord; Jesus introduced men to the realm of God's love. John's followers trembled at the thought of coming punishment; the multitudes who came to Jesus were healed and received abundance of life, for in him dwelt the glory of the new age.

7

Andrew

JN 1.35-42; MK 1.16-18 (MT
4.18-20); MK 3.14-18 (MT
10.2; LK 6.14; ACTS 1.13);
JN 6.1-11; 12.20-25;
MK 13.3-5

*He first found his brother Simon,
and said to him, "We have found the
Messiah" (which means Christ). He
brought him to Jesus.*

JOHN 1.41-42

ANDREW FIRST APPEARS in the New Testament as a disciple of John
the Baptist. One day soon after Jesus' baptism, Andrew and another
disciple stood near the bank of the Jordan with their gaunt and
rugged master. While the three men talked together Jesus passed
by. Seeing the man from Nazareth, the Baptist ceased speaking to
gaze after the retreating figure. His disciples noted John's silence and
his thoughtful expression. They saw his eyes light up as he cried out,
not in his usual thundering tone of denunciation, but in a voice of
surprised triumph, "Behold, the Lamb of God!"

Astonished by the Baptist's exclamation, the two disciples asked
each other, "Who is this passerby?" To find out they followed Jesus
at a fast pace in order to overtake him. Perhaps he heard their approaching footsteps, for when they were near, he turned around to
face them.

"What are you seeking?" he asked with a friendly smile.

Though they were welcomed rather than rebuffed, the two young
men stood tongue-tied before him. What were they really seeking?
It was impossible for them to put the substance of their dreams into
a simple answer. They wanted to find the Lord and experience life
to the full, not waste their years in futility. They were seeking someone who could show them how to do this. Yet at this moment, while
the stranger waited for them to speak, they were sure of but one

thing—of their desire to talk with Jesus. Accordingly, they replied with another question that was, in effect, a request for an interview, asking him, "Teacher, where are you staying?"

Jesus, looking into their eager faces, perceived that these young men were not seeking superficial answers, nor were they interested only in momentary excitement. They were deeply serious about whatever it was they desired. Graciously he invited them to his dwelling, saying, "Come and see."

One of the two men was Andrew, a fisherman from Bethsaida. Andrew had become dissatisfied with the tedious routine and simple pleasures of his fisherman's life. Despite the fact that he lived in a thriving Greek city situated near the northern shore of the Sea of Galilee, he was a Jew. But, unlike some of his Jewish contemporaries, he was not so set in his ways nor so obstinate in defending his ancient faith that he did not continue to seek new answers to old problems. Possibly his keen-minded Greek friends had stimulated his natural quickness of mind and given him enthusiasm for fresh ideas. Ready to follow any path leading to greater fulness of life, he had come to the Jordan to hear John preach.

For a while the emotional fervor of the Baptist's religious movement and its uncompromising moral demands satisfied Andrew. Then he saw that John's preaching was a prelude to something greater; it was a preparation for the Messiah's coming. Thereafter Andrew's thoughts centered on the One who was to appear. When would he come? What would he be like? Perhaps this Jesus of Nazareth, whom John called the "Lamb of God," would have news of the Messiah.

According to the Fourth Gospel, it was the tenth hour, or four o'clock, when John's two disciples followed Jesus to his dwelling. (Is this one of those unimportant, but exact details that an eyewitness is likely to include in his report of an event?) Until the day ended at sunset, Jesus talked with Andrew and his companion. The subject of their long conversation must have been the coming Messiah, for, on leaving Jesus' dwelling, Andrew searched among the crowd at the Jordan for his brother Simon and having found him exclaimed, "We have found the Messiah! We have found God's anointed One, the Christ!"

Was this not the first confession of Christian faith and was not Andrew the first recorded Christian missionary?

The Synoptic Gospels of Matthew, Mark, and Luke indicate that the disciples did not become convinced of Jesus' Messiahship until later in his ministry. But, as this story shows, John's Gospel, which is more the interpretation of a message than the chronicle of a life and which is generally even less concerned with chronology than are the Synoptics—John's Gospel ascribes belief in Jesus' Messiahship to Andrew at the time of his first meeting with the Master.

However long it was before the disciples' faith matured, Andrew's personal allegiance to Jesus began with this encounter at the Jordan. Later, after Andrew and his brother moved their home from Bethsaida to Capernaum, Jesus called these two fishermen to be his disciples, giving them a mandate to bring men to him as, on that first day at the Jordan, Andrew had brought his brother, Simon Peter. Though Peter became the more prominent of the two and his name is always first in the New Testament lists of the disciples, Andrew's name usually appears immediately after his brother's.

Andrew was a likeable man of wide sympathies and so much common sense that he was good at solving human problems. On several occasions that are recorded in the Gospels, his role was more important than his brother's. The first of these occasions was the feeding of the five thousand hungry people. They had followed Jesus to a deserted place on the eastern shore of the Sea of Galilee in the vicinity of Bethsaida. The story is of a miracle wrought by Jesus, the only one mentioned in all four Gospels. In John's Gospel, though not in the Synoptics, Andrew plays a leading part in the story.

When the need of the hungry multitude became apparent to all, Jesus asked his disciple Philip, "How can we feed these people?" Philip may at this time have kept the common purse. Being a native of Bethsaida, he would know about markets in the neighborhood.

Philip shook his head in dismay at the Master's question. "Forty dollars," he sighed, "would not buy enough bread for each person to have even a small amount."

Was forty dollars all that the common purse contained? If so, Philip's reply could indicate, not a negative approach to difficulty, or a plodding, unimaginative mind entangled in statistics, but actually a generous nature willing to spend everything he had for others.

When Andrew learned of the problem, he was undaunted by its magnitude and, being of a more sanguine nature than Philip, immediately searched for a solution. In the hungry crowd milling restlessly around on the fresh, green grass, he found a boy with five small barley loaves, no larger than cakes, and a couple of pickled fish. It was doubtless his picnic lunch prepared earlier that spring day by his mother. Barley, which ripened before the wheat, was at this season a staple in the diet of the poor.

The boy agreed to share his lunch, so Andrew brought him to Jesus. Andrew had found at least a token solution of their problem—a boy generously willing to divide his own lunch with others. The lad is unnamed and unknown except for this moment when he offered Jesus his loaves and fishes in an act that reflects some of the Master's own unselfishness and concern for others.

Then it happened, the miracle or "sign" so difficult to reconstruct on a factual, historical basis, but so significant to the early Church in its efforts to understand who Jesus really was. "Jesus then took the loaves, and when he had given thanks, he distributed them to those who were seated; so also the fish, as much as they wanted" (John 6.11). Thus the five thousand people were fed.

The fact that the lad's loaves were of barley brings to mind other miraculously multiplied barley loaves. These were so small that three or four of them were hardly sufficient to satisfy a hungry person (cf. Luke 11.5). Yet the prophet Elisha took twenty barley loaves, only enough for five or six people, and distributed them to one hundred men. Amazingly, as the old story in 2 Kings 4.42-44 narrates, there was more than enough bread to satisfy all the men.

The story of the feeding of the five thousand has other scriptural overtones. It reminds one of the manna which the Lord gave to the

Israelites in the wilderness. The rabbis of Jesus' time taught that the faithful would again be given heavenly manna in all the inexhaustible abundance that is characteristic of God's generosity. This would take place when the Messiah appeared. Did Andrew and the others wonder if that time had now arrived? Was this meal in the desert place the messianic banquet with Jesus as the host?

Though questions like these may have occurred to the disciples, they did not comprehend the full meaning of the event, "they did not understand about the loaves" (Mark 6.52). At the time they failed to perceive that this "sign" proclaimed that Jesus Christ can abundantly supply the needs of those who believe in him. According to the Fourth Gospel, the Master himself taught this truth when he said, "I am the bread of life; he who comes to me shall not hunger, and he who believes in me shall never thirst" (John 6.35).

Later, at the Last Supper, Jesus *took* bread, *blessed* it, *broke* it, and *gave* it to them using the same actions that are recorded of him in the feeding of the five thousand. On the earlier occasion, "taking the five loaves and the two fish he looked up to heaven, and blessed, and broke the loaves, and gave them to the disciples to set before the people; and he divided the two fish among them all" (Mark 6.41, cf. 14.22). The striking verbal similarity in the report of the two events indicates that Mark understood the miracle in the desert as a prelude to the sacramental meal of the Last Supper. To those with eyes to see and hearts to understand, both events revealed Christ's inexhaustible gifts of life and love.

Not long after bringing the boy with the loaves and fishes to Jesus, Andrew introduced a group of Greeks to his Master. These Gentiles were converts to Judaism and had come to Jerusalem to attend the Passover. There they heard about Jesus and, hesitating to approach him directly, went to Philip. Possibly they were his friends and came, as he did, from the Greek city of Bethsaida.

"Sir, we want to see Jesus," they said to Philip.

This simple request put Philip in an awkward position. He did not want to offend these men, yet he knew that Jesus had so far confined his mission to Jews. Would the Master welcome Gentiles? Philip, being a cautious man, consulted Andrew. Friendly, broadminded Andrew had more self-confidence than Philip and was perhaps more deeply understanding of the Master. Andrew's advice to Philip was to take the problem directly to Jesus himself.

This advice proved to be a happy solution to Philip's quandary, for, when the two disciples told their Master that members of an alien race were seeking him, he welcomed the Greeks as the first fruits of his world-wide kingdom. Initially announced to the Jews, God's kingdom was for the Gentiles also. Seeing these Greeks, few though they were in number, as the vanguard of many people who would come to him, Jesus exclaimed in exaltation, "The time has come for the Son of man to enter into his glory!"

As Jesus said these words, did Andrew and Philip recall Daniel's vision?

> There came one like a son of man . . . .
> And to him was given dominion
> and glory and kingdom,
> that all peoples, nations, and languages
> should serve him;
> his dominion is an everlasting dominion,
> which shall not pass away.
>
> DANIEL 7.13-14

Christ's glory was to be his cross and his dominion, the realm of love. Jesus tried to explain this paradox to the Greeks and to his disciples, showing them that his death would be his triumph. To do this he used a simple figure of speech. "Truly, I tell you that unless a grain of wheat falls into the earth and dies, it remains merely a single grain of wheat; but if it dies, it will bear a good harvest."

Andrew was puzzled by this teaching and also fearful of the upheavals that he believed must usher in the new era. One day he privately questioned the Master concerning the future. With him were Peter, James, and John. The five of them stood on the Mount of Olives looking across the Kidron valley toward the temple standing in all its splendor upon Mount Moriah. The disciples could not imagine a cataclysm so great as to cause the enormous stones of the temple to be thrown down, yet Jesus had said of them, "Not one stone shall be left upon another."

"When will this age end?" asked Andrew and the three other disciples, dreading the time of calamity, yet longing for the triumphant coming of God's kingdom. "When will these things happen?" they asked. "What sign will there be that the age is ending?"

Jesus answered them at length, closing his discourse with a warning to be alert. "Watch," he charged them.

After the crucifixion and resurrection, Andrew was among those in the upper room in Jerusalem who experienced the coming of the Holy Spirit. This is the last time he is mentioned in the scriptural record, though legends concerning his later life abound. They state that he preached in the region north of the Black Sea, bringing to Christ, as he once brought his brother, the peoples living in what is now Russia. Because of these legends he became the patron saint of Russia. He is the patron saint of Scotland also. His symbol is an X-shaped cross on which, according to tradition, he suffered martyrdom.

8

Philip

JN 1.43-46; 6.5-9; 12.20-24;
14.8-11; MK 3.18 (MT 10.3;
LK 6.14; ACTS 1.13)

> *God, Who first ordered Light to shine in darkness has flooded our hearts with His Light. We now can enlighten men only because we can give them knowledge of the glory of God, as we see it in the face of Jesus Christ.*
> 2 CORINTHIANS 4.6 (J. B. Phillips translation)

PHILIP HAD MANY of the qualities frequently associated with thinkers rather than doers. As the stories of the feeding of the five thousand and the coming of the Greeks show, he was often unwilling to act until he had thoroughly analyzed a situation. He seems to have lacked confidence in himself and was more apt to think about a problem than to act upon it, to dwell on difficulties rather than on possible solutions. He sought proof. He wanted to be sure. But there was another side to Philip's nature—he was deeply spiritual. It was this that finally drew him into Jesus' orbit.

A stanch Jew, obedient to the ancient Law of his people, Philip was well versed in the Scriptures. Hearing that the Baptist was announcing the imminent coming of the Messiah, Philip had responded to John's call to repentance and baptism. Throwing his usual caution to the winds, he had packed his traveling bag and, possibly joining Andrew and Peter, made the journey from Bethsaida down to the Jordan. There Philip had first seen Jesus.

Even after a wave of excitement about Jesus swept through the whole group of Andrew's and Peter's friends from Bethsaida, Philip seems to have remained unmoved, standing apart, interested in all that was said, yet not sure enough about the new prophet to commit himself. This was Philip's way, though it must have exasperated impulsive Peter and quick-thinking Andrew. It was fruitless for them to argue with him; he needed time to examine the evidence concerning Jesus and compare it with scriptural prophecies.

While the unhappy man hesitated, torn between his natural caution and a growing sense that the hour of Christ's coming was at hand, Jesus himself took the initiative. On the eve of his departure for Galilee, he went in search of Philip. Here was a man, Jesus perceived, who, despite his deliberation was neither slow of mind nor indifferent, but capable of reaching great depths of spiritual insight. Philip was able to penetrate the barrier of superficial doubt and tap the very sources of certainty. He had the qualifications for becoming an outstanding disciple.

When Jesus found Philip, he spoke two words to him. They were a command and at the same time an invitation—the earliest reported invitation to discipleship: "Follow me."

Philip instantly accepted this call, for his heart was already prepared. His previous uncertainties were swept away by an incoming tide of joy. He longed to share his experience with others, for his was a genuine discipleship that would express itself in bringing people to Jesus.

Nathanael was the first man he brought to the Master. The story of this encounter belongs primarily to the chapter about Nathanael, but it reveals a changed Philip, no longer standing outside the circle of Jesus' friends. He was now actively committed to the Master's cause.

From the first day, Philip's story is one of growth. The feeding of the five thousand showed him that he was more aware of human difficulties than of divine power. When, to his surprise, Jesus welcomed the Greeks, Philip saw that he had placed too narrow limits on the Master's message. During Jesus' last week Philip's faith reached a new summit.

In his study of the Scriptures, this disciple must have been impressed by the aspiration of the psalmist who wrote,

> As a hart longs
> for flowing streams,
> so longs my soul
> for thee, O God.
> My soul thirsts for God,
> for the living God.
> When shall I come and behold
> the face of God?
>
> PSALM 42.1-2

Whenever Philip recited these verses to himself, he asked the psalmist's question, unaware that it had already been answered. Was he not already drinking from the flowing stream? Did he not behold the face of God? But Philip was uncertain. His old desire for proof assailed him. Centuries earlier, the great prophet of the Exile had promised men a divine vision.

> And the glory of the Lord shall be revealed,
> and all flesh shall see it together.
>
> ISAIAH 40.5

Philip thought that now, if ever, the hour had come for God to reveal himself unmistakably to men. Choosing a time when the Twelve were alone with Jesus, Philip made his request, speaking not only for himself, but for his fellow disciples. "Lord," he said, "show us the Father and then we shall be satisfied."

If only they could see God, the loving Father, every man's doubt would vanish in the peace of absolute certainty. Such was their desire. They asked, of course, for the impossible—physical proof of spiritual reality. Meanwhile the truth for which Philip wanted visible evidence was already present to the eyes of faith.

Jesus glanced quickly from one to another of the expectant faces of his disciples who sat in silence awaiting his reply. Patiently and with infinite kindness, though there must have been disappointment in his voice, Jesus replied to Philip. "Have I been with you all this time and still you do not know me, Philip?"

No one spoke, though all of them might have said, "We do know you, Master. You teach us truths no man ever taught us before. You have forgiven us and healed us and led us into a new realm. We have committed our lives to you. But show us now the Father of whom you speak."

In the hush of the upper room where they all sat, Jesus said,

"He who has seen me has seen the Father; how can you say, 'Show us the Father'? Do you not believe that I am in the Father and the Father in me? The words that I say to you I do not speak on my own authority; but the Father who dwells in me does his works. Believe me that I am in the Father and the Father in me; or else believe me for the sake of the works themselves."

JOHN 14.9-11

Philip's story, the story of an intelligent man transformed by Christ's power into a hero of faith, is found only in the Gospel of John. The Synoptic Gospels merely list his name with those of his fellow disciples, while Acts mentions him among those who, having witnessed the resurrection and the ascension, were endowed with the Holy Spirit.

According to legend, Philip, after zealous missionary activity, suffered martyrdom at Hierapolis in Asia Minor. His triumphs over evil are symbolized in art by a vanquished dragon crouching at his feet. He is usually depicted holding a staff surmounted by a cross indicating his preaching journeys. Undoubtedly on these journeys he proclaimed the truth that he had learned as Jesus' disciple and he inspired many with his faith in "Christ, who is the likeness of God" (2 Corinthians 4.4).

9

Nathanael–Bartholomew

JN 1.45-51; 21.1-7; MK 3.18
(MT 10.3; LK 6.14; ACTS
1.13)

"Can any good thing come out of Nazareth?"

JOHN 1.46

NATHANAEL LIVED in Cana, a Galilean village built on a hill overlooking a marshy reed-filled valley. The name "Cana" means "place of reeds." In this small community, only a few miles from Nazareth, Nathanael sat alone one day under his fig tree. According to the rabbis, a fig tree provided a suitable place for a man to read and meditate upon the Scriptures. Nathanael was studying these books when a group of travelers entered Cana. Though he heard their voices, he did not look up, surmising that the visitors were coming for a wedding soon to be celebrated in the village. He had more important things on his mind than curiosity about strangers.

In the cool shade afforded by the fig tree's broad leaves, he continued his reflections upon the sad condition of Israel suffering, as she had been for many years, under foreign rule. From time to time he unrolled his well-worn scrolls, searching the sacred books for prophecies of the Deliverer. Like the people who had thus far recognized Jesus as the Promised One of God, Nathanael was both expectant and informed.

Philip was among the new arrivals in Cana. They included Jesus and the disciples who had traveled with him from the Jordan up to Galilee. It was Philip, the onetime diffident man, who, upon seeing Nathanael under the fig tree, walked toward him. Were the two already friends? Or is it possible that when Philip noted the scroll of the Law from which the Cana man was reading, he recognized a fellow intellectual and felt drawn to him?

"We have found him of whom Moses and the Law and also the prophets wrote!" exclaimed Philip, breaking into Nathanael's meditation. For all its impulsiveness, the announcement was keyed to the clearly demonstrated interests of the man under the fig tree.

Startled by the interruption and perhaps somewhat annoyed by it, Nathanael stared at the excited traveler standing in the hot sunshine just beyond the tree's shade and wondered, "Who may this person be of whom the traveler speaks?" Nathanael's mind seethed with questions. Rolling up his scroll, he rose, his interest showing in the rapidity of his actions. These signs encouraged Philip to complete his declaration, "He of whom Moses and the prophets wrote is Jesus of Nazareth, the son of Joseph."

Nazareth! The very name pricked the bright bubble of Nathanael's hope. He knew the place well—a miserable village, only a few miles distant, with dusty streets, dark hovels, and unimportant people. He laughed scornfully at the idea that one as important as the Messiah could come from such an unsuitable village. "Can anything good come out of Nazareth?" he asked, turning his back on Philip to enter the house.

Philip winced at the question, but his new-found certainty withstood even this derisive attack. Though tempted to argue, he checked himself, knowing the toughness of prejudice. Anyway, he knew he had a better weapon than words. Only recently he had discovered that to believe in Jesus one must know him. Good-naturedly and with an echo of the Master's own graciousness, Philip called out to Nathanael, "Come and see."

As Philip led an unwilling Nathanael to Jesus, the Master saw them coming and recognized the true character of this man of Cana. However haughty or prejudiced he seemed, he was basically a sincere, fairminded person, straightforward and upright of heart as befitted a faithful Israelite.

"Behold, here is a true descendant of our father Jacob-Israel!" exclaimed Jesus as the two men approached. Then as an afterthought, he added, "And there is no deceit in him!"

Unlike the ancient patriarch Jacob-Israel, Nathanael employed no deception or trickery to gain his ends. He might at times be quick-tempered and scornful, but never dishonest. He was, in the psalmist's words, a man

> . . . who walks blamelessly, and does what is right,
> and speaks truth from his heart.
>
> PSALM 15.2

At Jesus' exclamation, Nathanael looked up in astonishment. "How do you know me so well?" he asked, realizing that this stranger had divined his inmost nature.

"While you were sitting under the fig tree, even before Philip spoke to you, I saw you."

How far this stranger's attention ranged, thought Nathanael, how true his understanding! No man he had ever known before possessed such insight. Philip had been right in his confidence that one whose mind was already prepared by meditation and prayer would perceive that Jesus was indeed the Holy One of God.

The story must be greatly compressed, for with extraordinary speed the truth dawned upon Nathanael and he exclaimed, "You are the Son of God! You are the King of Israel!"

This man of Cana, having wrestled with his initial scorn and disbelief, as Jacob of old had wrestled with the angel at Peniel, perceived the reality concerning Jesus. Again, he was like Jacob who at Bethel saw a ladder joining earth to heaven.

"Truly, I say to you," Jesus declared, "all of you will see greater things than you have beheld today. You will see heaven opened and the angels of God ascending and descending upon the Son of Man." In effect, Jesus was saying that the ancient symbol of Jacob's ladder joining earth to heaven was to be superseded by Christ himself. Henceforth he would be the bridge across the chasm dividing men from God. He would link the inexhaustible riches of God's grace with men's need, thus overcoming their desolating sense of estrangement from the Lord. Paul expressed the same idea when he said of Christ, "Through him we have obtained access to this grace in which we stand, and we rejoice in our hope of sharing the glory of God" (Romans 5.2).

Nathanael appears once more in the New Testament. His second story, like the first, is found only in the Fourth Gospel. The event took place soon after the resurrection. With six other disciples he spent a night fishing in the Sea of Galilee but caught nothing. At daybreak a stranger hailed them from the shore and directed them to cast their net on the right side of the boat. Tired and discouraged though they were, they decided to do as the stranger advised. Soon their catch was so heavy that they could not haul it into their boat without tearing the net. Then it dawned upon one of the disciples who the figure on the beach was. "It is the Lord!" he exclaimed. Thus Nathanael, in company with Peter, Thomas, James, John, and two other disciples—all men whom the Lord commissioned as apostles —thus the man of Cana saw the risen Lord.

Who was Nathanael? Strangely enough, for he was clearly outstanding, his name does not appear in the lists of the twelve disciples, nor is he mentioned anywhere in the Synoptic Gospels or in the Book of Acts. One naturally associates his name with that of Philip, who introduced him to Jesus. Philip's name in the Synoptic lists is always accompanied by that of a certain Bartholomew about whom nothing is known. Was Bartholomew another name for Nathanael? Some commentators think it is possible that Bartholomew, a family name meaning "son of Tholmai," was Nathanael's second name and that the vividly portrayed Nathanael of the Fourth Gospel is the same man whom the Synoptics list as Bartholomew.

Despite the New Testament's silence concerning Nathanael-Bartholomew's later life, there are legends of his journeys to various lands. These stories tell how he accompanied his old friend Philip on several missionary journeys and later went with Thomas to India. Nathanael-Bartholomew is numbered among the martyred apostles.

His symbol is a knife, the supposed instrument of his flaying. All these legends may well be the work of pious imagination. Nathanael himself is better remembered as the honest man of Cana who prepared himself by study and prayer to perceive the glory of the Son of God.

IO

Wedding Guests at Cana

JN 2.1-11

"I came that they may have life, and have it abundantly."
JOHN 10.10

TORCHLIGHT FLICKERED in Cana's dark streets. To the lively accompaniment of flutes, deep-throated voices sang a traditional song while the bridegroom escorted his betrothed from her father's home to his own. Onlookers watching the festive procession joined the chorus of the groom's friends in the wedding chant:

> What is that coming up from the wilderness,
>   like a column of smoke,
> perfumed with myrrh and frankincense,
>   with all the fragrant powders of the merchant?
> SONG OF SOLOMON 3.6

The veiled bride, crowned with myrtle leaves, sat proudly erect in her swaying litter as it was carried in the midst of her procession. She was decked in jewels, some of them borrowed for the occasion. After she passed, the fragrance of her perfume lingered in the evening air. At the bridegroom's house his parents gave the bride an age-old blessing amid rejoicings of the wedding guests, both relatives and friends. The next morning the week-long festivities began.

At some point in the celebrations the bridegroom sang one of the old wedding songs handed down from generation to generation.

> You are beautiful as Tirzah, my love,
>   comely as Jerusalem,
>   terrible as an army with banners.

Turn away your eyes from me,
   for they disturb me—
Your hair is like a flock of goats,
   moving down the slopes of Gilead.
Your teeth are like a flock of ewes,
   that have come up from the washing. . . .
Your cheeks are like halves of a pomegranate
   behind your veil.
      SONG OF SOLOMON 6.4-7

There were also traditional songs for the bride to sing.

The voice of my beloved!
   Behold, he comes,
leaping upon the mountains,
   bounding over the hills.
My beloved is like a gazelle,
   or a young stag.
SONG OF SOLOMON 2.8,9

No one present could remember a happier wedding than the one in Cana. Was this the reason, perhaps, that the guests stayed on and on, singing, dancing, propounding riddles, and feasting, reluctant for this bright interval in their drab, monotonous lives to end? Merriment swept among the guests like a summer breeze. The joy of the wedding couple was reflected on the faces of their guests. But there was something else that raised the hearts of everyone present. Jesus was there. He was no specter at the feast, no gloomy figure casting a pall over the festivities with sternly disapproving looks, for wherever he moved among the guests, gaiety seemed to follow him, talk became more animated, smiles brighter, laughter heartier. It was not coarse or cruel laughter, but the expansive kind that banishes anxiety in a glow of happy fellowship.

The wedding festivities were being managed by the master of ceremonies, sometimes called the steward of the feast, who was a friend of the bridegroom host. As the steward surveyed the merry company he noted that everything was going well. He saw that Mary of Nazareth was there with Jesus and several other members of her family. Some of Jesus' disciples accompanied him. Nathanael, of course, had been among those originally invited, but doubtless Peter, Andrew, John, and Philip were unexpected guests. Despite the fact that they were strangers, all had been welcomed by the bridegroom. The infectious high spirits of the Master and his disciples obviously enlivened the feast, while the presence of Jesus seemed to bless the marriage. There was happiness and laughter, there was enough food and drink for everyone—at least for a while.

Earlier, the bridegroom had perhaps hesitated to invite Jesus to the wedding lest, in his new role as a religious leader, he frown upon the merrymaking. He had recently arrived from the Jordan where he had been with John the Baptist, the well-known ascetic who disapproved of wine drinking. At the wedding feast the bridegroom and his friend noted that Jesus' ways were different from those of the Baptist. Jesus ate and drank, rejoicing in the fruitfulness of the earth from which the Lord brought forth

> wine to gladden the heart of man . . .
> and bread to strengthen man's heart.
> PSALM 104.15

Jesus' enemies would one day accuse him of being a glutton and a drunkard—angry words to use against one who was merely not an ascetic. But his friends saw him at the wedding feast demonstrating the characteristics of the new age to which he summoned men. John the Baptist's disciples beat their breasts, fasted, and mourned. Jesus' disciples ate and drank and rejoiced with their Master in human joys. "I came," declared Jesus, "that they might have life, and have it abundantly" (John 10.10). In later years his followers were to declare, "And from his fulness have we all received, grace upon grace" (John 1.16).

The marriage feast went on and on until finally, as we already know, there was no more wine and Jesus' mother told him of it. At this point, the story of a Galilean wedding becomes a revelation of Christ's power to transform and enrich life.

Six stone water jars stood empty at the door. They were used to store water for ritual purification, because in this household no one ate without first ceremonially washing his hands. A guest's feet were also washed and many other ablutions performed. The jars were of stone, not earthenware, for the Jews believed that stone remained rittually "clean," while earthenware easily became contaminated by the evil feared to be lurking everywhere.

Gesturing toward the jars, Jesus bade the servants, "Fill them with water." This command required arduous labor on the part of these co-workers in Jesus' first recorded miracle, for water had to be fetched from the village well and brought in dripping pots to fill the great stone jars.

"Now, pour some out and take it to the master of ceremonies," he instructed them.

When this was done, the steward tasted the liquid but did not know it had been poured from a water jar. Now that the feast was near an end he expected that this wine would be of poor quality, for good wine was always served first when palates were keen; the inferior wine was kept for the last. "But you have kept your best wine for the end!" the steward exclaimed to the bridegroom, savoring the excellent drink the servants had brought him.

The story states that the master of ceremonies did not know the source of the new wine, but the servants knew. This situation must have been temporary, for such a marvel as water transformed into wine could hardly have been concealed from the wedding party.

This "sign" or miracle was to Jesus' followers a revelation of his power and, according to the record, in this hour "his disciples believed in him" (John 2.11).

Moses had struck water from a rock. Elijah caused a widow's oil jar to remain full during a famine. Jesus, as Lord over nature, transformed the water of Jewish ritual into the new wine of his Gospel. The meaning is clear—wine symbolized joy, the characteristic note of Jesus' message. As the taste of water is to wine, so is the old religion to the new life Christ gives to those who come to him.

II

Nicodemus

JN 3.1-17; 7.45-52; 19.39-42   *"Unless one is born anew, he canno,*
see the kingdom of God."
                                                JOHN 3.3

NICODEMUS' FOOTSTEPS echoed in the dark streets of Jerusalem. It was night and few people were abroad to see his muffled figure hurrying furtively through narrow byways to the house where Jesus was staying. Ever since he had heard of the new teacher and wonder-worker from Galilee, he had been eager to meet him. Because Nicodemus enjoyed great public esteem, both as a Pharisee and as a member of the sanhedrin, the ruling body of the Jews, he dared not be seen with Jesus. In seeking out the Galilean therefore, Nicodemus went secretly and at night.

His learned and powerful colleagues in the sanhedrin regarded Jesus as an ignorant preacher from the provinces. According to their standards he was untrained in the Law, in which they were undisputed authorities. Moreover, by coming to Jerusalem to preach, he seemed to them to lack proper respect for their jurisdiction. To these men, Jesus was a troublesome fellow whose popularity threatened their political and religious authority. Self-righteously the Pharisees and Sadducees whispered among themselves that something must be done to end this challenge to their power. Some way must be found to silence Jesus.

Nicodemus did not agree with the majority of his narrowminded colleagues. Being a Pharisee, and therefore slightly more receptive to new ideas than the conservative Sadducees, he tried to have an open mind about Jesus. Was it possible, Nicodemus wondered, that the Lord who once spoke through the prophets, was today speaking through Jesus? Clearly, much that the Galilean said had the ring of truth.

At this thought Nicodemus quickened his pace. Through him there blew, as it were, a wind of the spirit, beating against the conventionality of his calling. Scrupulously obeying the Law and making all the required ritual sacrifices, he had done everything expected of a Pharisee. Because of his wide-ranging knowledge of the Scriptures, he was regarded as an outstanding religious authority of the day. In any society he would have been considered a good and learned man. Yet Nicodemus knew that all this was not enough. Something was lacking. Instead of being content with his life, he was uneasy and dissatisfied. He dreamed of limitless horizons shining in the glorious light of God, but all he saw from his summit of learning and wealth, of power and esteem, was a circumscribed and threateningly dark world. His heart was heavy. Night reigned over him, but he longed for the day.

When he arrived at the house where Jesus was lodging, Nicodemus greeted the Master with all the polished courteousness of a man of the world at ease in all circumstances. The Pharisee's opening words were diplomatic but fundamentally sincere. "Master," he said, "we know that you have been sent from God to teach us, for no one could perform your wonderful works unless God were with him."

Beneath his tactful, well-mannered greeting, Jesus perceived the man's genuine desire, his longing to find the something more that transfigures life. Like the crowds, Nicodemus had first been attracted by Jesus' miracles, but this Pharisee was more than a seeker after fresh marvels. With this man's rigid habits of mind, he would be a difficult person to teach. Barricaded as he was behind pride and self-sufficiency, only a change of heart would bring him what he sought. He needed to become open-hearted and humble again like a child. Then he would reach out to God and in so doing find that the Lord was already searching for him.

With extraordinary incisiveness Jesus recognized the Pharisee's spiritual sickness and quickly prescribed a cure. "Truly, truly," declared Jesus to emphasize the bold figure of speech he was about to use, "unless a man is born again, he cannot even see the kingdom of God."

Not even see God's kingdom and he was a Pharisee! Nicodemus was shocked and hurt. It seemed to him that Jesus ignored all his spiritual attainments. He had worked hard at being a good Pharisee. His moral attainments must earn him some preferential treatment in the kingdom of God. A new beginning indeed! This talk about being born again, he thought, was nonsense. Irritably Nicodemus ridiculed Jesus' words by asking, "How can a man be born again when he is old? Can he enter his mother's womb a second time to be born?"

Jesus ignored the ill-natured absurdity of the question, knowing that Nicodemus had a basic difficulty. He could not see how a man can bring about so great a change of heart within himself that he becomes a new person. He needed to see that repentance comes first, that a man must be baptized, "born of water" to signify his inner cleansing. Some decisive break with his past must be made, for the kingdom of God does not evolve gradually and naturally from a lower order, but comes only when the Holy Spirit grants new life. "Born of the Spirit" describes the experience of entering upon newness of life.

Listening for statements to contradict, rather than truths to ponder, Nicodemus failed to understand the Master's patient explanations and asked him fretfully, "How do these things happen?"

"How can you, a famous teacher in Israel, remain ignorant of these matters?" countered Jesus.

As a representative of the people of God and an interpreter of the Scriptures, Nicodemus should have known that for centuries Israel's holy men had taught that a person must be born of water and spirit in order to enter God's kingdom. Had not the prophet Ezekiel made this truth plain? Speaking for the Lord, Ezekiel had said, "I will sprinkle clean water upon you, and you shall be clean from all your uncleanness. . . . A new heart I will give you, and a new spirit I will put within you; and I will take out of your flesh the heart of stone and give you a heart of flesh. And I will put my spirit upon you" (Ezekiel 36.25-27).

One of the penitential psalms had cried out for cleanness of heart and newness of life.

> Create in me a clean heart, O God,
>   and put a new and right spirit within me.
> Cast me not away from thy presence,
>   and take not thy holy Spirit from me.
>
> PSALM 51.10-11

Nicodemus did not want a new spirit. He desired all the blessings of God to be showered upon him just as he was. He wanted heaven on his own terms.

Though half-convinced by the teachings of the man from Nazareth, Nicodemus remained unwilling to act. He was afraid to risk his official standing by openly becoming one of the socially inferior and often unkempt group around Jesus. At the end of his night interview, Nicodemus rose and left the Master's presence to walk thoughtfully through the dark and silent streets of Jerusalem to his home.

"I am the light of the world," Jesus was to declare; "he who follows me will not walk in darkness, but will have the light of life" (John 8.12).

Nicodemus did not choose to walk in the full "light of life" as an avowed follower of the Galilean teacher, but this interested Pharisee became a secret disciple. While carrying on his customary activities, studying and teaching the Law, disputing with his colleagues, voting in the council, he tried to use his influence in the sanhedrin to aid Jesus. His position remained ambiguous and he soon discovered how feeble his help really was.

One autumn day when Jesus was in Jerusalem for the Feast of Tabernacles, the sanhedrin sent temple police to arrest him. The officers were so moved by Jesus' words that they returned to the council empty-handed, excusing themselves for their failure to carry out orders by exclaiming, "No man ever spoke like this man."

The insubordination of the police hired to carry out their commands angered the Pharisees. Judging religious matters was the prerogative of the sanhedrin, not the police.

"Is this pretender leading you astray as he does the unthinking mob of common people?" the religious leaders asked the police. "Do you not see that none of the authorities and not one of the Pharisees believes in Jesus? This crowd, this Jerusalem rabble, is ignorant of the Law. Do not let them influence you, for there is a curse upon them."

The one Pharisee who secretly believed in Jesus could no longer keep silent. The council's decision to arrest Jesus and the intemperate harangue violated Nicodemus' sense of fair play. Bravely he raised a lone voice against prejudgment, reminding his colleagues of justice and due process of law. "Does our law judge a man," he asked them, "without first giving him a hearing and finding out what he has done?"

Though Nicodemus made merely a plea for judicial fairness, the other Pharisees turned on him as if he were openly defending Jesus. Sarcastically they asked, "Are you, too, from the contemptible province of Galilee?" Then, adding scorn to their sarcasm, they advised him, who was one of the leading scriptural authorities of the day, "Search the Scriptures and you will see that no prophet is to come from Galilee."

Was Nicodemus present later when the sanhedrin voted to condemn Jesus for blasphemy? Surely, if this secret friend of the Master had listened to the proceedings, he must have protested, though his voice would have been drowned out by angry cries demanding Jesus' death.

Nicodemus appears only three times, all in the Fourth Gospel. On the third occasion it was too late for him to help Jesus, for the Master had already died upon the cross. Nicodemus could only pay his last respects to a lifeless body. He purchased spices for Jesus' burial—myrrh and aloes in such large quantities as only a wealthy man could afford. Torn by remorse and fear, he brought his costly offering to Golgotha where he helped Joseph of Arimathea lower the body from the cross and bury it in a nearby rock-cut tomb. This final act of devotion to the Master required courage in a city that only hours before had echoed to savage cries of, "Crucify him!"

On this sorrowful note the story of Nicodemus ends. Did this hesitant Pharisee find ultimate certainty in the light of the resurrection? Did faith transmute his remorse and despair into joy? Did Nicodemus finally, through belief in Christ, learn of the Father's love and experience the truth of the words which climax the story of his nighttime interview with Jesus? Those words sum up the message of Jesus and contain the quintessence of the Gospel.

For God so loved the world that he gave his only Son, that whoever believes in him should not perish but have eternal life. For God sent the Son into the world, not to condemn the world, but that the world might be saved through him.

JOHN 3.16-17

12

The Samaritan Woman

JN 4.4-43   *"I who speak to you am he."*
                                                JOHN 4.26

THE NOONDAY HEAT was intense. It burned through the woman's thin sandals as she hurried along the road, balancing her water jar on her head. She was a woman of Samaria, the country situated between Judea and Galilee and inhabited by a mixed race. Pure-blooded Jews despised the Samaritans whose fathers long ago had worshiped heathen gods. The scribes and Pharisees of Jerusalem condemned the Samaritan religion for its deviations from normal Judaism.

The woman was on her way from her home in Sychar to draw water at Jacob's well nearby. Reaching this historic spot, which was surrounded by a thick screen of bushes, she rested for a few minutes in the welcome shade. Jacob's well was in a ten-mile long valley whose grain fields, vineyards, plum and pomegranate orchards, and olive groves shimmered in the bright light of midday. Gazing upward, the woman saw the forbidding, gray limestone mass of Mount Gerizim rising in rugged majesty more than two thousand feet into the cool upper air. It was a sacred mountain crowned with a temple built as a rival to Jerusalem's temple. The Samaritan structure was now in ruins, having been destroyed by the Jews more than a century earlier.

According to Samaritan belief, God dwelt on Mount Gerizim, but the Jews, sure that Jerusalem founded on Mount Zion was the Lord's habitation, sang,

For the Lord has chosen Zion;
  he has desired it for his habitation:
"This is my resting place for ever;
  here I will dwell, for I have desired it."
                        PSALM 132.13-14

Again they expressed their belief in a song.

On the holy mount stands the city he founded;
  the Lord loves the gates of Zion
  more than all the dwelling places of Jacob.
Glorious things are spoken of you,
  O city of God.
                        PSALM 87.1-3

These verses were never sung in Samaria, for the Psalms and all the other books known as the Writings as well as the books of the Prophets were not included in the Samaritan Bible. It was a short volume containing only the Pentateuch.

Mount Gerizim, rising higher than its sister peak Mount Ebal, remained for the Samaritans the most sacred place on earth. They called it "the First of Mountains" or "the House of Angels" and taught their children that Adam had been formed of Gerizim's dust and that here he built the first altar to God. Noah, Abraham, and Jacob were all said to have come to this mountain, while Moses commanded that six tribes were to stand here for the blessings (Deuteronomy 27. 11-12). On Ebal, Joshua renewed the covenant between Israel and the Lord (Joshua 8.30-35). Finally, the Samaritans believed that the Messiah would first appear in glory upon the summit of Mount Gerizim.

The irreconcilable beliefs concerning Jerusalem and Mount Gerizim, and the unorthodox elements of the Samaritan religion caused so much hostility between the two peoples that they no longer communicated with one another. Their enmity frequently broke out in violence.

These disturbing matters were far from the Samaritan woman's mind that noon as she concentrated upon her task. It was a rigorous one requiring strong arms and a strong back. She let down into the well a rope from the end of which dangled a leather bucket. Her rope was very long, the well being more than a hundred feet deep, cut through turf and underlying rock to a spring that perpetually bubbled up at the bottom. As soon as her bucket filled with water, she must haul it up, dripping from the depths, and pour its cool contents into her clay jar.

Though she could easily have obtained water from one of the surface streams flowing nearer her home, she evidently preferred Jacob's well despite the extra toil it cost her. The place had sacred associations and perhaps its water seemed better to her than that from other sources. By coming at noon, as she did this day, she avoided the gossiping women of Sychar who usually drew water in the cool of evening. Had their hostility and self-righteousness hurt her so that she now preferred to draw water alone?

Today she suddenly saw that she was not alone. Partly concealed by the thick bushes, a traveler rested in the shade. She was sure that he would not speak to her, for Israel's men of wisdom had explicitly discouraged talk between men and women, declaring, "He that talks much with womankind brings evil upon himself." Furthermore, according to Jewish law in the Talmud, a man was not to speak with a woman in a public place, even if she were his own wife. Added to these prohibitions was the fact that the stranger was a Jew, evidently passing through Samaria on the shortest and most direct route from Jerusalem north into Galilee. No Jew would talk unnecessarily with any Samaritan, man or woman.

With merely a scowl in the stranger's direction, the woman turned and without a word resumed her work. Soon she began hauling up her long rope while the water plopped from her brimming bucket into the depths of the well.

The stranger suddenly broke the silence. "Give me a drink," he said.

Resting her heavy bucket on the stone curbing, the woman looked at the man in surprise. "How does it happen," she demanded, "that you who are a Jew asks for a drink from me, a Samaritan—and a woman?"

Anywhere else the wayfarer's request would have been regarded as perfectly natural, but not in Sychar. There it encountered a veritable jungle of inherited prejudices, hostilities springing from diverse religious customs, and centuries-old antagonisms between two groups that were actually quite closely related, but too different to be friends. Idolatrous practices introduced into Samaritan religion long ago by Babylonian colonists seemed to the Jews to taint everything in Samaria and make even a water container ritually unclean. The woman gazed in amazement at a Jew who was willing to risk ceremonial contamination by drinking from her water jar. Was this man unaware of the insuperable barriers of race, religion, and sex that divided them? There was something appealing, however, in his request. It was like a bridge thrown across the abyss separating Jews from Samaritans.

Ignoring the woman's question, the stranger spoke about some mysterious "living water" that *he* could give to *her*.

Intrigued by this, but bewildered by his talk of the gift of God and of his own identity she asked a practical question. "Sir, I observe that you have no rope nor bucket and you can see that this well is deep. Where will you get this living water of which you speak? Are you greater than our ancestor Jacob who dug this well?"

The traveler noted the woman's perplexity but continued, "Every one who drinks of this water will thirst again, but whoever drinks of the water that I shall give him will never thirst; the water that I shall give him will become in him a spring of water welling up to eternal life" (John 4.13-14).

Psalmists and prophets, most of them dwellers in arid lands, had long used the word "water" to convey the idea of God's life-giving energy, but poetic language like this confused the literal-minded Samaritan woman. If she had heard the Psalms sung and the books of prophecy read Sabbath after Sabbath in her synagogue, she might have understood the wayfarer's words and heard in them overtones of Jeremiah's prophecy from the Lord.

"For my people have committed two evils:
   they have forsaken me,
the fountain of living waters,
   and hewed out cisterns for themselves,
broken cisterns,
   that can hold no water."

JEREMIAH 2.13

Water was merely water to her, a daily necessity obtained only with toil. She had never said of the Lord, "With thee is the fountain of life" (Psalm 36.9). Nor had her heart stirred at the invitation, "Ho, every one who thirsts, come to the waters" (Isaiah 55.1). Her life was indeed a broken and dry cistern.

"Sir," she begged, disregarding the overtones of Jesus' words and thinking merely of her own convenience, "give me this wonderful water of which you speak, so that I will never be thirsty again nor have to come this long distance to draw water."

"Go, call your husband and then return here," directed the stranger, implying, perhaps, that his gifts are not for selfish enjoyment but to be shared.

The woman now faced a quandary—whether to admit her shame or conceal from this traveler her many marriages. No matter how outwardly poised she tried to be, sooner or later the facts of her irregular life came to light and her inner chaos was revealed. Trying to evade her present difficulty, she replied, "I have no husband."

True as this statement was, the wayfarer perceived what kind of life she lived. "You have had five husbands," he told her, "and you are not married to the man you now have."

Embarrassed, the woman changed the subject, first complimenting the stranger on his insight and then quickly raising an unanswerable theological problem.

"Sir, I see that you are a prophet!" she exclaimed ingratiatingly. "Please answer my perplexity. Our ancestors worshiped on this mountain," she declared, gesturing toward Mount Gerizim, "but you Jews say that people ought to worship in Jerusalem."

This dispute between Jews and Samaritans had reached a stalemate, with each side entrenched behind scriptural authority. The traveler avoided entanglement in a fruitless wrangle involving geography, Scripture, and theology, by raising the question to a higher level where it ceased to be a problem at all. He declared that the place where men worshiped God was of no importance.

At the heart of the dispute concerning Jerusalem and Gerizim was an inadequate idea of God. Only a true understanding of the Lord could heal this schism. The Samaritan sect worshiped a God they did not fully know, for they had only the Pentateuch's conception of him. But the Jews, taught by the full range of the sacred books known as the Prophets and the Writings as well as the Law, worshiped in the light of the whole religious tradition of Israel. Theirs was the living God of righteousness who, as the prophets taught, demanded righteousness of men. For the Jews, only religion joined with the morality of the prophets produced the good life. On this basis Christ's kingdom was founded. In it the differences between Jews and Samaritans would be abolished, with all men standing on an equal footing as worshipers in spirit and in truth.

Balancing her brimming water pot on the well curb, the Samaritan woman listened with deep attention while the man before her said,

"But the hour is coming, and now is, when the true worshipers will worship the Father in spirit and truth, for such the Father seeks to worship him. God is spirit, and those who worship him must worship in spirit and truth."

JOHN 4.23-24

The valley was filled with a noonday hush, interrupted only by the tinkling sound of distant streams and a slight rustling of leaves in the olive groves. The meadows lay green and silent beneath the hot sun. From time to time a faint sound punctuated the stillness as a drop rolled down the sides of the woman's water jar and splashed into the deep well.

The woman frowned in her effort to imagine a religion not bound to a particular place, a particular book, and a particular people, but the effort to understand the charter of spiritual liberty to which she had just listened was too much for her.

Looking at the wayfarer, she smiled as she attempted to bring this conversation, already far beyond her comprehension, to a close. "I know," she said, "that the Messiah who is called Christ is coming. When he comes he will explain all these things to us."

Quietly came the reply, "I who speak to you am he."

These words may express more than their surface meaning. Surely, they point far beyond the semireligious, semipolitical Messiah expected by first-century Jews. Jesus' mysterious affirmation, "I am he," doubtless preserves an authentic statement he used in order to explain his true nature. The words have a long history in the Scriptures. In the ancient Song of Moses, the Lord declared:

> "See now that I, even I, am he,
> and there is no god beside me."
> DEUTERONOMY 32.39

This affirmation, echoing God's revelation to Moses at the burning bush, "I AM WHO I AM" (Exodus 3.14), occurs repeatedly in the Old Testament, never more memorably than in verses from the great exilic prophet,

> "You are my witnesses," says the Lord,
>   "and my servant whom I have chosen,
> that you may know and believe me
>   and understand that I am He.
> Before me was no god formed,
>   nor shall there be any after me.
> I, I am the Lord,
>   and besides me there is no savior. . . .
> I am God, and also henceforth I am He."
> ISAIAH 43.10-11,13

May we not conclude that in applying to himself the ancient formula, "I am he," Jesus indicated who he really was and explained to those who were familiar with scriptural language the mystery of his person? Was he not saying that where he is there is God also?

Awed by Jesus' announcement, the woman became silent, her arguments and all her attempts to introduce a new subject at last ended. The amazing revelation she had just heard shattered her previous ideas and filled her with a sense of gratitude and devotion. She felt her old self swept clean away as she entered a new realm of being. The change in her was to be typical of those who beheld Christ's glory and found new life in him. She could not keep her experience to herself, but felt impelled to share it with all who would listen, publishing it far and wide, as had the shepherds, Anna, Andrew, and Philip.

In a symbolic gesture, for she had now found the inexhaustible fountain of living water and no longer suffered thirst, she left her brimming water jar near the well and hurried off to Sychar. There she roused those dozing in the noonday shade with her summons, "Come, see a man who told me everything I have ever done! Can he be the Christ?" Though convinced that he was, she was not dogmatic nor did she express her opinion as an assured fact. Like Philip, she issued an invitation to come and see.

Her neighbors and fellow townspeople were so amazed by the transformation of the woman from a sullen creature to one bubbling over with friendliness, that they quickly rose and followed her.

Jesus saw them coming down the road in their white garments and exclaimed to his disciples, who had rejoined him at the well, "Lift up your eyes and see, the fields are already white for harvest!"

It was, of course, a spiritual harvest, a harvest of souls for the Lord. During the next two days Jesus remained at Sychar with his new Samaritan friends. In the beginning their belief in him rested upon the testimony of the woman, but soon they attained to faith securely grounded upon their own experience. "We have heard him with our own ears," they announced to the woman who had first made Christ known in Samaria, "and we are now sure that this is indeed the One who will save the world!"

III

WHEN HE BEGAN

TO PREACH IN GALILEE

13

Simon Peter

JN 1.40-42; MK 1.16-18
(MT 4.18-20; cf. LK 5.1-11);
MT 14.22-33; MK 8.27-38
(MT 16.13-28; LK 9.18-26);
JN 6.66-69; MK 9.2-8
(MT 17.1-8; LK 9.28-36);
MK 14.29-31, 66-72
(MT 26.33-35, 69-75;
LK 22.31-34, 54-62;
JN 18.15-18, 25-27);
JN 20.1-10; LK 24.34;
JN 21.1-19; ACTS 1-5,10

"Simon, son of John, do you love me?"... And he said to him, "Lord, you know everything; you know that I love you." Jesus said to him, "Feed my sheep."

JOHN 21.17

SIMON PETER was fishing. With his brother Andrew he waded into the shallow, offshore waters of the Sea of Galilee at Capernaum. The morning was sunny with a gentle breeze ruffling the intensely blue surface of this so-called sea that is actually a lake of fresh, pure water. Shaped like a pear, it is thirteen miles long and eight miles across at its widest. Many people believed that God loved this beautiful expanse of water more than any other sea in the world. Capernaum was situated on its northwestern shore near the place where the Jordan River, flowing down from the north, empties into the lake.

Peter tossed his circular, weighted net into the air with a skillful, whirling motion and watched it fall cone-shaped beneath the waves. At each cast it imprisoned multitudes of darting creatures, for schools of fish were swimming in the shoals beneath the sparkling surface. The fishing was good this morning. Already Peter's and Andrew's partners in a nearby boat had caught a full load and were riding at anchor, mending their nets that had been torn by the weight of their catch.

The brothers Peter and Andrew had formed a partnership with Zebedee and his two sons James and John, pooling their fish in order to sell them more profitably. Theirs was a thriving business. Sometimes these five energetic and capable men, with the help of hired workers, would dry and salt their fish and transport them to inland markets as far away as Jerusalem.

Looking up from his net, Simon Peter saw a solitary figure striding along the beach toward them. The man's gait and the way he held his head gave, even at a distance, an impression of quiet power. Instantly Peter's face lighted up and his heart beat a little faster as he recognized Jesus. What would the Master say to them today, he wondered, joyfully anticipating some challenging or astonishing statement like those for which Jesus was already well known.

Simon Peter had first met Jesus not long before at the Jordan when his brother Andrew had brought him to the Master. That was the occasion on which Jesus had given him a new name, inappropriate at the time, but one of which he would finally be worthy.

"So you are Simon, the son of John," Jesus had said, looking intently at the strong, young fisherman standing before him. "Henceforth you shall be called a rock, you shall be called Cephas."

In Aramaic, the language spoken by Jesus, Cephas means rock, a name signifying dependability and strength. Its Greek equivalent, *Petros,* is the name generally given to Simon in the original Greek text of the New Testament. English versions translate *Petros* as Peter.

After the first encounter with Jesus at the Jordan, the two brothers doubtless returned briefly to their native city of Bethsaida where they had been brought up in the Jewish traditions of their father, John. In Bethsaida, however, this heritage seems to have been enriched by a cosmopolitan outlook. The two boys had made friends with Gentile boys, speaking Greek with them. The language opened to them the whole world of Greek culture. Even their names, Simon and Andrew, were Greek, for surprisingly enough, their father had not given them Aramaic names. This Gentile background may well have influenced Peter in later years to champion world-wide Christianity.

Shortly after their first meeting with Jesus, the brothers moved with their families a few miles southwest of their old home in Bethsaida to the lakeside town of Capernaum, attracted, no doubt, by its teeming offshore waters. Peter bought or built a new home at Capernaum. The Gospels record one or two occasions when Jesus was a guest in his house. After the wedding at Cana, he, too, seems to have made Capernaum his headquarters.

From here he set out on his earliest preaching missions through the villages and towns of Galilee accompanied, perhaps, by Peter and Andrew. At first they went along as friends of Jesus, procuring food and lodging for him and his party and helping him to manage the crowds. But more and more as these two young fishermen were caught up in enthusiasm for the kingdom of God, they desired to be its heralds.

Even in the quiet intervals when the brothers returned from one of the Master's missions and resumed their fishing, they could not forget Jesus. He seemed to be the true man beside whom all others appeared inferior. He dominated their thoughts. His teachings seemed to them to reduce the chaos of the world to ordered beauty. His mysterious greatness, so different from that of John the Baptist, awed them. What, they wondered, was the secret of his oneness with God? If they became his disciples, would he teach them this secret? The role of a disciple would, they knew, be an exacting one, but they soberly counted its cost, or as much of it as they could then foresee. They were now ready, if Jesus wanted them, to devote their lives to him.

All these thoughts were in Peter's and Andrew's minds on the sunny morning at Capernaum while they stood knee-deep in the shallows, their nets in their hands, waiting for Jesus to approach along the beach.

Across the water his clear voice rang out. "Come, follow me," they heard him call, "and I will make you fishers of men!"

For Peter and Andrew the sun suddenly shone brighter and the waves seemed to lap the shore with a more joyful rhythm. This was the moment for which they had waited. Everything else had been a prelude to it. Now they would share in Jesus' life as his intimate friends and help him establish the kingdom of God. Behind them lay their ordinary lives as Galilean fishermen, fathers of families, householders in Capernaum, while ahead stretched dazzling prospects. Jesus promised to make them fishers for the souls of men so that all those destined for the heavenly kingdom might be gathered up for the Lord as in a great net.

The words "fishers of men" had long ago been spoken in connection with threatened judgment upon Israel. Jeremiah had prophesied, "Behold, I am sending for many fishers, says the Lord, and they shall catch them [the people of Israel]. . . . And I will doubly recompense their iniquity and their sin, because they have polluted my land . . ." (Jeremiah 16.16,18). But the two Galilean fishermen knew that Jesus used the words "fishers of men" in a different sense from that of Jeremiah. The Master did not intend that Peter and Andrew should catch men for judgment or punishment. These two disciples were to rescue men from ignorance and sin and guide them to the heavenly kingdom. It was to creative, saving work like this that the brothers were called. In their hour of dedication, Peter and Andrew waded ashore, carefully folded their nets, which they would not be using for a while, and fell into step beside the Master.

On that sparkling morning in Capernaum, young Peter could not have forseen all that lay ahead of him, the joy and the heartbreak, the despair and the ineffable hope, culminating in a sublime sense of the ultimate reality of God's love. All of this is recorded in the more than one hundred and fifty references to him in the Gospels, the Acts of the Apostles, and some of the Letters. As an outstanding disciple, not only chief of the inner group of three composed of himself and James and John, but spokesman for the whole company of the Twelve and, after the resurrection, the first leader of the primitive Church, Peter is more often mentioned in the New Testament than any other person, except Jesus himself. While the stories of other followers of the Master must often be reconstructed from brief records, Peter's story is so generously documented that to tell it adequately would require an entire book. His personality, however, can be sketched from a few revealing episodes.

The one in which Peter attempted to walk on the water reveals this disciple's complex character and symbolizes both the strength and the weakness of his faith. Legendary elements doubtless color this story. Matthew, the only evangelist to narrate the episode (14.28-31), here presents a portrait of Peter that is in essential agreement with Peter's character as delineated in the other Gospels. All show him as a courageous, loyal, unpredictable, and occasionally wavering follower of Jesus. If Peter's nature sometimes had the unstable quality of water, it was more often of fire and rock.

It was a wild, dark night at sea. Peter and the other disciples, having left Jesus behind on the shore, were crossing the lake when a sudden storm broke upon them. This is a common occurrence on the Sea of Galilee, encircled as it is by lofty hills. The tempest stirred up such turbulent waves that the disciples' open fishing boat was violently buffeted. Fear was mingled with their sense of awe at this manifestation of God's power.

> The voice of the Lord is upon the waters;
>   the God of glory thunders. . . .
> The Lord sits enthroned over the flood;
>   the Lord sits enthroned as king for ever.
>
> PSALM 29.3,10

Toward morning, while they still fought the wind and waves, the frightened men saw Jesus walking toward them over the water.

"Courage," he called to them. "It is I: have no fear."

Impulsively Peter shouted into the tempest, "Lord, if it is really you, bid me come to you on the water."

"Come!" said Jesus.

Climbing out of his boat, Peter took a few steps, his eyes on Jesus.

Then, as the dark waves seemed to menace him, he glanced fearfully at the wild fury of the gale and began to sink. "Lord, save me!" he cried.

Immediately stretching out his hand, Jesus caught his terrified disciple and said, "O man of little faith! Why did you fear? Why did you not trust me?"

As this story shows, Peter was the most human of men, ever aspiring in spirit, yet continually enmeshed in the net of existence. The stories told of him record his extraordinary spiritual daring and his frequent failures. After being found wanting and receiving pardon, he always tried again, all the while demonstrating the reality of God's forgiveness and God's amazing grace in using so imperfect a man to carry out the divine purpose.

One day while Jesus and his disciples were traveling near the northern borders of ancient Israel where the tribe of Dan had settled centuries earlier, they came to Caesarea Philippi. It was a comparatively new city, having been built twenty or thirty years before by Herod Philip in territory bequeathed to him by his father, Herod the Great. The city occupied a magnificent site on the southwestern slope of Mount Hermon. This highest peak of the rugged, well-wooded Anti-Lebanon range rises in snow-capped splendor nearly ten thousand feet and on clear days its white crown is reflected in the blue waters of the Sea of Galilee some fifty miles away. Protected on the north by the great mountain barrier, Caesarea Philippi looked southwest over the fertile Huleh plain. Groves of evergreens grew on the city's plateau, while oaks, olives, hawthorns, and oleanders flourished in the neighborhood. Philip named the city for Tiberius Caesar and himself and built a shining white marble temple in honor of the deified Roman emperor. Not far away, in a cave from which issues the clear stream that is one of the main sources of the Jordan, the god Pan was worshiped.

Many evidences of paganism in this region—heathen altars, votive images, marble statues of naiads of the streams and satyrs of the woods—all these must have dismayed the disciples. It was here that Jesus gathered them around him and asked his penetrating question, "Who do men say that I am?"

During Jesus' ministry in Galilee, people had often discussed who he was, advancing various theories which the disciples now reported to him. Herod Antipas, half-brother of Herod Philip, no doubt suffering from guilt because he had executed John the Baptist, feared that Jesus was that stern, wilderness prophet returned from the dead. Other people thought that Jesus might be the prophet Elijah. Jesus dismissed these popular attempts to explain the mystery of his person and, gazing steadily at his disciples, asked them, "But who do *you* say that I am?"

No one spoke for a moment while they all recalled the weeks and months spent tramping the roads of Palestine and visiting innumerable villages with this man. They had seen him hungry and weary; they had heard him proclaim the good news to eager crowds; they had watched him heal the sick; they had camped many a night with him beneath the stars. Who was he? The eleven waited, as they often did, for Peter to voice their thoughts. They trusted his insight in matters like this, knowing that he was usually the first to find adequate words for their convictions.

Peter's close human fellowship with Jesus had convinced him of the greatness of this man from Nazareth. In him Peter found justice, mercy, and love incarnated. Jesus seemed to hold the key to life's meaning, even to be himself that key. Peter believed that the Master was the One sent from God to free his people. In an outpouring of enthusiastic devotion, Peter expressed the faith of himself and his fellow disciples, exclaiming, "You are the Messiah, the Anointed One, the Christ!"

"Blessed are you, Simon, son of John!" cried Jesus. "No man taught you this truth, but it was revealed to you by my heavenly Father."

In Matthew's account of this incident, a much discussed passage adds a statement that is capable of various interpretations.

"And I tell you, you are Peter, and on this rock I will build my church, and the powers of death shall not prevail against it. I will give you the keys of the kingdom of heaven, and whatever you bind on earth shall be bound in heaven, and whatever you loose on earth shall be loosed in heaven."

MATTHEW 16.18-19

Peter's role was unique and his magnificent labors to establish the Church were outstanding. His faith that Jesus is the Christ of God was the rock on which the Church was built. But other apostles, as well, were foundation stones of the holy city of God. "And the wall of the city had twelve foundations, and on them the twelve names of the twelve apostles of the Lamb" (Revelation 21.14). Christ, however, is the cornerstone of his Church, which is

the household of God, built upon the foundation of the apostles and prophets, Christ Jesus himself being the cornerstone, in whom the whole structure is joined together and grows into a holy temple in the Lord; in whom you also are built into it for a dwelling place of God in the Spirit.

EPHESIANS 2.19-22

As for the "keys of the kingdom," they became Peter's symbol and a sign of his authority. This authority to "bind" and to "loose" belonged not only to Peter but, according to Matthew 18.18 and John 20.23, to all the apostles.

Despite Peter's confession at Caesarea Philippi, he was then far from understanding its full meaning, for the idea of a Messiah victorious over every enemy still lingered in his mind. Jesus' victory was to be of a different kind. To many people it would appear a defeat rather than a triumph. Even the disciples needed to be prepared for the shock of coming events. Lest the Twelve interpret his Messiahship falsely, Jesus forbade them to proclaim it. Then he patiently began to teach them the meaning of all that would soon take place—his rejection, suffering, death, and his rising again after three days.

Peter, with all the intensity of his passionate nature, repudiated the idea that Jesus must suffer. It was inconceivable to him that the

Messiah should die. This must not—it could not—happen. Peter, sure that his own ideas were right and those of Jesus false, took his Master by the hand to emphasize the importance of what he was about to say. With great vehemence he rebuked Jesus for saying that rejection and death awaited him.

Overconfident and still basking in the Master's recent words of blessing, Peter was unprepared for Jesus' sharp reproof of a worldly point of view. "Out of my sight, tempter," he cried, "get behind me, Satan! For you are not on the side of God but of men."

After this Jesus began to teach them the cost of discipleship, saying, "Whoever wants to come with me must leave self behind, take up his cross, and follow me. Whoever tries to save his life will lose it; but the man who loses his life for my sake and for the Gospel will save it."

When these and other hard teachings began to cause dismay among the multitudes, many half-hearted adherents, unwilling to pay the price of discipleship, withdrew from Jesus. Watching the crowds deserting him, the Master turned sorrowfully to the Twelve. "Will you also leave me?" he asked.

Instantly Peter, his voice deep with emotion, answered for them all. "Lord, who else could we go to? Your words bring us that for which we have long waited—they show the way to everlasting life. We believe and we know that you are the Holy One of God." So declared not a self-willed, worldly man but Peter the Rock.

Even after such moments of insight, Peter was sometimes torn by doubt. How could Jesus be the Christ if his life were to end in shame and suffering? Peter was still struggling with this paradox when Jesus took him aside and, with James and John, led him to the top of a mountain to pray. On the summit the three disciples saw their beloved Master transfigured, radiant with divine glory so that even his garments shone with a whiteness no dyer could give them. Peter saw in the brightness two great men of Israel's past talking with Jesus of his approaching death. The shining figures were those of Moses and Elijah, the first representing the Law and the second, the prophets. Awed by this vision, Peter impulsively proposed, "Master, it is good that we are here. Let us build three shelters, one for you, one for Moses, and one for Elijah." He wanted to prolong the vision and remain in the glory of God's presence, safe upon the mountaintop where he need not face the dark crisis of which Jesus had spoken. Though Peter's very human wish was not granted, he received on the mountaintop heavenly confirmation of the confession he had made at Caesarea Philippi. Out of the bright cloud of divine glory enveloping them, he heard a Voice that said, "This is my beloved Son; listen to him."

Of all the stories told of Peter, perhaps the best known is that of his denial. While the disciples were eating the Last Supper with their Master, he warned them all, but especially Peter, that they faced temptations. "Simon, Simon," Jesus said, using his old name rather than the one that compared him to a rock, "Satan claimed his right to sift you all like wheat, but I have prayed for you that your faith may not fail." Then, looking directly at Peter, Jesus commanded him, "When you have turned back again to me, strengthen your brethren."

"Turn back again to Jesus!" repeated Peter, horrified at the thought he would ever turn away from him in the first place. Declaring his loyalty, Peter said, "Lord, I am ready to go with you to prison and to death!"

"I tell you," replied Jesus, who understood Peter's contradictory qualities, his bravery and cowardice, his faith and doubt, his wisdom and unthinking impulsiveness, his unreliability in a crisis, yet his great reserves of inner strength, "I tell you, Peter, the cock will not crow today before you have three times denied that you know me."

Before cockcrow of the momentous Friday, Peter not only failed Jesus in the Garden of Gethsemane but he denied him three times. In the darkness among the olive trees, instead of strengthening his Master with his prayers, Peter slept through Jesus' agonized struggle to accept God's will.

"Are you asleep, Simon?" Jesus asked of the heavily breathing figure huddled in his cloak. "Could you not keep awake for a single hour? Watch with me all of you and pray that you may not enter into temptation. I know that your spirit is willing, but your flesh is weak."

Jesus' arrest soon followed. Peter, keeping a safe distance between himself and the soldiers, trailed them back to Jerusalem and into the courtyard of the high priest's palace where Jesus was tried. The court-yard was dark and cold. While Peter waited, warming himself at a bonfire, one of the palace serving maids, seeing his face illuminated by the flames, recognized him and accused him of being Jesus' disciple.

"I do not know what you mean," Peter replied. She accused him a second time, but Peter merely repeated his first declaration.

Some of the bystanders then began to taunt Peter, saying, "You certainly must be one of them, for your harsh speech betrays the fact that you are a Galilean."

Dawn was now at hand. With an oath Peter made his third denial, "I do not even know this man of whom you speak." Immediately the cock crowed and at this reminder of Jesus' words, Peter came to himself and, knowing that he had failed his beloved Master, he broke down and wept.

The Gospels contain no record of Peter during the crucifixion and the burial of Jesus, nor on the following day, the Sabbath—days which the Galilean fisherman must have spent in utter despair. Not only was everything he had hoped for and labored for destroyed, but he knew himself to be a failure.

Before dawn of the first day of the week, he heard someone knocking on the door of his Jerusalem lodgings. In great alarm he opened the door to Mary Magdalene who had run all the way from Jesus' tomb. Peter saw that she was trembling and in great distress. "They have taken the Lord out of his tomb," she panted, "and we do not know where they have laid him."

Who would steal the Lord's body? Some nefarious plot must be afoot. Peter could not endure the ultimate horror of his Master's body being desecrated and, instantly pulling himself together, he ran to the tomb. Another disciple, younger than himself, accompanied him. The other disciple (was he John?) outran Peter and reached the tomb first.

Breathless from running, Peter arrived soon after his companion and, like him, saw that the huge stone blocking the entrance had been rolled away. Who could have done this? It could not have been the women. Being bolder than the younger man, Peter ventured into the burial chamber. Distraught though he was, he observed in exact detail the position of the grave cloths. Something was strange about them. If Jesus' body had been stolen, would not the cloths have been flung aside? But he saw that though they were empty, they did not seem to have been touched. It was as though the body had passed through them leaving them to collapse. The linen napkin that had swathed his head still lay in its round shape in the place where Jesus' head had been. The burial cloths seemed like a chrysalis from which a butterfly had emerged. Peter did not understand the meaning of this phenomenon until later.

Returning with a heavy heart to the house where he was staying, he was by turns puzzled, fearful, grieved. He did not know that his companion, having followed him into the tomb, had perceived that the grave cloths indicated an amazing truth. A material body had here been transformed into a spiritual body. This truth dawned on Peter slowly as memories of his Master took possession of his mind.

He remembered how Jesus had named him Cephas and had summoned him to discipleship, how he had fed the multitudes, walked on the water, taught the crowds, healed every kind of disease, and appeared transfigured on the mountain. Always Jesus had maintained his perfect, unbroken communion with his heavenly Father. Surely such a person could not die, Peter declared to himself. The idea brought him up short. Such a man had not died! He was one with God, and death could not claim him. As Peter was to say a few weeks hence, "God raised him up, having loosed the pangs of death, because it was not possible for him to be held by it" (Act 2.24).

On the first Easter Day to which he had awakened at Mary Magdalene's knock, Peter's extraordinary insight was vindicated when he encountered his risen Lord. Though the story of this event is not narrated in the Gospels, two ancient records testify to the fact that it took place. The oldest record, written by the apostle Paul about twenty-five years after the event, states what he had doubtless learned as early as A.D. 33 or 34 at the time of his conversion. Paul wrote:

> For I delivered to you as of first importance what I also received, that Christ died for our sins in accordance with the scriptures, that he was buried, that he was raised on the third day in accordance with the scriptures and *that he appeared to Cephas* [Peter], then to the twelve. Then he appeared to more than five hundred brethren at one time, most of whom are still alive, though some have fallen asleep.
>
> I CORINTHIANS 15.3-6

This statement by Paul to the church at Corinth is corroborated by a sentence in Luke's Gospel, a mere fragment of an untold story. It is the witness of the eleven and those gathered with them. "The Lord has risen indeed, and has appeared to Simon!" (Luke 24.34).

The resurrection of Christ became the keystone of Peter's faith. His experience of the living presence of his Lord erased the shame of the crucifixion and validated Peter's great confession at Caesarea Philippi that Jesus was the Christ. Peter and his companions saw Christ's resurrection victory over evil and death as the final sign that God prevails.

Unlike the story of Peter's first encounter with the risen Christ, of which only the two fragments quoted above survive, the last meeting between this disciple and his Master is narrated in great detail in the final chapter, or appendix, of John's Gospel. On this occasion, as at his call to discipleship, Peter was fishing. We have already learned of the failure of this night's fishing in the story of Nathanael-Bartholomew, one of the six men in the boat with Peter. When the discouraged men acted upon the advice of a stranger who called to them from the beach, their nets became filled with fish. Because of this abundance, one of the disciples exclaimed to Peter, "It is the Lord!"

Hearing this, Peter impetuously jumped into the shallow water and waded ashore while his companions followed in their boat, dragging the heavy net. On the beach they saw fish broiling over a charcoal fire. Nearby there was bread.

"Bring some of the fish you have just caught," said the stranger. Then he invited them all, saying, "Come and have breakfast."

When he took bread and broke it and gave it to them, they knew from his familiar words and gestures that the stranger was indeed their Master and their risen Lord. Yet all of them hesitated to question him.

After breakfast Jesus asked his chief disciple, "Simon, son of John, do you love me more than these others do?"

Peter replied, "Yes, Lord, you know that I love you."

"Then feed my lambs."

Three times in all, corresponding to Peter's three denials, Jesus asked the same question, "Simon, son of John, do you love me?"

The third time, Peter was hurt. Yet, remembering his weaknesses and confident that Jesus understood him, he replied, "Lord, you know all things; you know that I love you."

For the third time Jesus repeated his symbolic command, "Feed my sheep," bidding him, as on the day long ago when he was called to discipleship, "Follow me."

The way in which Peter carried out his Lord's command is narrated in the first twelve chapters of the Acts of the Apostles. These are heroic chapters showing the great heights of courage and leadership to which this disciple attained. Because he was always himself in need of forgiveness, he was well qualified to lead the society of the forgiven which is the Church of Christ.

There were many reasons for Peter's pre-eminence in the Church, but the ultimate one was his continuing fellowship with his Lord. This strong bond governed his life and permeated his relations with other people. Peter's example may well have been the basis for this advice to the Christians of Philippi, "Let your bearing toward one another arise out of your life in Christ Jesus" (Philippians 2.5, New English Bible).

The *Acts of Peter,* a third-century document of doubtful historical value, contains an account of Peter's meeting with his Lord on the eve of the apostle's death in Rome. Though the story is fictional, it shows the same, very human Peter known to us in the Scriptures, a man still self-willed and impulsive as of old, yet loyal to the end.

Peter, according to this legend, was in Rome during one of the persecutions of Christians. Fearing that he would be put to death for his faith, he disguised himself and fled from the city at night along the Appian Way. In the darkness he met Jesus coming toward him.

"Lord," cried Peter, "where are you going? *Domine, quo vadis?*"

"I go to Rome to be crucified."

"Are you being crucified again?"

"Yes, I am being crucified again."

Peter came swiftly to himself. Unwilling for his Lord to suffer in his place, the old disciple turned around and returned to Rome where on the following day he was martyred. At his own request he was crucified head downward, not considering himself worthy to die in the same manner as his Lord.

Peter's statement of faith, whether written by him or for him, rested not only upon the shining marvel of the mountaintop transfiguration, but upon his intimate, eyewitness knowledge of his Lord.

For we did not follow cleverly devised myths when we made known to you the power and coming of our Lord Jesus Christ, but we were eyewitnesses of his majesty. For when he received honor and glory from God the Father and the voice was borne to him by the Majestic Glory, "This is my beloved Son, with whom I am well pleased," we heard this voice borne from heaven, for we were with him on the holy mountain.

2 PETER 1.16-18

14

James and John

MK 1.19-20 (MT 4.21-22;
LK 5.10); MK 3.17; 9.2;
LK 9.51-56; MK 10.35-45
(MT 20.20-28); MK 9.38-40
(LK 9.49-50); JN 21.1-2;
ACTS 1.12-14; 12.1-3;
GAL. 2.9
The Beloved Disciple:
JN 1.35-39; 13.23-26; 19.26-
27; 20.1-9; 21.7

And going on a little farther, he saw James the son of Zebedee and John his brother, who were in their boat mending the nets. And immediately he called them; and they left their father Zebedee in the boat with the hired servants, and followed him.

MARK 1.19-20

SOUTHWARD THROUGH Galilee journeyed a large group of Jesus' disciples and followers accompanying their Master to Jerusalem. At the head marched two young men chosen to lead the company across the Samaritan border and along the hazardous roads of that unfriendly country. The two were James and John, the fishermen sons of Zebedee of Capernaum.

With long swinging steps James and John strode confidently forward setting a difficult pace for the older men and the Galilean women to follow. James and John felt jubilant this day: they were sure of their mission and fired with zeal for their Master. Every movement of their lithe, young bodies expressed verve and enthusiasm. Because they expected that when Jesus reached Jerusalem he would be acclaimed Messiah, each mile that brought the brothers nearer the Holy City heightened their sense of exaltation.

The thought of crossing Samaria awakened no foreboding in James and John, for they knew that the Samaritans, no less than the Jews, looked for the One who was to come in the name of the Lord.

The brothers were sure that the people of Samaria would welcome Jesus as the Messiah. Had not the woman at Jacob's well and the inhabitants of Sychar already declared him to be the Savior of the world?

Jesus, however, was prepared for Samaritan hostility. This was often directed against Jewish pilgrims bound, as were these travelers, for one of the great religious festivals in Jerusalem. Galilean pilgrims usually journeyed by the safer though longer route on the far side of the Jordan, through Perea and on by way of Jericho to the Holy City, thus avoiding Samaria altogether. Jesus had set his course directly through this land seething with ill will against the Jews. But while his company was still crossing Galilee, he had taken the precaution of sending two messengers across the border to arrange for the first night's lodging in unfriendly territory.

James and John, on their march across Galilee, passed through the luxuriant Valley of Jezreel which was enlivened that morning with bird songs and the sound of water flowing in the valley's many streams. The beauty of the landscape provided a pleasant accompaniment to the brothers' thoughts. A gentle breeze stirred the ripening grain, flowers of many hues opened their petals to the sun, sheep grazed contentedly in the lush grasslands, and the orchards and vineyards were in blossom. To the south the travelers saw the rugged skyline of Samaria, through whose mountain passes and fertile valleys their road continued south into Judea and on to the Holy City. Today Samaria's mountains appeared misty-blue against the more intense blue of the sky, giving to the whole scene the poetic quality of one of the psalms.

> The hills gird themselves with joy,
> the meadows clothe themselves with flocks,
> the valleys deck themselves with grain,
> they shout and sing together for joy.
> PSALM 65.12-13

The Valley of Jezreel, with its western arm called the Plain of Esdraelon, abounded in history. The brothers remembered that Deborah and Barak defeated Sisera, the Canaanite king, at Megiddo. Gideon routed the Midianites encamped near Mount Moreh at the edge of the plain. On the heights of Mount Gilboa overlooking the valley, Saul and his son Jonathan, in a battle with the Philistines, met their death. The Valley of Jezreel in years gone by had echoed to the clatter of King Ahab's speeding chariot; Naboth's vineyard was located here; and the prophets Elijah and Elisha, staffs in hand, crossed and recrossed the plain on missions for the Lord.

Stirred as James and John were by such memories, more recent events occupied their thoughts. Since the sunlit morning, months ago, when Jesus had encountered them mending their nets in a boat anchored offshore at Capernaum, the brothers had been part of an extraordinary movement. Like their friends Peter and Andrew, they had eagerly accepted Jesus' summons to discipleship, though it meant leaving their father Zebedee with the hired helpers in the family's fishing boat. Thereafter the brothers had accompanied Jesus on his preaching missions. All that they saw—sick people cured by Jesus' power, devils cast out, the blind given back their sight, the despairing given hope—all these wonders convinced them that God was moving mightily in the affairs of men and that his kingdom was at hand.

After Peter's great confession at Caesarea Philippi, "You are the Christ," and after the shining glory of the transfiguration, James and John became impatient for the climax of their Master's ministry. They believed that their present journey was his royal progress up to the Holy City to claim his appointed throne.

Yesterday, when he set his face to go to Jerusalem, the awesome solemnity of his manner as he spoke of his coming rejection and death had cast a momentary shadow over them all. Was he really a king on the eve of his accession, they wondered, puzzled by the strangeness of his words. But once on the road, the brothers' buoyant spirits returned. As they approached Samaria they talked of the exalted roles that would surely be theirs in Christ's coming kingdom. Bound as they were by the thinking of their own time, they had thus far failed to understand what Jesus meant when he spoke about the nature of his coming victory and the character of his reign.

At the Samaritan frontier their road entered a pass between the hills, and the border village of Engannim came into view. Here the brothers halted while two men approached.

"These are our messengers returning!" John exclaimed, anticipating the triumphant reception the men had surely arranged for Jesus in Samaria.

As the men drew nearer, John saw the troubled expressions on their faces. They shook their heads warningly, motioning Jesus to turn back. What had happened?

Their story was soon told. The people of Engannim had scoffed when Jesus' emissaries claimed that he was the Messiah.

"He is no Messiah!" declared the Samaritans. "If he were, he would remain here to restore our temple on Mount Gerizim. Whoever travels on to Jerusalem is an enemy of Samaria."

It was useless for the messengers to argue. "Begone, you hated Jews," shouted a crowd of angry villagers, picking up stones with which to enforce their command. "We want none of your kind here."

Enraged by this reception, James and John shook their fists toward the inhospitable village. Even Elijah, they thought, had suffered no greater indignity on the occasion when soldiers had come to take him prisoner. Then, according to the legend in 2 Kings 1.9-12, the old prophet had invoked fire from heaven to consume the soldiers. Avenging fire—that was what the Samaritan insult merited, James and John decided. They could do no better than follow Elijah's example.

"Master," they shouted, their faces contorted in fury, "do you want us to call down fire from heaven to burn up all these evil Samaritans?"

Jesus turned toward his two hot-headed disciples and looked at them sadly. They had failed him, but not because they lacked loyalty or were deficient in zeal. Though they possessed these two qualities to a high degree, they still had not grasped the purpose of his mission. Their vehemence prevented them from seeing the basic quality of his life. He was a man of peace, a Savior to whom avenging fire was completely alien. Jesus rebuked his two overzealous disciples and, according to a statement recorded in several ancient manuscripts, said to them, "You do not know what manner of spirit you are of; for the Son of man came not to destroy men's lives but to save them" (Luke 9.55, footnote).

Chagrined by their failure, James and John accepted their Master's rebuke, following him when he and his company turned around and approached Jerusalem by another route. It may have been after this incident that Jesus gave Zebedee's sons their nickname "Boanerges," meaning "sons of thunder."

John's intense, almost blind, loyalty to his Master sometimes made him intolerant of anyone outside the circle of Jesus' chosen companions. One day this disciple encountered a stranger, an exorcist, who, by invoking the name of Jesus, cured people afflicted with mental sickness. This use of his Master's name as a magic formula was unauthorized and it made John angry. He failed to perceive that God's grace was actually working through the stranger enabling him to relieve scores of sufferers. Rudely pushing his way through the crowd John confronted the exorcist.

"We forbid you to heal in the name of Jesus," he cried. "You have no right to use his name since you are not one of us—you are not a disciple."

John was so pleased with his successful defense of the Master's reputation that when he reported this incident to Jesus he expected to be commended. But instead of a smile he saw only dismay on Jesus' face.

"Do not stop this stranger from curing any sick people he can," Jesus commanded John, who had yet to learn his Master's unlimited compassion and his complete freedom from exclusiveness. "No one performing a mighty deed in my name," he declared, "can, at the same time, say anything against me. For he that is not against us is for us."

On another occasion, when James and John were again traveling toward Jerusalem, they drew apart from their fellow disciples and, in voices pitched too low to be overheard, discussed Jesus' coming kingdom.

"Will he sit upon a throne?" asked James, trying to imagine what it would be like when they reached the Holy City.

"If he does, then which of us will be given the two chief seats, the one on his right and the one on his left?" John wondered aloud.

James was quick to catch his brother's meaning. "Yes, it is none too soon to decide which of us Twelve will become the two most important men of his realm."

The brothers agreed that the chief seats were theirs by right. The sacrifices they had made for Jesus and their loyalty to him entitled them, they felt, to this reward. It would be clever, they decided, to have these seats assigned to them without delay—before Peter and the others might claim them.

Taking Jesus aside, the brothers begged him, "Master, we want you to grant our request."

Jesus looked at his two disciples. "What do you want me to do for you?" It was the question he often asked of those who came to him.

"Give us the chief seats," John demanded, his voice hard with calculation.

"Let one of us sit on your right hand and the other on the left when you occupy the throne of glory in your kingdom," added James.

"You do not know what you are asking!" exclaimed the Master.

His disciples still did not understand the nature of his kingdom. By making their selfish request for worldly power, the brothers showed how far they were from understanding their Master's mission and the quality of his life.

Quickly Jesus challenged them, asking if they were able to drink his cup of suffering and to be baptized with him in the dark waters of humiliation and death. All too easily, for their eyes were focused upon renown, the confident young men replied, "We are able."

Jesus explained that he had no authority to give them the chief seats they desired. In his realm greatness is not a favor that can be bestowed but a quality that is developed through service and sacrifice. His throne was to be a cross; his glory would be revealed in his sacrifice. Jesus knew, however, that in the end James and John, having at last overcome their selfish search for eminence, would one day drink the cup of martyrdom and enter into true glory.

News of the request made by Zebedee's sons spread like wildfire to the other disciples, producing jealousy and discord among them. To halt this insidious growth and teach his followers what he expected of them, Jesus declared, "Whoever would be great among you must be your servant. . . . For the Son of man also came not to be served but to serve, and to give his life as a ransom for many" (Mark 10.43,45).

The Gospel of Matthew, possibly in order to minimize the self-seeking of James and John and thus protect the reputations of these great apostles, gives a slightly different version of the incident. Matthew attributes the request for the chief seats, not to the men themselves, but to their mother. Thus her sons escape blame for worldliness, while their mother appears only as an overambitious parent asking the best for her children.

This mother's identity is a biblical puzzle. Matthew 27.56 states that she and two women companions, Mary Magdalene and Mary the mother of James and Joseph, witnessed the crucifixion. Zebedee's wife was there, doubtless because of her devotion to the Master, a devotion no less deep than that of her two sons. The parallel account in Mark 15.40 also mentions three women at the cross—Mary Magdalene, another Mary, and a certain Salome. Were Mark's three women at the cross the same individuals as those described by Matthew? We cannot be absolutely sure of this, but if they were, then Zebedee's wife of Matthew's account is Salome in Mark's version.

John 19.25 opens a new avenue of speculation concerning Zebedee's wife. "But standing by the cross of Jesus were his mother, and his mother's sister, Mary the wife of Clopas, and Mary Magdalene." Here again, in addition to Jesus' mother, are three women, two of them apparently the Marys of the other two accounts. Again assuming that John's three women witnesses are the same as those given in Matthew and Mark, it would appear that the third woman, Mary of

Nazareth's sister, was the same person as Salome and Zebedee's wife. According to this identification, James and John would have been cousins of Jesus, a relationship that might explain their request for the chief seats. We lack proof, however, that the three evangelists, Matthew, Mark, and John, were describing the same three women at the cross, so their identity remains uncertain. Furthermore the Gospels and the Book of Acts nowhere mention any kinship between Jesus and his two outstanding disciples, James and John.

The Gospels portray these two young fishermen as very human in their failure to understand Jesus. Their faults are not glossed over but honestly shown; in fact there seems to be an emphasis on their weaknesses. Thus, as is the case with Peter, in reading their story we see two men rather than a pair of improbable figures wearing halos. In addition to their other shortcomings, James and John fell asleep during the night in Gethsemane and fled at Jesus' arrest. (It is possible, of course, that their flight had been prearranged by the Master to ensure that his mission survive his death.) Despite these candidly related stories, the sons of Zebedee were men whom Jesus found worthy to be his closest companions. If their full story were known, it would undoubtedly contain innumerable acts of devotion and courage confirming our impression of these disciples as men of unusual dedication and deep spiritual perception. Both brothers witnessed the glory of the risen Christ (Luke 24.33-36; Matthew 28.16-17; John 21.1-2) and in the following months and years of stress and danger, they became pillars of the early Church. Much of Christianity rests upon their witness and their faith.

James' life ended shortly before A.D. 44 during the reign of Herod Agrippa I, grandson of Herod the Great and friend of the Roman emperor Caligula. Agrippa, in an attempt to curry favor with his Jewish subjects by persecuting the young Church, imprisoned Peter and, as Acts 12.1-3 records, had James put to death by the sword. James, at his death an outstanding leader of the Church, is the only one of the twelve disciples whose martyrdom is recorded in the Bible.

It inevitably brings to mind Jesus' words to him, "The cup that I drink you will drink; and with the baptism with which I am baptized, you will be baptized" (Mark 10.39).

Zebedee's son James is often called James the Great to distinguish him from another James, also one of the Twelve. A sixth- or seventh-century legend, which conflicts with the record of his early death in Jerusalem, credits James the Great with establishing Christianity in Spain, where the city of Santiago was named for him. Because of his alleged pilgrimages, a pilgrim's staff, a traveler's gourd of water, and a scallop shell became his symbols.

His brother John's chief symbols are an eagle typifying soaring inspiration and a book representing the Gospel bearing his name. Like James' mission to Spain, John's authorship of the Fourth Gospel, as well as of the three Letters of John and the Revelation, is a time-honored belief deeply imbedded in Christian thought and memorably expressed in many works of art. Though the very complex problem of the authorship of the five New Testament books ascribed to John cannot be discussed here, we should note that most modern scholars do not credit John the son of Zebedee with the actual writing of these books.

Another puzzling question remains concerning the disciple John whose story in the three Synoptic Gospels and the Book of Acts we have already sketched. Was this John the same person as the beloved disciple who often appears in the Fourth Gospel? The Synoptic Gospels do not speak of the disciple whom Jesus loved, while John the son of Zebedee is never mentioned by name in the Fourth Gospel. Is the John of the Synoptic Gospels the same person as the beloved disciple of the Fourth Gospel? Though many people assume that this is so, we have no certain proof that it is.

John 1.35-39 is often considered to be the first reference to the beloved disciple, though he is not actually mentioned as such in these verses. He is merely designated as Andrew's companion when these two men heard John the Baptist exclaim, as Jesus passed by, "Behold, the Lamb of God!" If the unnamed man of this story was the beloved disciple, his friendship with Jesus, like that of Andrew and of Peter, spanned the Master's entire ministry.

At the Last Supper, where Mark states that only the Twelve were present, the disciple whom Jesus loved is specifically mentioned for the first time. The Master and his disciples were reclining at the table in the Eastern manner, supporting themselves on their left arms so that their right hands were free to take food. Possibly Judas, as treasurer of the company, reclined in the honored place at Jesus' left. The other privileged position on his right was occupied, not by Peter, but by the beloved disciple. This man by turning his head, came so close to Jesus that the two of them could whisper together without being overheard.

After Jesus made his shocking declaration, "One of you will betray me," Peter, seeing the advantage of the beloved disciple's position at the table, induced him to question Jesus secretly. Accordingly, this intimate disciple turned toward the Master to say in his ear, "Lord, who is it?"

"It is the one to whom I shall give this morsel after I have dipped it in the dish." So saying, Jesus gave a piece of bread to Judas on his left, in itself a courteous gesture toward an honored guest, but to the beloved disciple an ominous portent.

Later that evening, after Judas had betrayed Jesus, Peter followed his Master at a distance "and so did another disciple" (John 18.15). This unnamed man was clearly a person of some consequence, having friends in the highest religious circles of the Holy City, for it is reported that he "was known to the high priest" and "he entered the court of the high priest along with Jesus," apparently unchallenged, "while Peter stood outside at the door" (John 18.15-16). Was this mysterious disciple the beloved disciple? The record does not say. It seems difficult to identify a man of influence in Jerusalem's priestly circle with Zebedee's fisherman son from Galilee.

At the crucifixion, the affection and abiding trust between Jesus and the disciple whom he loved is vividly revealed. We already know from Mary's story that as Jesus was dying he entrusted his mother to the beloved disciple's care. The moment is portrayed in innumerable paintings and sculptures being undoubtedly one of Christendom's most familiar scenes—Jesus hanging on the cross while near him stand two people he especially loved, his mother and the beloved disciple. Almost without exception the captions read: Crucifixion with the Virgin and St. John.

On the third day after the crucifixion, when the beloved disciple learned from Mary Magdalene that Jesus' tomb was empty, he ran with Peter to the sepulcher. After Peter emerged from the rock-cut burial vault and departed, the beloved disciple entered it. He, too, saw the empty grave cloths, but could not understand why they lay as they did until the truth of what had taken place suddenly dawned on him. Then the beloved disciple knew that Jesus had risen; he was not dead. This is the first recorded instance of such faith among the disciples.

This faith became a certainty to the beloved disciple one dawn after he had fished all night with Peter, Nathanael-Bartholomew, and four other disciples. We already know how, on that occasion, a stranger spoke to them from the shore directing them to cast their net on the right side of the boat. At sight of the miraculous abundance of fish that they hauled in, the beloved disciple, with the quick perception he had displayed at the tomb, pointed to the stranger on the beach and cried, "It is the Lord!"

In the four stories of this nameless man—during the Last Supper, near the cross, at the tomb, and on the Sea of Galilee—he is portrayed as an ideal disciple without the human failings of John, James, and Peter. Though the Fourth Gospel presents the disciple whom Jesus loved as well-nigh perfect, some flesh-and-blood person must have been the model for this portrait. Who was he? We may never know beyond a doubt, because the question is enormously complicated. John the son of Zebedee was greatly revered in the early Church, not only as one of its "pillars" but as an intimate friend of Jesus. It is possible, though with our present knowledge we cannot prove it, that the Fourth Gospel's portrait of the beloved disciple is based on John's personality as it was idealized by the first Christians.

15

Certain People Whom Jesus Healed

MK 1.21-45 (MT 8.1-4,14-17;
LK 4.31-41; 5.12-15);
LK 17.11-19

*God anointed Jesus of Nazareth
with the Holy Spirit and with power;
. . . he went about doing good and
healing all that were oppressed by
the devil, for God was with him.*

ACTS 10.38

THE SERMON in Capernaum's synagogue on a certain morning was different from an ordinary Sabbath discourse during which old men frequently nodded and the young stirred impatiently. Today everyone in the congregation sat up straight, listening intently, for the customary preacher with his tiresome, rambling exposition of the Scriptures was silent and Jesus was preaching. His words were far from dull. They had the freshness of the morning breeze blowing in from the Sea of Galilee. They sparkled like rippling waves in sunlight. He spoke with power. He spoke with authority. His personality electrified his listeners. His words imparted courage to despairing men and women who were afraid of life.

Instead of citing the stale opinions of long-dead authorities, as many other preachers did, Jesus gave his own message. Though this glowed with originality, Jesus was by no means ignorant of the Law's ancient interpretations. He was well acquainted with traditional wisdom, but his own message was new and vital. "You have heard that it was said to men in years gone by . . . but I say to you . . ." he often declared, going on to explain some aspect of the Law. Such independence in preaching was novel to audiences accustomed to the traditional commonplaces of droning rabbis. Jesus, moreover, did not use lifeless words long ago drained of meaning for the average person. He spoke in vivid, often dramatic terms about matters that affected everyone. Day-to-day problems of living, troubles, aspirations, life's deepest concerns—all these were his subjects.

He did more than talk. Everyone knew that he was not only a speaker but a doer. He did not ignore evil or merely talk about it; he attacked it. People perceived in him the love and power of God which he proclaimed. The congregation knew that the forces of evil must inevitably collide with the holiness of Jesus. Men and women in the Capernaum synagogue that morning, expecting a showdown between Jesus and the omnipresent demons, sat forward, listening, watching.

Suddenly the Sabbath hush was rent by an unearthly cry. It came from a deranged man well known for the strange, chaotic voices that spoke through his lips. These voices were believed to come from evil spirits within him. They were demons at war with God and were thought to have invaded the wretched man's personality, destroying its unity and leaving him a helpless mouthpiece for their tortured utterances. People listened to him with a horrified curiosity that was mingled with respect, being half convinced that some message hidden from normal men might lurk in the madman's words.

"Jesus of Nazareth," cried the demented man, speaking in behalf of all the evil spirits within him, "what is there between you and us? What will you do? Have you come to destroy us?" It was as though the demons trembled in the presence of one in whom they recognized the power to ruin them.

Jesus waited, calm and silent. He made no impatient gesture nor did he request the synagogue officials to remove the insane man so that he might finish his sermon. He would deal with these evil forces —that would be his sermon.

"I know who you are," shrieked the madman pointing to Jesus. "You are the Holy One of God."

With a strange sensitivity, born perhaps of his affliction, the demoniac divined Jesus' secret, his unbroken unity with God. It was a secret Jesus was unwilling to have proclaimed in this way.

"Be quiet and come out of him," the Master commanded the demons.

At this the wretched man became convulsed and cried out. It seemed as if his unclean spirits struggled against Jesus' holiness. Finally, in obedience to a higher power the demons departed, leaving the man sane.

In that devil-haunted world, exorcisms were often accomplished by incantations and magic, practices forbidden in Jewish religion but frequently resorted to by men and women battling desperately against strange forces that seemed to threaten them on every side. If some in the congregation that Sabbath day assumed unthinkingly that Jesus was merely a clever magician using occult powers, other people, watching him more closely, observed that he employed no magic formula and uttered no incantation, but restored the insane man to sanity simply by the power of a spoken word. In order to make himself understood by his contemporaries, Jesus acted within the framework of ideas current in his day, treating the man as if possessed by a demon. But, as this story shows, Jesus transcended the magical practices of the time.

"Has a wonder-worker come among us?" the people of Capernaum asked one another. The disciples and some of the wiser members of the congregation knew that the healing was not accomplished by a magic trick nor was it a mere marvel; rather, it was a sign of the authority and power of Jesus. The cure of the demon-sufferer demonstrated more conclusively than any sermon that God was present among them.

Greatly impressed by the healing of the madman in the synagogue, Peter and Andrew with James and John returned with their Master to Peter's home, which may have been Jesus' temporary headquarters in Capernaum. At the house all was in confusion, with members of the household running hither and thither because Peter's mother-in-law was ill and suffering from a high fever.

The commotion made by the five men returning from the synagogue roused the sick woman. When she attempted to leave her bed to help her daughter with the midday meal, she found that she was unable to do so. Her head throbbed and her body seemed on fire. Peter and his wife became so alarmed that they appealed to Jesus.

Immediately he went to the sick woman's bedside and, taking her by the hand, assisted her to her feet. At his touch her fever departed, enabling her to stand unaided. Feeling completely well again and with none of the exhaustion that usually follows a fever, she wasted no time in recounting the details of her illness, but energetically began to prepare and serve the midday meal.

To Peter, the episode became one more demonstration of Jesus' extraordinary power to heal. As for Peter's mother-in-law, may she not be counted among those "who have tasted the heavenly gift, and have become partakers of the Holy Spirit, and have tasted the goodness of the word of God and the powers of the age to come" (Hebrews 6.4-5)?

At this time others besides the demoniac and Peter's mother-in-law were healed in Capernaum. When the sun set behind the western hills and a trumpet blast announced the Sabbath's end, people were freed from the laws forbidding them to carry burdens or walk more than the two thousand paces of a Sabbath day's journey. Many who had waited impatiently for this moment now brought their sick to Jesus. Mothers carried fretful babies, children led blind parents, the helpless were borne on pallets or hammocks, the mad were brought in chains. All the pain and wretchedness of the town seemed gathered in a sea of suffering at Peter's door. Perhaps, as the disciples struggled to keep order in the crowd and darkness deepened, they lighted torches lest a sick child should be accidentally trampled underfoot. The flickering light illuminated faces etched by misery but now shining with joy, for many, when they felt the touch of Jesus' healing hand, went away cured.

Early next morning Jesus left Capernaum to escape its importunate multitudes, for his healing mission was subordinate to his mission to teach the reality of God's love. As he journeyed, he met a leper on the road. Though the man may have suffered from some other less serious skin complaint than the dread affliction today called Hansen's disease or true leprosy, he had evidently been declared a leper by the priests and compelled by the Law (Leviticus 13.46) to dwell alone or with other sufferers like himself in an isolated house outside the town. He lived by begging, especially from travelers on the highway. He was required to cry out a warning to passersby, "Unclean, unclean," so that people would not touch him and become infected. (In ancient times and even until quite recently, leprosy was mistakenly believed to be highly contagious.)

Seeing Jesus coming down the road and knowing him to be the new healer of whom every traveler from Capernaum spoke, the leper ran and knelt before him and begged, not for alms, but for healing. Despite the fact that leprosy was then believed to be incurable, the leper, his eyes bright with faith, cried to the Master, "If you want to, you can cure my uncleanness."

While Jesus' companions recoiled in horror, knowing it was unlawful to touch a leper, the Master stretched out his hand and placed it upon the man, declaring, "Indeed, I want to heal you. You are now clean again."

Before continuing his journey, Jesus gave the healed leper two commands. He was not to rush home to his family but must first show himself to the priest who, as health officer of the community, would legally certify to his cure (Leviticus 14.2). Next, Jesus charged him not to spread abroad news of his recovery. The leper, however, heedless of the harm he might do to the Master's mission, did not deny himself the satisfaction of talking far and wide about his amazing cure. As a result of the man's disobedience, news of Jesus spread like wildfire, causing the sick to besiege him in every town he entered, so that he was forced to remain in the country.

Though Jesus doubtless cured many other lepers, only Luke's Gospel contains another story of such an occurrence. Jesus was traveling toward Jerusalem when ten lepers from a leper colony, situated, as was customary, outside a village, shouted to him from the distance, saying, "Jesus, Master, have pity on us."

It was a common cry in those days, but one frequently unheeded by travelers absorbed in their own affairs or callous to the sight of disfigured bodies and pitiful cries. Alert as Jesus was to evidences of human misery, he instantly saw these ten men suffering a living death.

"Go and show yourselves to the priests," he called to them, "for you are now cured." As the ten lepers walked along the road, they felt wholeness invade their bodies and they knew that Jesus had healed them.

Rejoicing in their unexpectedly good fortune, nine of the men hurried off to have their cures certified by the priests, but the tenth man paused on the road and turned back. He was a Samaritan and therefore, in Jewish eyes, a foreigner, but Jesus' compassion had embraced him as well as the other nine. Moved by gratitude for his healing, the Samaritan poured out thanks to God and prostrated himself at the Master's feet.

Jesus, commenting on the ingratitude of the nine lepers, asked, "Were not ten men healed? Where are the other nine? Is there no one but this Samaritan to give thanks to God?"

Turning to the Samaritan, whose gratitude was an evidence of the man's inner poise and spiritual health, Jesus said to him, "Rise and go your way; your faith has made you well."

The tenth leper and many others whom Jesus healed knew, with the psalmist of old, that the only suitable response a man can make to God's love and God's healing is thankfulness.

> O give thanks to the Lord, for he is good;
> for his steadfast love endures for ever!
>
> PSALM 107.1

16

The Paralyzed Man Who Was
Lowered through a Roof

MK 2.1-12 (MT 9.1-8;
LK 5.17-26)

Bless the Lord, O my soul,
and forget not all his benefits,
who forgives all your iniquity,
who heals all your diseases, . . .
who satisfies you with good as long
as you live
so that your youth is renewed like
the eagle's.
PSALM 103.2-3,5

NEWS THAT Jesus had returned to Capernaum was soon announced
to a young man lying upon his bed, helpless with paralysis. The
whole town buzzed with talk, for many people, having listened to
Jesus' sermon in their synagogue a few Sabbaths earlier, were eager
to hear him again. They wanted to see him challenge evil and bring
healing of both body and mind to the sick. The scribes and Pharisees
were beginning to oppose the new prophet and conflict was in the air.
But this made less impression on the paralyzed young man than his
friends' accounts of the wonderful cures wrought by Jesus. In the
Master's presence people seemed to enter upon a new existence, free,
joyful, and as far removed from their ordinary selves as day is from
night. The young man, hearing footsteps in the street as crowds
began to run toward Jesus, felt the excitement everywhere. Lively
expectation sprang up within him when four of his friends offered to
carry him to the house where Jesus was staying.

Whether this house was Jesus' own home, as has been suggested, or Peter's makes no difference to the story. It was evidently a one-story dwelling with a flat roof reached by an outside stairway. Though large as Galilean houses went, it was not nearly large enough to accommodate all who wanted to see and hear Jesus. Those who came to him filled all available spaces inside the building, blocked the door-way, and stood outside, massed in the courtyard, scarcely breathing in their eagerness to catch every word the Master spoke within the house.

A slight disturbance in the street momentarily diverted the attention of those in the courtyard. Four men carrying the paralyzed man on his thin mattress or pallet, seeing the crowd barring their entrance to the house, gently lowered their make-shift stretcher to the ground and dis-appeared. The young man closed his eyes and moaned, fearing that his bearers had deserted him. His friends' faith in Jesus' power to cure him had given him a momentary vision of himself walking again, but now he knew it was not to be. He felt that he had been foolish to entertain so false a hope. Long ago he had sinned and God con-tinued to be angry with him. That, he believed, was the root of his tragedy. It was absurd to look for a cure in the face of divine wrath.

Meanwhile his four bearers attacked the problem of bringing him to Jesus. The dense crowd made their task difficult though not impossible. Three of the bearers climbed to the flat roof and very carefully made an opening in it slightly larger than the pallet. The fourth man went off to procure ropes. Opening a hole in the roof was fairly easy, Palestinian roofs usually being constructed from saplings and brush or bundles of reeds. These were covered with a layer of clay that was flattened by rolling with a heavy, circular stone. After baking for several days in the sun the clay roof became hard and strong. (The roof tiles mentioned only in Luke's version of the story were doubtless a concession to Gentile readers unfamiliar with Galilean building methods.)

When his friends raised the paralyzed man's pallet and carried it up the outside staircase to the roof top, he was so dazed and frightened that he clung feebly to the sides of his mattress for support. Slowly, carefully, he was lowered, by means of ropes fastened around his pallet, through the hole in the roof and gently placed on the floor at Jesus' feet.

The wretched man's eyes sought those of the Master and, seeing in them compassion and understanding, he all but cried out, "Who can heal such a man as I? I am guilty and condemned to remain outside God's mercy in this grievous affliction from which I suffer." Though he actually spoke none of these words, he felt that Jesus understood how heavily his guilt weighed upon him.

The Master looked up at the four men peering through the hole in the roof, their faces lit by the sun and inwardly illuminated by faith. Then he bent down to the man on the mattress and spoke with the tone of authority that the people of Capernaum had heard before, "My son," he said, using an affectionate form of address, "My son, your sins are forgiven."

The young man sighed. He knew he needed forgiveness even more than a cure. Through his helpless body surged a tide of hope bringing with it a sense of well-being. Forgiven for all that was past and thus released from evil's bonds, he knew he had reached the point of healing.

In the crowded room tension was high. People hardly breathed, expecting a miracle. The scribes, however, stirred impatiently. Though everyone else was standing, these learned men had taken the only seats, confident that these were their due. From these best places they could easily see and hear everything. At Jesus' words of forgiveness, the eyes of the scribes narrowed and their lips formed the dread word, "Blasphemy." Only God, they knew, could forgive sins.

> "I, I am He
>   who blots out your transgressions for my own sake,
>   and I will not remember your sins."
>   ISAIAH 43.25

Yet they heard this young teacher of Nazareth usurping one of God's prerogatives and taking upon himself the forgiveness of sins. The scribes looked at one another, deeply annoyed. Who was this man that he should be so presumptuous? Why did he speak blasphemy?

Words could be dangerous and some day they knew that they would have to deal decisively with this young prophet who so freely promised divine forgiveness. They decided, however, that today Jesus was pretending. His words were merely talk. He could no more forgive this paralytic than he could heal him. The crowd would soon see that this new teacher was only a charlatan.

Jesus quickly discerned what they were thinking and challenged them with a question, "Why are you entertaining such thoughts about me? Which do you think is easier, to speak words of forgiveness, or to cure this man?"

Then, turning to the paralytic lying troubled by the animosity in the room, the Master cut through the tense atmosphere with his command, "Rise, take up your pallet and go home!"

The scribes were on the point of speaking but their words froze on their lips when the young man rose awkwardly to his feet, picked up his mattress, walked through the hushed throng and out the door. A chorus of thanks to God arose from the crowd within the house and from the four men on the roof so that the whole place echoed with voices glorifying the Lord for his saving and healing power. Though the scribes remained silent, bitterly biding their time, the paralyzed man, his friends, and many people of Capernaum, knowing that Jesus had wrought a marvel before their eyes, exclaimed, "We have never seen anything like this before!"

The cure demonstrated to the hostile scribes the reality of Jesus' forgiveness and his authority to forgive. It also raised a question they were too dull to answer truthfully: Who then is this prophet from Nazareth?

17

Matthew-Levi

MK 2.13-17 (MT 9.9-13;   *"I did not come to judge the world*
LK 5.27-32); MK 3.18   *but to save the world."*
(MT 10.3; LK 6.15)   JOHN 12.47

IN AN AGE of grasping and unprincipled public officials, Levi's occupation was lucrative. He was a tax collector or, as it is sometimes called, a publican. He served the interests of his superiors—and of himself—not those of the people. In the Roman empire the privilege of collecting taxes in each district was awarded to the highest bidder. Competition for this privilege was keen because collectors could demand more than Rome actually levied and pocket the difference. The money wrung from hapless taxpayers minus the revenues forwarded to the imperial treasury in Rome often amounted to a considerable sum. It was this that made taxgathering profitable. Though the district tax official, who was usually a Roman, reaped the largest rewards, even at such local levels as Capernaum, an official like Levi did not have to remain a poorly paid underling but could amass a fortune and live in a large house. There he could entertain his many friends in princely style. Cooperating as he did with Rome, Levi, the son of Alphaeus, became more prosperous than many of his fellow Jews.

Though wealthy, this tax collector was deeply troubled. His Jewish neighbors regarded him as a traitor in the employ of Rome and hated him for skimming off the wealth of their country and sending it abroad. Taxpayers feared him for his unjust demands. The scribes and Pharisees despised him for breaking the holy Law and classed him with thieves, harlots, murderers, and the heathen—excommunicated sinners all. This hurt Levi, for he was a sensitive man. In his own heart he despised himself, knowing that he was indeed disloyal to his own people, the chosen of God. It amounted to disloyalty to the Lord himself. This thought undermined Levi's peace of mind and caused him to be at war with himself. When people opposed him, he shouted at them. His sleep was troubled and hard lines etched his face. His wealth was costing him too much.

Capernaum was a toll station on the famous road linking Egypt with the East, the road called "the way of the sea" (Isaiah 9.1). Much of the commerce of antiquity was carried along this route, which from time immemorial had served as a military highway for Egyptian, Assyrian, Babylonian, and other conquering armies. By Levi's day the Romans had paved it and regulated its commerce. They stationed soldiers to defend the caravans using it from surprise attacks by robber bands. From Damascus the road ran south, crossing the Jordan River by a ford below Lake Huleh, skirting the shores of the Sea of Galilee near Capernaum, and continuing southwest through the pass at Megiddo and on to the Mediterranean coast and Egypt beyond. A branch road led south from Megiddo to Jerusalem.

The tax office at Capernaum levied customs on goods transported over this great highway and also collected local taxes on the thriving fishing industry of the town. Peter, Andrew, and the family of Zebedee doubtless paid their taxes at this office. Levi must have been busy from morning until night sorting, weighing, and counting many different kinds of coins, keeping his account books, and writing his reports for Rome. He had to argue with reluctant taxpayers, threaten those who refused his demands, and always make sure that he himself received a generous share of the revenues. Though hard and exacting, the work was no problem to Levi for he was an able man and well educated for the time. As he stamped the money bags with Roman seals, however, he often sighed, remembering that he was a Jew in the employ of the heathen. By associating with Gentiles he had made himself unclean in pious eyes. How could he break out of his servitude to Rome? Would the Lord ever forgive him for making a foreign conqueror's yoke heavier upon the chosen people of God? Feeling alienated from all that meant most to him, he often prayed,

> Have mercy on me, O God, according to thy steadfast love;
>   according to thy abundant mercy blot out my transgressions,
> Wash me thoroughly from my iniquity,
>   and cleanse me from my sin!
>
>   PSALM 51.1-2

Jesus' arrival in Capernaum made a difference to Levi. He listened while the Master spoke those revolutionary words, so disturbing to the scribes and Pharisees—words that seemed to turn the established religious order upside down. He heard Jesus proclaim the beginning of God's reign in the hearts of men. Furthermore, he saw proof in the Master's wonderful works that this era had arrived. When respected citizens of Capernaum like Peter, his brother, and the sons of Zebedee left their fishing to become Jesus' disciples, Levi knew that something unusual was afoot.

The people around Jesus welcomed the tax collector to their company. Many of them were like him, "lost sheep of the house of Israel," living outside the exclusive little society of the righteous. In that society, composed mainly of scribes and Pharisees, a man was judged righteous if he wore a ritual fringe on his garment, refrained from speaking to Gentiles, performed all the ceremonial washings, and obeyed hundreds of other similar regulations governing minute details. To Jesus' friends such matters seemed of trifling importance. They rejoiced to hear the Master speaking of the Heavenly Father, not as a stern judge scanning the account book of each man's merits and demerits, but as a shepherd glad to find his lost sheep.

From the beginning Moses had taught the people of Israel that God had redeemed them and given them the Promised Land to enjoy, not because they had earned it or deserved it, but because the Lord is himself righteous and loving. "Know therefore," declared Moses, "that the Lord your God is not giving you this good land to possess because of your righteousness; for you are a stubborn people. . . . you have been rebellious against the Lord" (Deuteronomy 9.6-7). The

prophets continued this teaching, celebrating the goodness of God
and his spiritual gifts freely given.

> Thus says the Lord who made you,
>   who formed you from the womb and will help you:
> Fear not, O Jacob my servant . . .
> For I will pour water on the thirsty land,
>   and streams on the dry ground;
> I will pour my Spirit upon your descendants,
>   and my blessing on your offspring.
>
> ISAIAH 44.2-3

By Levi's time this doctrine had been relegated to the attic of men's
thinking in favor of a new idea, preached by the Pharisees, that
heavenly blessings must be bought with a price, that men must earn
their own salvation. As Paul, a Pharisee himself, was to say, these
men were "ignorant of the righteousness that comes from God, and
seeking to establish their own" (Romans 10.3). But accumulating
enough merits to balance his many sins as a taxgatherer did not appeal
to Levi. He thought the effort doomed to failure, as indeed Paul later
proclaimed, "For no human being will be justified in his [God's]
sight by works of the law" (Romans 3.20).

In Jesus' preaching Levi heard a fresh and glorious note reaffirming
the ancient prophetic insight and proclaiming the outgoing love of
God for all men regardless of their merits. It was a heart-warming
truth. After hearing Jesus tell his story of the Prodigal Son, Levi
recognized himself as the prodigal; the Pharisees, with their conscious
rectitude and their earned merits, as the elder son; and God as the
forgiving, ever-loving father.

Levi had made himself tough and hard, believing that this was the
only way to succeed in a cruel world. But beyond the undeniable
cruelty of things as they are, he began to feel the warmth of God's
forgiveness and of his salvation freely offered to sinner and righteous
man alike. Soon the hard lines in Levi's face melted, his manner became more friendly and relaxed, and his associates sometimes saw
him smile.

One day Jesus entered the tax office at Capernaum in search of Levi whom he undoubtedly knew and had talked to on many occasions. Levi, sitting at his table counting the day's receipts, looked up in surprise wondering why the Master had come. From this encounter between the two men only a brief command survives. It includes, however, a world of meaning, being both a coveted invitation and a summons that Levi was ready to obey.

"Follow me," said Jesus.

Immediately Levi arose and in that hour became Jesus' disciple. He settled his accounts, turned in his books, and renounced his calling once for all. Unlike fishing, taxgathering was not an occupation to which a man could return from time to time.

Soon afterward Levi gave a great feast at his house for Jesus. Among the guests invited to meet the Master were Levi's old associates from the tax office and other Jews who had become careless in obeying the Law. Jesus sat down to eat at Levi's table with all these guests, knowing exactly what kind of people they were.

The Pharisees thought that to share a meal with godless men living outside the Law was a shameless act. In their self-conscious rectitude they were shocked that a religious teacher would soil his reputation in this way. "What will this man from Nazareth do next?" they asked. First he had presumed to forgive sins. Later he called a notorious revenue agent to be his disciple. Now he ate with tax collectors and sinners. "Why does he do these things?" cried the Pharisees in dismay as, one by one, Jesus set aside the requirements of their intricate code of righteousness and seemed to turn their religion upside down.

In answering the last charge against him, Jesus explained the nature of his mission. He had not come to establish a special community, an exclusive little enclave of good people. This was the goal of the Essenes and the Pharisees. Jesus' mission was to open God's kingdom to all, and to welcome especially those, like "the lost sheep of the house of Israel," whose need was greatest. "Those who are well," he explained, "have no need of a physician, but those who are sick; I came not to call the righteous but sinners" (Mark 2.17).

Levi's name is not found in any of the lists of the Twelve, for it occurs only in Mark's and Luke's stories of the tax collector's call and of the banquet in his house. In Matthew's Gospel the Capernaum tax collector is named, not Levi, but Matthew (9.9). This Matthew is listed among the twelve disciples in the three Synoptic Gospels. From these records it would appear that Levi and Matthew refer to the same man who, like Simon Peter and others, was known by two names.

Aside from the vividness of his call, Matthew-Levi remains a shadowy figure of whom little is known. In art he is frequently shown as one of the four evangelists. He holds a pen or the Gospel that bears his name, though sometimes the money bag of his taxgathering days is depicted. His symbol is a winged man, in token of the First Gospel's account of Christ's incarnation.

Matthew's authorship of the First Gospel, long a traditional belief, is by no means certain. According to Papias, an early bishop of Hierapolis in Asia Minor, writing about A.D. 130, "Matthew compiled and arranged the *logia* in the Hebrew language and each one interpreted them as best he could." What did Papias mean by *logia*? If, as some scholars believe, he meant the sayings of Jesus, then Matthew may have compiled the document used as a basis for the Gospel of Matthew. A large part of this Gospel consists of the discourses of Jesus. Other scholars, however, translate *logia* as oracles, meaning Old Testament prophecies foretelling Christ. The First Gospel contains more than sixty of these, which may well be from a collection originally made by Matthew-Levi of Capernaum. Whatever this disciple wrote, or inspired others to write, he remains one of those few who knew Jesus intimately and in whose once soiled heart the light of God shone, enabling him to witness to the glory that is in Christ.

18

Three Whom Jesus Healed on the Sabbath

MK 3.1-6 (MT 12.9-14;
LK 6.6-11); LK 13.10-17;
14.1-6

*And he said to them, "The sab-
bath was made for man, not man for
the sabbath."*

MARK 2.27

EATING WITH SINNERS was not the only accusation the Pharisees
brought against Jesus. Probably their most serious charge against him
was that he broke the law concerning the Sabbath day. One Sabbath,
doubtless in Capernaum, they tried to trap him in the act of violating
this holy ordinance.

As was his custom, Jesus set out for the synagogue to attend the
usual holy day service of prayer, praise, scripture reading, and sermon, all ending with Aaron's benediction

The Lord bless you and keep you:
The Lord make his face to shine upon you, and be gracious to you:
The Lord lift up his countenance upon you, and give you peace.

NUMBERS 6.24-26

Before the time came for the ruler of the synagogue to pronounce
these ancient words, Jesus' enemies planned to show him up to the
whole congregation as a Sabbath-breaker. To that end they had made
sure that a man with a withered hand would be present.

The Sabbath law was explicit. "You shall keep the sabbath, because
it is holy for you; every one who profanes it shall be put to
death; whoever does any work on it, that soul shall be cut off from
among his people" (Exodus 31.14). Would healing the man's
withered hand be considered work?

Such extremely rigid upholders of the Law as the Essenes said that it was better to let a man drown than to profane the holy day by performing the work necessary to save him. Humane rabbis conceded, however, that if a person's life were in danger help could be given him. Curing a man was considered work. Obviously an atrophied hand was not a matter of life or death; consequently, the Pharisees argued, Jesus would be guilty of law-breaking if he healed the man's hand this morning.

Quietly the man with the shriveled hand entered the synagogue and sat down on one of the rear benches. His affliction may have resulted from an ordinary injury or some cruel Roman punishment; it might also have been congenital or psychological in origin. Whatever its cause, it made him unable to work and therefore dependent on charity. The people of Capernaum knew him well, having often given him alms.

"Will Jesus heal him today?" members of the congregation asked each other, half eager for, yet half dreading the controversy that would surely ensue. They knew that the Master had already exorcised an unclean spirit and healed Peter's mother-in-law on the Sabbath. Would the hawk-eyed Pharisees sitting smugly in their front-row seats this morning prevent Jesus from exercising his well-known compassion?

As a distinguished guest, the Master had been invited to read the Scripture lesson and comment on it. All eyes were upon him when he stood up. Acutely aware, as he always was, of those around him, he instantly saw the man on the back bench and understood his need.

"Stand up and come here," commanded Jesus in a voice of such authority that silence fell upon the assembly while the man walked forward. The Pharisees' grim faces broke into satisfied smiles. Jesus seemed to be falling into their trap.

According to the canonical Gospels the disabled man said nothing. Nevertheless, a fragment preserved by the fourth-century Church father, Jerome, quoting from the lost apocryphal *Gospel according to the Hebrews,* records this plea: "I was a stonemason working for my living with my hands. I implore you, Jesus, restore me to health, so that I do not have to beg for my food."

Jesus took in the whole situation at a glance. Turning from the afflicted man before him, he confronted the hostile Pharisees. The smiles suddenly vanished from their faces.

"Is it right to do good on the Sabbath or to do harm?" he sternly questioned them. Receiving no reply, he continued, "Is it right to save life or to kill?"

It was they who were trapped now, not he. The Pharisees could make no reply. How could they say that it is wrong to do good on the Sabbath? Everyone knew that to be able to do good, but to refrain, is equivalent to doing evil. Failing to save a life when one can do so is like killing. At heart they were not evil men and they were unwilling to be accused of inhumanity.

Jesus waited patiently for their answer, but no sound broke the oppressive silence in the synagogue. The Pharisees saw no escape from their dilemma. Jesus seemed to them to be flouting the very thing that preserved Israel's identity in the pagan world—her sacred Law.

The Sabbath was one of the chief pillars of the Law. According to the prophet Ezekiel, God had said, "Moreover I gave them my sabbaths, as a sign between me and them, that they might know that I the Lord sanctify them" (Ezekiel 20.12). The weekly day of rest and prayer had set its mark on Israel, making her different from other peoples by cementing her covenant relationship with God and by endowing her sons and daughters with the strength that holiness imparts.

Jesus' claim to freedom from Sabbath restrictions so that he might heal a man seemed, to the Pharisees, to undermine their very religion. They were fanatics in defense of existing values, not prophets with vision. They saw their doggedly defended world of Judaism seriously endangered by this revolutionary Galilean teacher. Though he claimed to have come to fulfill, not to destroy the Law, he had already breached their zealously guarded ramparts with his teaching of a new law and a new covenant. Now he was winning over the people of

Israel to his new message in which they found deeper peace in God than the ancient Law afforded.

The Pharisees continued to sit grim-faced and silent in their front seats. They refused to examine the strange new teaching that the Sabbath is made for man, not man for the Sabbath. The doctrine that man is superior to the Law made a mockery of all they had worked for. If they could not defend this citadel of Judaism against subversive new ideas, they could at least barricade their own minds and hearts against Jesus.

He looked searchingly at the Pharisees ranged against him before turning back to the man with the shriveled hand.

"Stretch out your hand!" Jesus commanded.

Impressed by the Master's courage in the presence of his enemies, the man obeyed. He felt blood begin to circulate and muscles flex in his useless hand. His was a test case indeed, demonstrating God's love and healing power. Far from destroying the Sabbath, Jesus had fulfilled its purpose. The holy day was ordained to bring men deliverance from evil and peace of heart, both of which Jesus had given to the man with the withered hand.

Frustrated in their plan to outwit Jesus, the Pharisees stormed out of the synagogue. Some day, they knew, they must destroy Jesus before he ruined their religion by substituting the welfare of individuals for the immutability of the Law. Moreover, if the healing they had just witnessed showed that Jesus shared in God's creative power, the wisest of the Pharisees realized that Judaism would eventually have to be transformed to encompass so amazing a truth.

Despite the Pharisees' continuing hostility, Jesus did not bow to their opinions. One day he encountered in the synagogue on the Sabbath a pitifully bent woman. She had endured the crippling affliction of a hunched back for eighteen years until there were few who remembered that she had once stood erect and walked as gracefully as anyone. Her "spirit of infirmity" is mentioned (Luke 13.11), indicating the current belief that some evil spirit had caused her spinal malady.

Jesus' radiant spirit and obvious vigor surely awakened in her that morning a desire to be cured. From her intense desire came hope. Then she remembered stories of the Master's compassion for the sick and his power to heal. "I know that he can drive out my evil spirit," she told herself.

Her faith must have been apparent to Jesus, but the story gives only the bare facts. "Woman," he said to her, "you are released from your infirmity." So saying he laid his hands on her, enabling her to stand straight. Her first words were of praise to the Lord.

Instantly the ruler of the synagogue sprang to his feet angered by this flagrant example of Sabbath-breaking. "There are six days on which men may legally work," he warned his congregation, referring to the fourth commandment of Deuteronomy 5.12-14, and adding, "Come to be healed on one of those days, not on the Sabbath."

Caught in the crossfire between the ruler and Jesus, the woman tried to edge away, but hearing the Master begin his fiery reply she tossed her head high and stood her ground.

"You hypocrites!" he thundered. "If you interpret the Law strictly, each one of you breaks the Sabbath when you untie your ox or ass from its stall and lead it to the watering trough. If a dumb beast can be loosed from its bond on the holy days, surely this daughter of Abraham, whom Satan has kept bent and crippled for eighteen years —surely she also can be released on the Sabbath to receive the blessing and peace God promises."

Jesus' argument was unanswerable. There was nothing for his opponents to do but move shamefacedly away while the healed woman joined with the congregation in giving thanks and rejoicing in the Master's marvelous act.

The Sabbath argument with the Pharisees continued. It was doubtless in another town that Jesus, again on the Sabbath, encountered a gravely ill man. On this occasion Jesus was not in a synagogue but in a Pharisee's house dining there as his guest.

The Pharisee was the ruler of a synagogue and had invited some of his friends to meet Jesus. All the food served to these guests had been prepared the day before so that no cooking need be done to profane the holy day with work. In this case other arrangements had also been made, arrangements to trap Jesus.

On entering the Pharisee's house, Jesus felt hostility in the very air. He had often been an honored guest in the homes of Pharisees and some of these religious leaders, like Nicodemus, were his secret adherents. On one occasion a group of friendly Pharisees, learning of a threat against Jesus' life, hurried to his side to warn him, saying, "Get away from here, for Herod wants to kill you" (Luke 13.31). But the Pharisees of this story were not friendly to the Master, all of them watching his every move with coldly critical eyes.

In one pair of eyes, however, he saw something different. They expressed the suffering and despair of a very sick man, the one who had been brought in to see if Jesus would heal him on the Sabbath. Some organic disease, perhaps of the heart, had caused fluid to accumulate in the tissues of this man's body, a condition called dropsy or edema. There was no unfriendliness in this sufferer's face, only a silent plea for help.

Jesus saw the trap that had been laid for him and his stern voice rang out over the crowded room, "Is it lawful to heal on the Sabbath," he asked, "or is it against the Law?"

The stony-eyed Pharisees looked away, not one of them daring to reply. Then Jesus, turning from his opponents, healed the wretched man and mercifully sent him home.

The story omits the harsh words that the Pharisees must have shouted at Jesus on this occasion and ends with his closing question, "If your ass or ox fell into a well, would you not immediately pull it out, even though the day were the Sabbath?"

Again a group of Pharisees, whose minds were too narrowly focused on the legal question of the Sabbath to perceive the meaning of the action they had witnessed, could make no reply. Their uncomfortable silence was itself an acknowledgment of the Master's intellectual and moral triumph.

In these three stories of healings on the Sabbath, though the Pharisees assume the role of adversaries, the real antagonist of Jesus is evil in its many forms. The message these stories convey is not so much Jesus' victory over the Pharisees as his triumph over the powers of evil. In curing the man with the withered hand, the woman with the bent back, and the sufferer from dropsy, the Master demonstrated that those who come to him are given a new life through the power and love of God that is in Jesus Christ.

19

The Official from Capernaum

JN 4.46-54; cf. MT 8.5-13
AND LK 7.1-10

*Then they cried to the Lord in their
  trouble,
    and he delivered them from their
    distress;
he sent forth his word, and healed
  them,
    and delivered them from destruc-
    tion.
Let them thank the Lord for his
  steadfast love,
    for his wonderful works to the
    sons of men!*
                    PSALM 107.19-21

"IF I CAN only reach Jesus in time!" murmured the distraught father to himself as his horse galloped toward Cana. The distance between his home in Capernaum, from which he had set out early that morning, and Cana, where Jesus was staying, was only about twenty miles, a day's journey for a foot traveler, but considerably less than that for a well-mounted rider. The father, being an official in the household of Herod Antipas, tetrarch of Galilee, rode a fast horse. Even so, the man's impatience to reach Jesus made the road seem endless. At home in Capernaum his son lay so desperately sick that the doctors had given him up. The father, however, entertained a hope that the new healer and prophet from Nazareth might be able to cure the boy's fever. Haste was essential, for the exhausted lad was already near death.

A little past noon the official reined in his panting horse at Cana and dismounted near Jesus. While the father begged Jesus to hurry to his son's bedside, a crowd gathered, curious to see what the Master would do. Surveying these idle onlookers, Jesus reproved them (as the plural pronouns and verbs of his recorded statement indicate) for their childish eagerness to behold new wonders and their lack of real interest in his message. "Will you never believe," he asked them, "unless you see signs and wonders?"

In his great need the father clung to his faith in Jesus' power to heal. Again he pleaded urgently, "Sir, come with me before my son dies!"

Perceiving how great was the father's faith, Jesus turned from the eager crowd and spoke in low tones to the desperate man. "Go, return to your home; your son will live."

Without hesitation the official mounted his horse and was soon riding back to Capernaum at a leisurely pace, quite different from the morning's wild gallop. He needed no proof that Jesus' words had already accomplished his son's healing because this new prophet had made an extraordinary impression on him. He had never before seen one in whom God's love was as evident as it was in Jesus. This prophet was clearly a man of power, a person close to God, a physician who could send forth his healing word to restore a stricken boy.

Before reaching home the father met his servants hurrying down the road toward him. Even before they spoke, he was confident that they would tell him, "Your son lives!"

"At what hour did he begin to improve?" asked the father.

"The fever left him yesterday at one hour past noon."

The father remembered that at the same hour Jesus had "sent forth his word," declaring, "Your son will live."

His son's recovery was the sign, the miracle, but the official already believed in Jesus' transforming, life-giving power. So, too, did the father's entire household when he told them all that had happened in Cana.

Who was the nameless official of this story told only in John's Gospel? Some commentators identify him with a certain Chuza described in Luke 8.3 as Herod's steward and the husband of Joanna. She was among the women who followed Jesus on his preaching tours and contributed of their wealth to further his mission. If Joanna's son was the lad restored to health by Jesus, it is easy to understand the motive for her later service to the Master.

Matthew 8.5-13 and Luke 7.1-10 contain two versions of a similar story. This one concerns a Roman centurion who begged Jesus to heal his sick slave. Scholars have suggested that Matthew's and Luke's narratives of the centurion and his slave and John's story of the official from Capernaum and his son are derived from the same original episode. However this may be, the Roman centurion is a distinctive personality among Jesus' friends. He is a Gentile, courteous even in the midst of his trouble and sensitively aware of the fact that a Jew like Jesus could not enter a Gentile home without becoming ritually unclean. The healing of this Roman officer's slave demonstrated that Christ came, as Simeon prophesied, not only as the glory of his people Israel, but also as the light to lighten the Gentiles.

IV

AS HIS FAME SPREAD

20

The Disciples

MK 3.13-19 (MT 10.2-4;
LK 6.13-16; JN 21.2;
ACTS 1.13-14); MK 6.7-13
(MT 10.1-25; LK 9.1-6);
LK 10.1-24; JN 17.6-26;
MT 8.18-22; LK 9.57-62

*". . . for I have given them the
words which thou gavest me, and
they have received them and know in
truth that I came from thee; and they
have believed that thou didst send
me. I am praying for them."*

JOHN 17.8-9

WHEN MATTHEW-LEVI resigned from his tax office, he joined a group
of six disciples. They included those whose stories have already been
told: the brother fishermen of Capernaum, Peter and Andrew, James,
and John; Philip from Bethsaida, and Nathanael-Bartholomew of
Cana.

These seven followers of Jesus were accepted without question
by the crowds that flocked to the Master, for people expected a religious leader to be accompanied by disciples. In those days a little
group of disciples comprised an informal theological school whose
members studied the Law under their rabbi's direction. As we have
noted, John the Baptist's disciples received rigorous training in fasting
and prayer while they helped him "prepare the way of the Lord."

Jesus' disciples believed that their roles were more demanding and
also more exalted than those of other disciples, for Jesus had made
them heralds of the reign of God. They were called to labor, not for
the Law with its many hair-splitting distinctions, but for the souls of
men.

These seven men doubtless recalled the story of the great prophet

Isaiah who, when Israel rejected him, entrusted his teaching to his disciples for safe-keeping, saying, "Bind up the testimony, seal the teaching among my disciples" (Isaiah 8.16). He hoped that, no matter what befell him, his message would be preserved by them against a future time when it could be openly proclaimed.

During the sunlit days in Galilee when multitudes surrounded Jesus, his disciples did not expect to have the duties of Isaiah's followers fall upon them, for they could not conceive of their Master's rejection. Though they often saw groups of scribes and Pharisees shaking their heads as they argued about the new Galilean teacher, the disciples met few common people who took this opposition to Jesus seriously. His words roused men from their drab existence. Weighed down, as most of them were, by disappointment with their lot, by a sense of guilt, and by ever present fear, they responded enthusiastically to his description of the glorious possibilities of their life as children of God.

Crowds came to him from far and near. Galileans rubbed shoulders with Judeans and Idumeans, while aristocrats from Jerusalem mingled with dwellers from beyond the Jordan and pilgrims from as far away as the great coastal cities of Tyre and Sidon. Above the joyful sounds made by the multitudes, high-pitched cries often rose from unclean spirits whose announcement, "You are the Son of God," could not be silenced.

Jesus' mission soon reached a turning point. It was time for him to demonstrate the fact that the new Israel, the new people of God, was already in existence. A hardy band of followers, men whose hearts God had already touched, separated themselves from the multitude at the seaside to climb a mountain with their Master. Among them were those whom Jesus later described in his prayer to his Father as "the men whom thou gavest me out of the world; thine they were, and thou gavest them to me" (John 17.6). Only to those from whose hearts God was not banished could Jesus teach the reality of God's love. It was men such as these that God gave to Jesus.

The band of followers scaled the mountain, perhaps steep-sided

Mount Tabor clothed in verdure and standing apart like a sentinel guarding the Valley of Jezreel. Each step seemed to bring them out of the valley of self-seeking and nearer to a pinnacle of dedication. Centuries earlier Moses had toiled up a different mountain to receive God's covenant with Israel on the top of Mount Sinai. Were not these followers of Jesus approaching the summit of a new Sinai where Jesus would bring into being the new Israel of God?

If the record of the event lacks those lively details which help to make many scenes in the Gospels seem real, it is filled with symbolic meaning.

And he went up into the hills, and called to him those whom he desired; and they came to him. And he appointed twelve, to be with him, and to be sent out to preach and have authority to cast out demons: Simon whom he surnamed Peter; James the son of Zebedee and John the brother of James, whom he surnamed Boanerges, that is, sons of thunder; Andrew, and Philip, and Bartholomew, and Matthew, and Thomas, and James the son of Alphaeus, and Thaddaeus, and Simon the Cananaean, and Judas Iscariot, who betrayed him.

MARK 3.13-19

These twelve men symbolize the twelve tribes of Israel. When Peter said, "We have left everything to follow you. What shall we receive?" Jesus in his reply referred to the symbolic meaning of the Twelve. "Truly, I say to you, in the new world, when the Son of man shall sit on his glorious throne, you who have followed me will also sit on twelve thrones, judging the twelve tribes of Israel" (Matthew 19.28).

Who were these Twelve, chosen from the larger group of Jesus' disciples? Each Gospel and the Book of Acts contains a list of their names, though John's list is fragmentary. These five lists (Matthew 10.2-4; Mark 3.14-19; Luke 6.14-16; John 21.2; Acts 1.13-14) are in virtual agreement. Various ancient manuscripts and translations give different forms of the names. Here we shall follow the Revised Standard Version.

The first seven men have already been identified. Stories of two others, Thomas and Judas Iscariot, will be told in later chapters. The three remaining disciples are little more than names.

James is the first of these. He does not act in any New Testament episode, hence his identification remains a puzzle. Frequently called James the Less to distinguish him from his better known namesake, James the Great, who was Zebedee's son, he must also not be confused with a third James who was Jesus' brother. Was James the Less, described as Alphaeus' son, possibly a brother of Levi-Matthew whose father is also called Alphaeus in Mark 2.14? We do not know. Mary, one of the Galilean women who witnessed the crucifixion, is called "the mother of James the younger" (Mark 15.40). Was she, then, Alphaeus' wife and mother of his son James? Again we are not sure. Matthew 27.56 names not only James but a certain Joseph as being her son. Father, mother, brother—all these relatives of James may be mentioned in the Gospels, yet this disciple's only certain relationship in the New Testament is with Jesus and the Twelve.

Little, again, is known of the next disciple, Simon the Cananaean or Zealot. Both descriptive terms have the same meaning, for Cananaean, an Aramaic word for "enthusiast," is equivalent to the Greek "zealot." Possibly Simon belonged to the fanatical, anti-Roman sect known as the Zealots. On the other hand he may have been merely zealous in upholding the Law.

The last of these three little-known disciples has a double name—Judas and Thaddaeus. Luke and Acts list him as Judas, the son of James, and this was probably his name. After Jesus' betrayal by Judas Iscariot, however, the name Judas became one of shame. This may have prompted Matthew and Mark to give him the descriptive name of Thaddaeus. He is doubtless the "Judas (not Iscariot)" mentioned in John 14.22 in connection with his question to Jesus, "Lord, how is it that you are making yourself known only to us, and not to the world?"

Judas-Thaddaeus here voiced the perplexity of many looking for a worldly Messiah. They asked, "Why does Jesus not compel the world to believe in him by some overwhelming display of his miraculous power? Why does he manifest his glory to so few?" The answer, of course, lies in the nature of God, in his omnipotence and in his love. Love does not compel. It does not violently overthrow the barriers of self-sufficiency, self-seeking, cynicism, and pride which men erect against God. Only to those in whose hearts love dwells, only to those who believe his word, can Christ unveil his glory. Judas-Thaddaeus with his fellow disciples belonged, however imperfectly, to the fellowship Jesus described, "If a man loves me, he will keep my word, and my Father will love him, and we will come to him and make our home with him" (John 14.23).

From Peter to Judas Iscariot, these are the Twelve. To them Jesus patiently explained the hidden meanings of his parables. In the profound yet simple words of the Lord's Prayer he taught them to pray, thus making real to them the nearness of God. He gave them examples of humble service, none so dramatic as washing their feet before the Last Supper. He counseled them in the duties of discipleship. He trained them in action, sending them out two by two with authority to cast out unclean spirits and preach repentance. Because they were sent abroad to preach and heal in his name the Twelve are called apostles, for an apostle is a messenger or ambassador.

Only Luke records the sending forth, two by two, of seventy disciples. The whole impersonal episode is rich in connotations. It brings to mind the seventy elders of Israel whom Moses appointed to help him and upon whom the Lord put a share of the spirit resting upon Moses (Number 11.16-25).

The symbolic number seventy conveyed to the Jews an idea of entirety and completeness. According to Genesis, chapter 10, the whole world contained seventy nations. This may be the connotation of seventy in Luke's narrative, for in both his Gospel and the Book of Acts, this evangelist emphasized the world-wide spread of Christ's message. Perhaps the story of the Seventy was set beside that of the Twelve to counteract any false notion that the apostles were sent only to Israel. It is clear, moreover, that Jesus had many more disciples than the Twelve, for these well-known men are specifically referred to in only about ten percent of the 230 Gospel references to Jesus' disciples.

The greatly condensed stories of three would-be disciples illustrate the cost of discipleship. According to Matthew, the first man was a scribe who, in a glow of enthusiasm, promised to follow Jesus wherever he went. But the scribe's face fell and he turned back to the comfort and security of his home when Jesus declared, "Foxes have holes, and birds of the air have nests; but the Son of man has nowhere to lay his head" (Matthew 8.20).

The second man, when invited to follow Jesus, begged off by saying he must first bury his father, perhaps meaning that he could not join the disciples until the old man eventually died and he had performed the sacred obligation of a son. This excuse revealed that the man's bondage to his home was greater than his allegiance to God's kingdom. Jesus' reply to this man is difficult to understand because of its figurative language. "Leave the dead to bury their own dead," he commanded; "but as for you, go and proclaim the kingdom of God" (Luke 9.60). Was this a dramatic way of saying that the spiritually dead, those who did not respond to Christ, could perform the excessively elaborate and prolonged burial rites then in vogue that often failed to express true mourning? But a disciple must give priority to his work for the Lord.

The third would-be disciple wanted to say good-bye to his family, as Elisha did when called to be Elijah's disciple (I Kings 19.19-21). Jesus perceived that this request for a delay cloaked the man's basic reluctance and half-heartedness. Such a person, the Master decided, was unfit for discipleship requiring absolute devotion. "No one who puts his hand to the plow and looks back," declared Jesus, "is fit for the kingdom of God" (Luke 9.62).

In the preface to John's Gospel, the belief of Jesus' disciples is expressed,

And the word became flesh and dwelt among us, full of grace and truth; we have beheld his glory, glory as of the only Son from the Father.

JOHN 1.14

This testimony contains the secret of the disciples' dedication to their Lord—they had known him at first hand as the Son of God. They were convinced that though the Father dwells in unapproachable majesty, in light too bright for human eyes, they had seen his Son whom he sent into the world. This was the basic belief of the apostles. It is stated in Jesus' great prayer no less than five times.

. . . they . . . know in truth that I came from thee; and they have believed that thou didst send me.

As thou didst send me into the world, so I have sent them into the world.

. . . that the world may believe that thou has sent me.

. . . that the world may know that thou hast sent me. . .

. . . these know that thou hast sent me.

JOHN 17.8,18,21,23,25

As Jesus was sent, so he sent forth his apostles to proclaim that the "grace and truth" they had witnessed in him reflected the glory of God. With all the resources at their command, his disciples guaranteed Jesus' divine credentials.

21

The Demoniac at the Lakeside

MK 5.1-20 (MT 8.28-34;
LK 8.26-39)

*"But if it is by the Spirit of God
that I cast out demons, then the kingdom of God has come upon you."*
MATTHEW 12.28

FROM A PORT on the Sea of Galilee's western shore, Jesus and his disciples set out on a six- or seven-mile voyage across the lake lying like a blue jewel amid its encircling hills. They embarked in a small fishing boat, perhaps the one belonging to Peter and Andrew, or the boat kept drawn up on the beach when crowds pressed dangerously close to the Master. Once Jesus had used this craft as a pulpit from which to preach to a multitude on the shore, but today he sailed in it across the lake.

Before long the voyagers landed on the western shore beneath towering cliffs glowing yellow in the afternoon sun. As the disciples scanned the heights above them, they saw the strange figure of a man gesticulating wildly as he rushed toward them. He was obviously distraught. The clanking of broken chains at his wrists warned Jesus' company that the approaching person was a madman who had burst from his fetters. The disciples wanted to push their boat into deep water again to put a safe distance between themselves and this frightening figure. They believed him possessed by evil spirits that had been strong enough to break the chains with which he had once been bound. If the man's friends and neighbors had failed to subdue him, what could strangers do but leave the tormented creature in the desolation of the cliffside caves and tombs, screaming and beating his body day and night?

The madman's raving made the eastern shore of the lake seem hostile to the disciples. It was foreign territory in any case, being the region called the Decapolis or Ten Cities, a federation of independent Greek cities under Roman rule. With their forums, baths, theaters, aqueducts, and temples, these cities were centers of Greek culture inhabited by Greek-speaking pagans whose customs and outlook were strange to the Jews. While the demoniac came nearer and nearer, the disciples looked longingly back across the lake toward the familiar green hills of Galilee.

Jesus seemed to have no fear of the madman and waited in quiet confidence for him to approach, never flinching at the furious uproar the creature made as he stumbled forward. When he reached Jesus on the beach, his true self seemed momentarily to control the evil forces within him and he acknowledged the Master's presence by kneeling at his feet. The demoniac's action appeared to be a wordless plea for healing and peace.

"You evil spirit," commanded Jesus, addressing the destructive force controlling the sufferer, "come out of this man and leave him!"

The terrified demon cried, "What do you want with me, Jesus, Son of the Most High God? Do not torment me."

Again, as with the unclean spirit in the Capernaum synagogue, this devil recognized Jesus' power to banish evil and knew that Satan's reign was threatened by one who established the kingdom of God.

"What is your name?" Jesus asked the demon. In antiquity a name was much more than an identifying label—it was itself part of a person's essential character and nature.

"My name is Legion," replied the malign spirit or spirits, "for we are a great host."

This reference to a dread Roman legion, with its six thousand heavily armed, fighting men, suggests that the man's derangement was overwhelming. It may also indicate that some terrible experience connected with Rome's military operations in this region had produced a mental breakdown in this man's sensitive nature.

"Do not send us away," the demons begged of Jesus, for they feared destruction if they were banished. Being evil they knew that they could not exist except as parasites upon the good. A herd of pigs was grazing on a nearby hillside. "Send us over to them," implored the devils, "and we will enter the swine."

At this point the story takes on the characteristics of a rollicking folk tale. Jewish peasants must once have laughed uproariously at the double twist with which it ends. The devils received their due when the swine into which they had been sent stampeded, hurled themselves over the cliff, and were drowned. At the same time pagan swineherds lost their beasts which were "unclean" according to Jewish Law.

News that the madman had been restored to sanity spread far and wide and people hurried to see for themselves what had happened. They found the one-time demoniac sitting composed and quiet, clothed, and in his right mind. Strangely enough this sight disturbed them more than the man's former insane behavior, to which they had become accustomed. They shrank from the sane man and from Jesus. If this stranger were powerful enough to overcome evil spirits, what else might he not do? They did not want him to remain in their region lest he declare war here against Satan's reign. Some of the prophets had foreseen a final conflict of the children of light against the children of darkness, but the people of this region did not want spiritual warfare to be fought in their country, so they urgently begged Jesus to depart.

As his boat was pushing off from shore, the former demoniac begged to go with him. Added to the man's very human desire to remain with Jesus was, perhaps, a paralyzing fear. He may have asked himself, "Is my cure real, or will another demon soon overwhelm me?"

On similar occasions, Jesus had commanded action. To the paralytic he said, "Take up your bed and walk"; to the leper, "Go, show yourself to the priest." In this case also, Jesus prescribed action capable of convincing the demoniac of the reality of his cure.

"Go home to your friends and family," directed Jesus, sending the man back to those who had been most deeply injured by his wild behavior, the very people hardest to convince of his cure. "Go, tell them," continued Jesus, "what the Lord in his great kindness has done for you."

The man stood quietly on the beach watching the sail of Jesus' boat until it was a dot on the blue expanse of the mountain-ringed lake. Then returning to his former home in one of the cities of the Decapolis, he told his story and all men marveled at his deliverance from evil.

> Then they cried to the Lord in their trouble,
>   and he delivered them from their distress;
> he brought them out of darkness and gloom,
>   and broke their bonds asunder.
> Let them thank the Lord for his steadfast love,
>   for his wonderful works to the sons of men!
> For he shatters the doors of bronze,
>   and cuts in two the bars of iron.
>
> PSALM 107.13-16

22

Jairus' Daughter and the Woman in the Crowd

MK 5.21-43 (MT 9.18-26;
LK 8.40-56)

*Heal me, O Lord, and I shall be
  healed;
save me, and I shall be saved;
for thou art my praise.*
                    JEREMIAH 17.14

AFTER LEAVING the Decapolis, Jesus sailed across the Sea of Galilee to its western shore. There he saw a friendly crowd lining the beach where his boat was to land. Unlike the Greeks who had asked him to leave their side of the lake, the Galileans of this region welcomed the Master. Here his message was bearing fruit. Many of his fellow countrymen, having opened their hearts to Jesus, had received abundant life from him.

In the sunshine of that Galilean morning, while a brisk wind tumbled lively waves upon the beach, Jesus' friends crowded around him glad to be in his presence. In their happiness they felt as though they were basking in God's smile. As Jesus began to speak to them, people gave him rapt attention, believing that he spoke the words of life.

Suddenly there was an interruption. One of the chief men of the town pushed through the listening throng on the beach. The crowd parted respectfully to let this synagogue official through, but many wondered what was on his mind.

"Has Jairus come to dispute with Jesus?" whispered one who knew that synagogue authorities everywhere, as well as the scribes and Pharisees, were hostile to Jesus.

"To me he seems more like a distraught man than an indignant official," the first man's companion replied under his breath. "See his furrowed brow and distracted air."

A third man joined the low conversation. "Did you not know that Jairus' only daughter lies at the point of death?" he asked. "Nothing can save her now, but Jairus must be asking help from this man of Nazareth. You know he is reputed to be a healer."

"We know, we know," responded the first man, vigorously nodding his head, "but it must have been hard for the ruler of our synagogue to humble his pride enough to beg the Master for his daughter's healing. What will the Pharisees think of him?"

While the men were still whispering, Jairus reached the center of the crowd and knelt at Jesus' feet. Fatherly concern had dissolved any doubts this responsible official may have entertained concerning the teacher from Nazareth. "Master," Jairus pleaded, interrupting Jesus' discourse, "my little girl is dying. I pray you, come and lay your hands on her and make her well so that she may live."

Would Jesus break off his address in order to hurry to the bedside of a twelve-year-old child, and a girl at that? Those watching him believed that Jesus faced a dilemma. Everyone had a solution for it.

"He must finish his discourse first. He might never have a crowd as large as this to talk to again."

"But the child will die."

"Well, she's only a girl, isn't she?"

"As if that matters to the Master!"

"Anyway, he could send one of his disciples."

The situation was no dilemma to Jesus who turned instantly and followed Jairus. The crowd hurried along with the Master, but his disciples closed in around him so that his progress through the town's narrow streets would not be blocked.

Halfway to the sick girl's house he halted abruptly. "Who touched my garments?" he inquired.

"Master," complained his disciples, "you see how we are jostled on all sides. It is impossible to say who touched you."

Jesus turned to look at those behind him. He knew that one of them had touched his garment because he had felt some of his healing power going forth from him. A timid woman stepped forward hesitantly.

She was pale and thin but, strangely enough, her clear, bright eyes indicated health. Only that moment she had been cured of the hemorrhage that had drained her strength for the past twelve years and had, during that long time, made her ceremonially unclean. When she touched the fringe of Jesus' garment, she had been made whole. Trembling with joy and no longer afraid of contaminating others with her ritual defilement, she approached Jesus and knelt at his feet.

"It was I, Master," she confessed, "who touched your garment."

Her story was quickly told. She said that all of her money had been spent on doctors whose treatments, far from helping her, served only to make her malady worse. Though there was no hope of a cure by human means, her faith in God's healing power remained strong. When she heard of Jesus, she believed that he could make her well. "I could be cured if I merely touched his garment," she had thought.

Approaching him near enough to do this was difficult, for the Law in Leviticus 15.25 stated that one with her malady was "unclean" and therefore forbidden to touch anyone. Today the presence of the crowd gave her a chance. Furtively she edged closer and closer to him from behind. Carefully, so as not to touch his person, she stretched out her hand and lightly brushed one of the four tassels ornamenting the four corners of his cloak. These symbolic tassels tied with a blue thread served as reminders of a Jewish man's obligations under the Law (Number 15.38-39).

After listening to the woman's story, Jesus blessed her, saying, "Daughter, your faith has healed you. Go in peace, forever free from your disease." There may have been other women whom he addressed as "daughter," but this is the only instance recorded in the Gospels. By using this intimate term he clearly endorsed this woman's faith which, venturing forth, had been met by the restoring power of God.

During this interruption Jairus waited impatiently. Every minute counted now, for his little girl's strength was rapidly ebbing. Yet, because his own anxiety had made him more sensitive to the troubles of others, he rejoiced in the woman's cure. It made God's healing power a vividly present reality. Seeing that in this hour God had come among his people to help them, Jairus was confident that the Master would reach his child's bedside in time

But it was not to be. Panting messengers arrived, having run all the way from his house. Their frozen expressions indicated to Jairus, even before they spoke, that the worst had happened.

Gravely the men announced, "Your daughter is dead. There is no need to bring the Master farther."

Not knowing what to do next, Jairus stood dazed in the middle of the road until Jesus, far from turning away, put his hand on the distraught man's arm and said, "Do not be afraid. Now is the time to hold firmly to your faith."

Dismissing the crowd and taking only Peter, James, and John with him, Jesus hurried with the sorrowing father to his house. When they arrived they found it already a scene of grief, with hired mourners weeping and wailing and musicians playing upon their flutes the doleful music of death.

"Why are you lamenting?" Jesus asked the noisy group. "The child is not dead—she is sleeping."

With a burst of rude laughter the professional mourners mocked him. No one could tell them about death; they knew it when they saw it. No doubt beneath their scorn lay jealousy of the authority he had taken upon himself in this house of death where they had been called to officiate. Their ridicule failed to shake Jesus' serenity. Abruptly he ordered them out of the house and, with only the child's father and mother and his three disciples, he entered the little girl's room.

She lay motionless on her bed, her eyes closed. Taking her hand, as if to impart some of his own vitality to her, Jesus spoke two words, saying, *"Talitha cumi."* They were the loving command familiar in Aramaic-speaking households when night ended and a new day awaited a young daughter's awakening. The words meant, "Little girl, wake up!"

At Jesus' command the child shook off her sleep, slowly rose, and began to walk around the room, all the while touching familiar objects, the bed and table, the chair and lamp. Scarcely believing their eyes, her parents watched her until Jesus told them to give her something to eat. When she ate a bowl of soup they were finally convinced that what they saw was real.

The story of Jairus' daughter is like a prism flashing a wide spectrum of meanings, one shading into another and all brilliant with the poetry of the Gospel. It is possible to interpret the story as one of healing from apparent death, for Jesus' words, taken at their face value, support such a view. To Christ's later followers, looking back upon the event after his resurrection, the raising of Jairus' daughter appeared to anticipate his own conquest of death and to undergird Paul's belief, "As in Adam all die, so in Christ shall all be made alive" (1 Corinthians 15.22).

To the crowds in Galilee the event gave further evidence that Jesus' ministry was one of power and that his message to John the Baptist had been true. The blind were receiving their sight, the lame were walking, the deaf hearing, and this morning a girl who had been pronounced dead was raised up. Jesus did not spend his time merely speaking comforting words or patching up life's ills, but he grappled with evil itself in all its manifestations of ignorance, despair, suffering, and death, and he made the miseries of men yield to the power of the living God. His fight would continue, but many Galileans saw that the victory was already his.

Finally, to Jairus and his wife one thing was clear. The healthy vigor of a once ailing woman and the laughter and footfalls of their young daughter testified that the Lord's healing power was available to his people.

23

His Brothers and Sisters

JN 2.12; 7.3-14; MK 6.2-6
(MT 13.54-58); MK 3.31-35
(MT 12.46; LK 8.19);
ACTS 1.14; I COR 9.5
JAMES: ACTS 12.17; 15.13;
21.18; GAL 1.19; 2.9,12;
I COR 15.7

*"Is not this the carpenter, the son
of Mary and brother of James and
Joses and Judas and Simon, and are
not his sisters here with us?"*

MARK 6.3

SITTING IN A FAMILY conference with his four brothers, Jesus listened patiently to their advice. Though they did not fully understand him at this time, which was about midway in his mission, they felt a keen sense of responsibility and deep affection for one who had been so close to them during their childhood years in Nazareth. They were proud of him. Because the wonders he was performing redounded to the glory of the entire family and gave them all a vicarious sense of importance, they were eager to promote his career. Consequently, on learning that many of Jesus' early followers were deserting him, the brothers discussed with him how he might regain his waning popularity.

Jesus was now preaching and healing in obscure Galilean villages. Though threats had been made against his life, his brothers knew him too well to believe that fear alone kept him in semihiding, far from Jerusalem where his enemies were concentrated.

"No one can win fame by preaching here," commented James, the eldest of the four brothers. "Galilee is such an out-of-the-way corner. All the important religious leaders live in Judea." Pointing to Jesus to emphasize his advice, James said, "You must proclaim your message there."

Joses, the second brother, instantly took up the argument, offering a practical plan to implement James' hard-headed advice. "Go up with us to the Feast of the Tabernacles in Jerusalem," he urged.

It was autumn. With the harvest now in, the brothers would soon join multitudes of pilgrims bound for Jerusalem's annual Feast of Tabernacles in memory of the forty years Israel once spent in the wilderness. This festival was a joyful renewal of the people's covenant with the Lord. On hillsides surrounding the Holy City each family attending the celebration would build a rustic shelter or booth of branches in which to sleep and eat during the feast's eight days. His brothers believed that this was an opportunity for him to display his power and win acclaim throughout Israel.

The third brother, Judas, now added his voice to the discussion, saying, "If you go to Jerusalem the crowds will see your wonderful deeds. No man works in secret if he wants to be known."

All the brothers nodded vigorously at this statement, which led Simon, the youngest, to ask a direct question, "Since you can perform wonders, why do you not let the world see them?"

"Why indeed?" chorused the four.

The Master looked from one to another. Their advice was sound, but it was based on worldly considerations. Did his brothers not know that Jesus was no publicity-seeker, no wonder-worker greedy for power? The devil had once dangled before Jesus a temptation similar to this one.

"Go up to the feast yourselves," said Jesus, "but I shall not go with you, for my time has not yet come."

He had replied in a similar way to his mother when she mentioned to him the lack of wine at the wedding feast, saying, "My hour has not yet come."

Both replies indicated his refusal to work wonders for his own glory. He never sought anything for himself. He needed to be free to act in his own way without family coercion, for his deeds required spiritual timing unknown to those with worldly ambitions.

Grumbling at Jesus' stubbornness, the brothers departed for Jerusalem sure that he was throwing away his best chance to dazzle the crowds. How could he be the Messiah if he would not show himself in Jerusalem? As the Fourth Gospel states, "even his brothers did not believe in him" (John 7.5)—did not yet envision his true glory.

Halfway through the Feast of Tabernacles, however, Jesus went to Jerusalem, not with the fanfare of a self-styled messiah, as his brothers had desired, but privately, almost secretly. Had he come as the Messiah, the religious authorities, who feared him and were on the alert for him, would have had just cause for action against him. But he entered the Holy City quietly, as a teacher and prophet against whom no legal accusation could be made.

Despite his precautions to avoid a tumult, his presence stirred up considerable excitement. He was criticized and defended, until it seemed that everyone knew about this man from Nazareth and held strong opinions concerning him. Some debated with him; some believed in him; others accused him; still others tried to have him arrested. Watching these events, his brothers must have been confused by the contradictory responses Jesus aroused.

Who James, Joses, Judas, Simon, and their sisters were is a question that has been debated for centuries. Besides the story told above, which is the only incident featuring the brothers, they are referred to eight times in the Gospels, Acts, and 1 Corinthians. James is mentioned seven additional times in Acts and in the Letters.

At the beginning of Jesus' ministry, after the wedding at Cana, as we noted in Mary's story, he went to live in Capernaum with his mother, his disciples, and his brothers. Here they all apparently made their home for a while.

Nazareth was, of course, the family's original home. In this village nestled among the southern Galilean hills, only twenty miles from Capernaum, Jesus' brothers and sisters had been born and raised and he himself had grown to manhood. The inhabitants of Nazareth knew all there was to know about Joseph and Mary's family, or so they thought. The facts, however, did not particularly impress them. When Jesus became famous, these people searched their memories but found few clues to his greatness. As children, many of them had played with Jesus and his brothers in the narrow main street, running and shouting, inventing games, and dodging laden donkeys. Jesus had often led a crowd of boys up the hill behind the village to catch a glimpse of the mysterious Mediterranean shimmering on the western horizon or of the blue Sea of Galilee enclosed within the mountains to the east. From their hilltop the boys marveled at the snow-capped majesty of Mount Hermon and the grandeur of the whole Anti-Lebanon range to the north. Villagers who used to encounter Mary at Nazareth's well recalled how proud she had been of her family. As for Joseph, most homes contained some sturdy household article made in his shop. Undoubtedly many of the people were related to Jesus. Were his sisters married and still living there and had his brothers wed girls from Nazareth?

Despite all this, or perhaps because of it, the men and women of Nazareth listened unsympathetically when Jesus came to preach in their synagogue.

"What is so unusual about him that all Galilee rings with his name?" men asked.

"Did he not sit beside us on these very benches when we recited our lessons here in the synagogue school?"

"Who taught him the message he proclaims?" asked others, filled with resentment against one they considered no better than they were.

Stories of the cures he performed elsewhere aroused their curiosity, but became merely a source of irritation when he failed to accomplish marvels at Nazareth. "Are we not important enough to have a miracle performed for us?" they complained, unaware that their own lack of faith was the reason Jesus could not demonstrate God's power to them.

Around the village well and outside the synagogue, critical voices were raised. "Is not this man our village carpenter?" people asked each other querulously. "Is he not Mary's son and the brother of James, Joses, Judas, and Simon? And are not his sisters living here with us?"

No one would have doubted that the people of Nazareth spoke the simple truth had it not been for the second-century dogma of Mary's perpetual virginity. This belief caused churchmen to wonder who these people called brothers and sisters could be. The natural interpretation of all New Testament references to Jesus' brothers is, of course, that they were truly his brothers. Because Joseph took Mary as his wife "but knew her not until she had borne a son" (Matthew 1.25) and Jesus is described as Mary's "first-born son" (Luke 2.7), the reader of these Gospels is prepared for the presence of younger children in the family of Joseph and Mary. Moreover, their existence underlines the reality of his humanity.

But the dogma concerning Mary required Church fathers to find some explanation other than the natural one for the relationship of Jesus to James, Joses, Judas, Simon, and their sisters. According to one view, they were Joseph's children by a former marriage and thus older than Mary's son. This belief, based on legends from apocryphal gospels which lack scriptural support, is held by some Protestants together with the Greek Orthodox and other Eastern Churches.

Jerome, the great fourth-century translator of the Bible into Latin, first proposed the view held by Roman Catholics. He believed that the brothers were actually cousins of Jesus. Arguing that the New Testament word "brother" may also mean "kinsman," Jerome supported his theory by elaborate interpretations of biblical evidence in the course of which he declared that these "cousins" were also disciples.

Wherever the truth lies, everyone agrees that humanly James, Joses, Judas, and Simon were very close to Jesus. If they were younger brothers and if their father Joseph died before they were grown, as we suggested earlier, Jesus may have had to undertake their support. Was this the reason he did not begin his public ministry until he was thirty? Perhaps, during his unrecorded years in Nazareth, he learned how to quiet a group of restless youngsters by telling them stories. It may have been thus that he trained himself in the art of story-telling, an art in which he was a consummate master.

However misguided the brothers' advice to Jesus about going up to Jerusalem, it reveals their strong sense of family loyalty, a loyalty that on another occasion prompted them to investigate the rumor that he was out of his mind. As we have already noted, they went with Mary to the crowded house where he was preaching, prepared to bring him home should the ugly rumor prove true. At this time, perhaps because they were unsympathetic to his mission, they had clearly lost touch with him. The proverb Jesus quoted at Nazareth surely applied to them, "A prophet is not without honor, except in his own country, and among his own kin, and in his own house" (Mark 6.4). Though they did not give him due honor, they acknowledged their duty as their "brother's keeper."

Good men of limited vision, it was hard for them to understand Jesus, living as he did in a different sphere from theirs. It was as though an eagle had been raised in a family of moles. After the resurrection their eyes were opened and they waited with Mary, the disciples, and the faithful women in the upper room in Jerusalem spending their days in prayer until the Holy Spirit was given to them. The final reference to the brothers as a group is in one of Paul's letters (1 Corinthians 9.5) in which he indicates that they were married and traveled with their wives spreading the good news of Christ in whom they finally believed.

For many years James, the eldest of the brothers, as abundant evidence shows, presided over the mother Church in Jerusalem. When Peter escaped from prison he immediately reported the fact to James. Three years after Paul's conversion on the Damascus road, he visited James in Jerusalem and fourteen years later was again received in the Holy City, this time by "James and Cephas [Peter] and John, who were reputed to be pillars" (Galatians 2.9). Later James sent emissaries to investigate the situation in Antioch and he presided over two Church councils.

The Book of Acts shows James' qualities of leadership, his ability to conciliate opposing viewpoints, his appreciation of those who differed from him, and his understanding of the needs of the Gentile world. Clearly his position in the Church was due to merit as well as to his relationship to Jesus. The ultimate basis of his leadership, however, rested upon his faith in the risen Christ who had appeared to him (1 Corinthians 15.7), thus sealing his final understanding of his brother's glory.

24

The Paralyzed Man at the Pool of Bethzatha

JN 5.1-18   *"Rise, take up your pallet, and walk."*
                                                                    JOHN 5.8

THE POOL of Bethzatha near the Sheep's Gate in Jerusalem was a
well-known place of healing. Its name was sometimes pronounced
Bethesda or Bethsaida. Scores of blind, lame, paralyzed, and diseased
people came here hoping that by bathing in the moving waters they
would be cured. An intermittent spring may have fed the pool and
caused its recurrent heaving and bubbling that people attributed to
an angel who was believed to "trouble" the water.

In the shade of the five porticoes that had been built around the
pool, sick people moaned on their pallets or stared with vacant eyes,
waiting for the water to become active. When that happened there
would be a rush for the steps leading into the pool. According to current belief, healing energy was released by the first stirrings of the
surface, but only one person could be healed at each moving of the
waters. Other sufferers had to wait for the next disturbance.

From his thin mattress a paralyzed man watched the mirror surface
break into motion again and again, but always someone else reached
the water first. The man had been helpless for the past thirty-eight
years, able only to drag himself painfully over the ground by his
arms. With no friends waiting to carry him into the pool at the right
moment, he had little chance of ever being cured. Nevertheless he
remained on his pallet beneath one of the porticoes, convinced that
some day he would walk away on his own legs.

One Sabbath day during a feast of the Jews, the paralyzed man became aware that a stranger was looking at him. This stranger did not stare with the bold curiosity of the usual passer-by, but with an expression that all but said, "I know of your suffering, for I share it with you, but I can help you, if you will!"

The man painfully changed his position. He was attracted by the stranger's vitality in such sharp contrast to his own weakness. A healthy person usually recoiled slightly from the sight of a crippled body or looked with disdain upon one whose helplessness was believed to be the penalty for his sin. But this strong and vigorous stranger seemed genuinely concerned with the paralyzed man's plight.

Suddenly he realized that he was being addressed. "Do you want to be healed?" came the stranger's question, warm and golden like the sun breaking through a dark cloud.

Did he want to be healed—he who had been unable even to stand up these many years! What a question it was! Yet in a moment he realized that the stranger's query showed extraordinary insight. After lying helpless for so long, was he indeed ready to take up the burdens of an active life? If he were cured, people would not give him special consideration; he would have to work for a living instead of lying all day beside the pool; he could no longer indulge in self-pity. But beyond all this he knew that by accepting a cure he would enter into a new relationship with God, the ultimate source of all health and soundness.

That was the challenge. For a moment he hesitated, expressing his irresolution in a complaint. "I have no friend to help me into the pool when the water moves," he told the stranger. Had that been part of his trouble all these years, his conviction that others were to blame for not helping him?

"Rise," commanded the stranger, sweeping aside the man's objection and bidding him do the impossible. "Rise, take up your pallet, and walk!"

With a great effort the invalid pulled himself erect only to discover that his legs were strong enough to bear his weight. To his amazement he found he could walk. More than that, he could carry a burden. Rolling up his mat, he hoisted it to his shoulder and, with a somewhat unsteady gait, he made his way through an astonished crowd, out of the portico, and into the street. What joy to be walking again, seeing the world from a man's height. In his great happiness he did not notice that his benefactor had slipped away from the crowd. The weight of his bed roll now bore down on his shoulder but it reassured him that he was indeed cured.

Before he had carried his conspicuous burden far, he encountered some zealous guardians of the Sabbath Law. They stopped him and asked, "Do you not know that today is the Sabbath? It is against the Law to carry your pallet today."

To one who for the first time in many years was experiencing fullness of life and joy, this trifling legal objection seemed ridiculous. Anyway, he was not to blame for Sabbath-breaking. "The man who healed me commanded me to do so," he explained.

"Who is he?" asked the Jewish legalists, though they must have had their own suspicions.

"I do not know," came the reply.

Continuing on to the temple he began to see his cure in the light of prophecy. Surely his healing pointed to the dawn of a new day when men would see the glory of God. Was his own body actually one of the signs pointing to the coming of the Lord?

> They shall see the glory of the Lord
>   the majesty of our God. . . .
> Then the eyes of the blind shall be opened,
>   and the ears of the deaf unstopped;
> then shall the lame man leap like a hart.
>   ISAIAH 35.2,5-6

Later, while walking in the temple, the man encountered Jesus and learned who had healed him. "See," exclaimed the Master, "you are now cured, whole in both body and soul!"

The man nodded vigorously and danced a few steps in sheer high spirits, testing the marvelous soundness of his once useless legs.

"But sin no more," Jesus warned him, "or something even worse than that from which you suffered might assail you."

As Jesus spoke, the healed man could all but see the ugly shapes of anger, resentment, envy, revenge, fear—the devils possessing men who are estranged from God. These were sin's companions and they could come to harm him again if he admitted sin into his life. But no evil could breach the citadel of his present joy.

Expecting the religious leaders who had questioned him to share his wonder and thankfulness, he hastened to tell them that it was Jesus who had cured him. This information raised a veritable hornet's nest of controversy, for the Jews immediately began to attack Jesus for accomplishing this cure on the Sabbath.

Again he faced the old charge of Sabbath-breaking. But in answering his opponents with the statement, "My Father is still at work and so I work too," he raised another issue—that of blasphemy. By associating his healing of the paralyzed man with God's ongoing acts of creation, Jesus seemed to his enemies to claim the attributes of deity, thus making himself God's equal. This was certainly blasphemy. His opponents paid no attention to Jesus' own statement, "The Father is greater than I" (John 14.28), but continued to base their case against him both on his disregard of the Law concerning the holy day and on blasphemy.

If Jesus infuriated the religious authorities by healing the man at the Pool of Bethzatha, the event gave his friends much to ponder. Acts like this dramatized the fact that he brought abundant life to those who turned to him in faith. It was clear that he was no ordinary miracle-worker playing upon the credulity of men. Who then was Jesus and how could he do his wonderful works? Jesus himself answered these questions. "The works which the Father has granted me to accomplish," he declared, "these very works which I am doing, bear me witness that the Father has sent me" (John 5.36).

25

The Widow of Nain and Her Son

LK 7.11-16   *Blessed are those who mourn, for
                                      they shall be comforted.*
                                      MATTHEW 5.4

NAIN WAS a pleasant town as the meaning of its name stated. It was situated in Galilee about six miles south of Nazareth on the lower slope of a hill called Little Hermon. The town's elevation afforded its inhabitants an extensive view of thriving groves of figs and olives and of the fruitful Plain of Esdraelon in the distance. The people of Nain counted themselves fortunate to live in such a delightful place. Today, however, though the sun was pleasantly warm and a gentle breeze from the west stirred the blue-green leaves of the olive trees, the people of Nain mourned. A young man of promise, the only son of a widowed mother, had died in their town.

In a society in which men were the only breadwinners, a widow's plight could become well-nigh desperate, as the old story of Ruth and Naomi testified. Those ancient widows of Judah lived precariously on charity and on Ruth's meager gleanings in the harvest fields until she remarried. The young man now lying on his bier had dutifully supported his widowed mother until today. Now that he was dead, to whom could she turn?

Most of the townspeople came to the funeral. The tragedy of a young life ended in its morning and of a woman left desolate touched the pity of all. Today this widow sorrowed, but no one knew who might be chief mourner in tomorrow's funeral.

Leaning upon the arm of a kindly neighbor, the widow stumbled through the town gate in a daze. Behind her came bearers carrying on their shoulders the wooden poles of her son's bier. They walked with measured steps along the road toward the cemetery situated, as the Law required, at some distance from town. The flute players and the mourning women were followed by the crowd moving in a slow procession to the sad music of death. The well-known dirge sung by the professional mourners awakened memories of other funerals. Life seemed only a sorrowful journey toward the grave and many wept with the widow.

Some of those in the procession must have remembered the story of the fiery prophet Elijah raising the widow of Zarephath's son from death. Following his master's example, Elisha had raised the Shunamite widow's son to life (2 Kings 4.18-37). Shunem was only three miles from Nain, on another side of Little Hermon, and the wonder of the ancient story of God's restoring love lingered in the neighborhood. Today, however, the people looked for no miracle of divine mercy, for the Lord seemed to be hiding his face. Where was there a living prophet whose mighty acts showed forth the presence of God with his people? Where could one see the glory of the Lord?

While those who bewailed death marched heavily out of Nain, a lively group of people, in startling contrast to the mourners, approached the town, singing as they went. They were an enthusiastic band of Jesus' disciples and followers traveling with him through Galilee to proclaim God's kingdom and to manifest its coming. No suggestion of darkness or death restrained the joyfulness of their voices or the lightness of their steps.

Inevitably the two processions met, Nain being a walled town with a single narrow road leading to it. Glancing up, the widow saw the strangers standing respectfully aside waiting for her son's bier to be carried past them. Then hearing the words, "Do not weep," she paused, surprised at the note of compassion in the stranger's voice, and she looked up into Jesus' face.

The bearers also halted, the wailing stopped, the flutes became silent. While the mourners of death and the heralds of new life waited, Jesus strode forward and, placing his hand upon the bier, commanded, "Young man, I say to you, rise up."

A long-drawn sigh came from the crowd and then everyone held his breath. Only Peter, James, and John had heard such words before when they had been addressed to Jairus' daughter. But even these three disciples were amazed when the dead man stirred, sat up, and began to speak. All eyes turned to Jesus. With a gesture like that of Elijah's when he descended from the upper room to give the once dead boy to his mother, Jesus presented the widow with her living son.

Holy fear now filled the people of Nain as they stood in awe before the empty bier. It was fear like that of the shepherds on a night long before when they saw the splendor of God's glory shining over Bethlehem. The young man's return to life signified that the Lord had indeed come among his people in all the power of his creative, restoring love. He had sent them this great prophet, as mighty as any of old, a prophet with divine authority to give sight to the blind, hearing to the deaf, life to the dead.

Taking her son's arm, the widow rejoiced as she recalled the words of a psalm,

> Thou has turned for me my mourning into dancing;
> thou hast loosed my sackcloth
> and girded me with gladness,
> that my soul may praise thee and not be silent.
>
> PSALM 30.11-12

The mourners stood irresolute for a moment before turning around to follow Jesus and his friends in a single joyful procession back to Nain. The flute players changed their tune and blew a lively one while all the people shouted, "A great prophet has appeared among us! God has visited his people."

26

The Sinful Woman Who Anointed Jesus

LK 7.36-50; cf.MK 14.3-9
(MT 26.6-13; JN 12.1-8)

*"Therefore I tell you, many as her
sins are, they are forgiven, for her
love is great; whereas he to whom
little is forgiven has but little love."*
LUKE 7.47 (MOFFATT)

BECAUSE THE WOMAN was well known in town, she crept furtively
along the street toward the house of Simon the Pharisee, holding a
fold of her cloak over her face to avoid being recognized. Accusing
glances or leering stares usually followed her when she appeared in
public, for she was a harlot.

She had not been invited to Simon's banquet—far from it, for no
Pharisee would welcome to his home a woman of her reputation.
She planned to mingle with the crowd of onlookers gazing through
Simon's open door and perhaps catch sight, among the invited guests
inside, of the new teacher and prophet, Jesus of Nazareth. She might
even drift unnoticed into the house itself and thus come near to the
man whose teachings had changed her life. At feasts like Simon's the
distinction between guests and strangers often became blurred when
onlookers were invited in to share food left over from the banquet.

On this occasion the woman was not trying to force her way into
a place where she was unwelcome, nor was she attracted by the hospitality freely offered to onlookers. She merely wanted to see Jesus.
Tightening her hold on the alabaster flask concealed beneath her cloak,
she hurried on. Was it foolish of her, she wondered, to plan her ges-

ture of thanks to one for whom she felt such deep gratitude? It could do no real good to anyone, least of all to him, but it expressed the love that overflowed her heart. Surely the Master, being the sort of person he was, would understand her motive and accept her homage.

But what would Simon say? Pharisees were so sternly righteous! They were good men, of course, but they upheld the Law so rigidly that sinners like herself lived in fear that they might someday invoke the rule in Deuteronomy (22.21) that harlots be stoned. But she took courage from a story she had been told about some scribes and Pharisees who brought an adulteress to Jesus for condemnation (John 8.3-11). He turned to the woman's accusers and said, "He who is without sin, let him be the first one to throw a stone at her." When they all crept away, Jesus said to her, "Neither do I condemn you. You may now go, but do not sin again."

When Jesus first preached in the town of Simon the Pharisee, the woman had watched from the edge of the crowd. He must be like one of the prophets of old, she thought, intrigued by his fiery earnestness and his integrity. She marveled that one with such power as his could be so simple in manner. His message held out to her the possibility of forgiveness. For the first time she saw that there could be for her an escape from the miserable trap in which she felt caught. She believed that, instead of being soiled and joyless, her life could one day become pure and shining.

"What makes Jesus so different from other religious people, especially the Pharisees?" she asked herself. One answer was obvious. The Pharisees carefully protected their own righteousness, avoiding contamination from sinners like herself, but Jesus welcomed sinners and all those upon whom the best Jewish society turned its back. Had not Jesus chosen a prominent publican, the tax collector of Capernaum, to be his disciple?

Feeling welcome, she had listened to Jesus whenever he preached. Soon his perfect holiness and purity made her conscious of her need for pardon and cleansing. "But I have nothing good to offer God in exchange for his forgiveness," she told herself in dismay. If the Pharisees were right in believing that a person's dealings with God were on a strict balance-sheet basis, so many good deeds meriting so much forgiveness, there could be no hope for such a great sinner as herself. She had no merits to cancel her transgressions and could never, according to the Pharisees, be counted among the righteous. "In God's sight I am bankrupt!" she cried, tormented by a sense of alienation from the Lord.

Once in her childhood she had felt herself accepted as a daughter of God, but that was long ago. Since then she had formed no permanent relationships with people and the very superficiality of her connections with others deepened her sense of estrangement from the central reality of life. Where could she turn for help?

She felt alone with the burden of her guilt. No one had ever taught her one of the great insights of her people that "No man living is righteous before thee" (Psalm 143.2). According to this, the most saintly Pharisee inevitably fell short of perfect uprightness, for

> If thou, O Lord, shouldst mark iniquities,
>   Lord, who could stand?
> But there is forgiveness with thee.
>
> PSALM 130.3-4

From Jesus the woman learned for the first time of God's forgiveness. One day, having decided to make the leap of faith and abandon her former life, she said to herself, "I will go to my heavenly Father, and I will say to him that I have sinned and am no longer worthy to be his daughter."

No sooner had the thought taken possession of her than she knew beyond a doubt that God had been in the shadow all the time, waiting to welcome her. Pardon and peace flooded her being. Her past was erased in her reunion with God.

Today the woman felt that she was a new person, no longer bound to her former profession. She was free, whole, joyful, scarred by her past it is true, but delivered from its bondage. Her self-respect had returned. Her own contempt for herself had been worse than all the enmity of others. Now she rejoiced in the new life that had been hers since she had become a follower of Jesus.

All this was in her heart when, peering through the open door, she saw Jesus eating at Simon's table. Contrary to Eastern custom, the Master had been received with little courtesy. His feet had not been washed or his head anointed. Moreover, Simon had failed to give him the warm greeting invariably accorded an honored guest. Did Simon see Jesus merely as an itinerant preacher, a social inferior to whom only scant attention need be paid? Had the Pharisee invited one whom he regarded as a poor man in order to gain merit for himself?

The woman took her alabaster flask from beneath her cloak and advanced boldly through the crowd of guests, servants, and curious bystanders milling around the dinner table. She knelt near Jesus and began to weep, remembering, in the presence of this holy man, her life of sin. Her tears fell on his feet, which she wiped with her long hair and kissed. She poured fragrant oil from her flask upon his feet, anointing him, as it were, with the oil of her gladness. Penitence, love, and, above all, thanksgiving were all mingled in her act.

Her mood of devotion lasted but a moment, for Simon soon caught sight of her. Frightened, she tried to melt into the crowd again, but it was too late. The host stared at her in affront while all eyes followed his. Pointing rudely to Jesus, Simon spoke, saying, "If this man were really a prophet, he would know what sort of woman this is who has just touched him. He would know that she is a sinner!" Simon was all but shouting, clearly enjoying a perverted sense of righteousness in condemning Jesus.

"Simon is right," agreed one of the other Pharisees. "This preacher cannot be a prophet. To allow this sinner to approach him shows him up as either a fool or a knave."

Painful though this exposure of her life of shame was, the woman was more distressed that Jesus had been accused and all because of her. To preserve his own reputation among these righteous Pharisees, he might, she thought, now turn angrily on her and order her away. She could not blame him if he did. Every man for himself—was not that the way of the world? She braced herself for his displeasure.

Jesus spoke, addressing Simon. Attention was immediately diverted from her and she was grateful to Jesus for rescuing her from embarrassment. "Simon," said Jesus, "I want to say something to you."

"What is it, Teacher?" asked Simon.

Everyone present, in their absorption in Jesus' parable, forgot that the sinful woman still stood in their midst. The point Jesus made in his story about the creditor and his two debtors was that he who is forgiven most, loves most. Simon had to agree to this truth, while the crowd applauded the Master's wisdom. All were now on his side.

Finally Jesus said to his host, as he gestured toward the woman, "Simon, do you see this woman? When I entered your house, you gave me no water for my feet, but she has washed them with her tears and dried them with her hair." He continued to compare the Pharisee's slights with the woman's kindness, ending with the statement, "Because her love is great, her sins, which are many, are forgiven. He who is forgiven little, loves little."

God's pardon had created love in her heart, a love as great as the depth of her conscious need. She was capable of love because she had accepted forgiveness.

Simon, his eyes flashing, rose and stalked away. He was outraged that Jesus had judged him less worthy than this notoriously sinful woman. Was he not a Pharisee? He knew he was a good man and he felt secure in his own righteousness. By his own efforts, by disciplined living, and by zealously upholding the Law he would continue to defend Israel and earn his own blessedness. He felt no need for forgiveness.

Jesus turned to the penitent woman, "Your sins are forgiven," he declared. "Your faith has saved you. Go in peace."

The penitent woman appears only in this one incident from the end of the seventh chapter of Luke. Medieval scholars searching for her identity, decided that she must be Mary Magdalene who is introduced in the beginning of Luke's eighth chapter. This identification rests primarily on the fact that these two women appear very close together in Luke's gospel, surely an inadequate reason for believing that the two are actually one woman. Their situations are completely different. Jesus cured Mary Magdalene, not of moral sickness, as he did the penitent woman, but of a grave bodily or mental disease. Mary was said to be a person "from whom seven demons had gone out" (Luke 8.2). This is not the description of a harlot. Mary Magdalene has long suffered from guilt by association—association on a page of the Bible. The alabaster flask, long hair, tears, and remorseful expression with which Renaissance artists invariably depicted her rightly belong to the nameless harlot who, in gratitude for her great pardon, anointed Jesus' feet in the house of Simon the Pharisee.

The Gospels of Matthew, Mark, and John contain parallel accounts of another woman who anointed Jesus, this time in Bethany on the eve of his triumphal entry into Jerusalem. As the Fourth Gospel identifies this second woman, not as a sinner but as Mary, the sister of Martha and Lazarus, the story of this anointing will be told in connection with the sisters of Bethany.

V

IN THE FINAL MONTHS

OF HIS MINISTRY

27

The Greek Mother of an Afflicted Daughter

MK 7.24-30 (MT 15.21-28)

*For there is no distinction between
Jew and Greek; the same Lord is
Lord of all and bestows his riches
upon all who call upon him.*
ROMANS 10.12

THE GREEK MOTHER was in great trouble. Her daughter's mind was deranged and doctors believed that her recovery was unlikely because hers was a case, they said, of demon-possession. All ordinary remedies were useless against such a deadly ill. The neighbors, attempting to be helpful, suggested calling in an exorcist or one of the wandering miracle-workers who appeared from time to time in the neighborhood. Often such people were successful in driving out evil spirits, but the mother was opposed to incantations and magic, fearing that they might do more harm than good. "If there were only someone who possessed power superior to that of evil itself, I know he could drive out my child's demon," she said, gallantly refusing to give up hope of a cure, yet worn out by her endless battle with the girl's disorder.

News reached Syro-Phoenicia, where the Greek mother lived, that a Galilean prophet was able to drive out evil spirits. "How could I ever take my poor daughter all the way to Capernaum where he is?" asked the woman of the neighbor who brought her the news of Jesus.

"Many dangerous miles lie between this land of Syria and Galilee of the Jews," agreed the friend.

"Anyway," added the Greek woman sadly, "his power cannot be for Gentiles like us."

Her background was complicated. She and her daughter lived near the Syrian coast in the region once known as Phoenicia, a proud maritime country dominated by its two great seaports of Tyre and Sidon. Long ago in the days of Abraham, the original Phoenician inhabitants of this coastal area were called Canaanites, being identified as the cursed descendants of Noah's son Canaan (Genesis 9.25). Because these people worshiped heathen gods, a great gulf had always separated them from God's people, the descendants of Abraham.

Three hundred years before this woman's time, Phoenicia had been conquered by the Greeks, who left their stamp upon it. Though the Romans had wrested this coastal strip from the Greeks and had recently incorporated it into Roman Syria, its inhabitants still spoke Greek, as did this woman, and worshiped Greek gods. Roman, Greek, Phoenician—there was nothing in the woman's complex background, she feared, to entitle her to help from one who belonged to the people of God and who preached the coming of his kingdom.

When she heard a rumor that Jesus had crossed the border between Galilee and Phoenicia and was staying in seclusion somewhere in her country, she saw her opportunity and made her plans. Entrusting her afflicted daughter to the care of a friend, she set out in search of the Galilean prophet. He was traveling along a road with his disciples when she encountered him. Immediately she knelt in the dust at his feet.

"O Lord, Son of David," she cried, using his messianic title, "have mercy on me, for my daughter is tormented by a devil."

Silence followed her plea. Nevertheless she did not give up hope, but followed the travelers, crying out as she went. Was Jesus testing her sincerity and waiting for some clear evidence of her faith?

The disciples tried to end the uncomfortable situation by begging Jesus to send her away, but he did not do so. She was a woman in need and his compassion went out to her.

Half to himself and half to his disciples, as though sounding them out, Jesus said, "I was sent only to the lost sheep of the house of Israel." The disciples nodded in agreement. The Gospel, they believed, must first be preached to the Jews, who would then open God's kingdom to the whole world. If Jesus embarked on a ministry of healing among the Gentiles, his disciples feared that he would not have time to complete his mission to the Jews.

From the men's expressions, the Gentile mother saw that her plea was almost hopeless, yet she still would not give up. At this critical moment, with the disciples' faces registering impatience, she remained balanced and calm. As she knelt again at the Master's feet, she begged persistently, "Lord, help me!"

"It is not fair," replied Jesus, "to take the children's bread and throw it to the dogs."

What was the tone of his voice? What gestures accompanied his seemingly harsh and unfeeling reply? Was he expressing the disciples' point of view? Was he testing her? Certainly the Greek woman did not interpret his answer as an unkind refusal. Perhaps she saw his smile and answered with one of her own, matching his half-humorous saying with a witty answer. "You are right, Lord; yet pet dogs under the table eat scraps left by the children!"

She smiled triumphantly, for she believed, beyond reason or evidence, in Jesus' power to overcome evil and his willingness to bestow God's best gifts upon Gentiles as well as Jews.

"Woman," exclaimed Jesus, responding to her spirited good humor, "you have great faith! What you desire shall be done." Then he pronounced the words she so greatly desired to hear. "The evil spirit has left your daughter."

The Greek woman hurried home to find her daughter lying quietly in bed, her demon departed and her torment ended. Like the Capernaum official's son and the centurion's servant, this girl was delivered from her affliction by one whom she never saw, one to whom distance was no barrier to the exercise of his healing power. The most noteworthy aspect of her cure was that she, a Gentile girl, was healed by a Jew. This healing symbolized, as had the coming of the wise men to Jesus' cradle, the extension of Christ's kingdom to all nations. The old mold in which men tried to contain God's saving power for Israel alone was broken.

28

The Deaf and Dumb Man

MK 7.31-37

*In that day the deaf shall hear
the words of a book,
and out of their gloom and darkness
the eyes of the blind shall see.*
ISAIAH 29.18

TO THE DEAF and dumb man of Mark's story the world was a silent, confusing place. Having been born deaf, he had never heard and tried to imitate the sounds that make up speech and so, when he attempted to express himself, he made ugly, incoherent noises. These seemed to his neighbors to be caused by an impediment in his speech, but there was nothing wrong with his vocal cords. He was dumb because he had always been deaf.

Fortunately the man could see and so he did not suffer from the totally dark and silent isolation of those, like Helen Keller of our day, who cannot make any meaningful contact with the world without long and patient training. Nevertheless the man of Mark's story, even with his enormous advantage of sight and with his other lively senses of smell, taste, and touch, lived with a formidable obstacle. In his day, the deaf were protected by Law, "You shall not curse the deaf or put a stumbling block before the blind, but you shall fear your God: I am the Lord" (Leviticus 19.14). But there were no special schools in which they could be taught how to overcome their handicap. Moreover, deafness had a stigma attached to it, for it was believed to be the work of demons as well as an evidence of sin.

The deaf man could see the stars, but who could teach him that they are God's handiwork? Who, for that matter, could tell him about the Lord God of Israel? Often, when people tried to help him, he recoiled from them in fear, not realizing that their overtures were prompted by friendliness. He had never heard laughter, singing, or a word spoken in love. Even prayer was unknown to him. Cut off from the comforting companionship of others, the deaf man lived more and more within himself, a prey to all the demons that flourish in continual loneliness. Behind his barrier of deafness, distrust and ill will possessed him. Life to him meant endurance, not happiness.

"If only someone could get through to this poor, unfortunate creature," sighed his neighbors, baffled in their attempts to aid him.

When Jesus arrived in their town, everyone hailed him as a great healer, news of his cures having preceded him. Among the marvelous acts reported were his casting out of the demon that had made a certain man speechless (Matthew 9.32-34; Luke 11.14-15) and his conquest of another evil spirit that had caused both dumbness and blindness (Matthew 12.22-24). Such wonders, the Pharisees declared, were due to the fact that Jesus was in league with the Devil. The Master answered this illogical charge with his question, "If Satan casts out Satan, he is divided against himself; how then will his kingdom stand?" (Matthew 12.26).

The deaf and dumb man's neighbors saw the unreasonableness of the Pharisee's charges. The fact that Jesus had restored speech to other afflicted people encouraged them to bring their friend to the Master. Though the man was troubled by the jostling of the crowd and frightened by the strangeness of the occasion and though he himself knew nothing about Jesus, the faith of those leading him must somehow have communicated itself to him. Certainly Jesus' personality made an impression on him as he stood bewildered and trembling before the Master, half desiring to run from the curious stares of the people around him, yet half eager to see what this amazing stranger would do.

Noting that the man acted like a frightened animal, Jesus took him aside to accomplish this healing in private. First he put his fingers in the man's ears, appealing to his senses of sight and touch and indicating what affliction was to be cured. The ancient sign language of spitting indicated the driving away of demonic forces. Jesus then touched the deaf-mute's tongue, signifying that his speech was restored.

The man and his neighbors waited motionless while the Master looked up to heaven and sighed. Some of the bystanders thought he prayed before he spoke his healing word, "*Ephaphatha*"—be opened!"

The airy syllables of this Aramaic command were the first sounds the deaf man heard as the barrier separating him from other men fell down at Jesus' word. In another moment the man's tongue was released and he was speaking, doubtless exclaiming with the bystanders, "How wonderful is all that Jesus does! He makes even the deaf hear and the dumb speak." This healing was symbolic of Jesus' power to open men's ears to the word of God and enable their lips to glorify him.

29

The Father and His Epileptic Son

MK 9.14-29 (MT 17.14-21;   *"I believe; help my unbelief!"*
LK 9.34-43)   MARK 9.24

THE FATHER CARRIED such a burden of despair that his faith in God had begun to waver. Month in and month out he had watched his son in the throes of epileptic seizures that caused the lad to grind his teeth and bruise himself as he cried out in convulsions. In those days doctors diagnosed this disorder of the central nervous system as demon-possession and the Greeks named it epilepsy, literally meaning seizure by an evil spirit. Though the father had tried various cures and magic incantations, none was potent enough to drive out his son's malign spirit. Was the power of evil stronger, he wondered, than the power of God? In his despair the father no longer offered praises to the Lord, for he questioned God's goodness and cried to him for help.

> I cry aloud to God,
>   aloud to God, that he may hear me.
> In the day of trouble I seek the Lord. . . .
> "Will the Lord spurn for ever,
>   and never again be favorable?
> Has his steadfast love for ever ceased?
>   Are his promises at an end for all time?
> Has God forgotten to be gracious?
>   Has he in anger shut up his compassion?"
>   PSALM 77.1,2,7-9

Reports reached the father of a prophet from Galilee who was performing works of mercy. Hopeless parents like himself had already obtained healing for their children from this Jesus of Nazareth. His disciples told of a Capernaum official's son, of Jairus' daughter, of a young man at Nain, and of a Greek woman's daughter, all of whom had been made whole by the Master. Even the disciples themselves had accomplished wonders. They anointed the sick with oil, cast out demons, and healed many.

Though believing that his son's affliction was incurable, the father brought the lad to the disciples because Jesus himself was absent from the neighborhood. A crowd gathered to watch these men exorcise the boy's demon, but when they failed to do so, everyone began to talk excitedly. Words filled the vacuum left when action failed. Each person explained his theory of the disciples' lack of success, the scribes even charging them with being in league with Satan. Sick at heart, the father led his son away from the futile argument.

Suddenly Jesus appeared, accompanied by Peter, James, and John, all striding down a mountain path. Instantly the scene changed as the crowd ran forward eager to welcome the Master. Something about him this day filled them with awe. Did the glory witnessed by his three disciples on the mountain of transfiguration still shine from his person?

Peter, James, and John came forward reluctantly, pained, perhaps, by the contrast between this scene of human need and frustration in the valley and the heavenly light that had enveloped Jesus on the mountaintop. Up there no pushing crowds invaded the solitude and silence in which God's voice had spoken; here heated voices argued and accused. There the glorious figures of Moses and Elijah conversed with Jesus; here a father and his pathetic son waited for him. There Jesus spoke with God; here he must confront a demon. Unlike his disciples, Jesus plunged confidently into the situation before him.

"What is your trouble?" he asked of the crowd. "What are you discussing?" The scribes were too deeply entangled in argument to frame an immediate answer, but the father's need was so real and pressing that he replied instantly. "Master, I am bringing my son to you, for he is possessed by a violent demon. I asked your disciples to cast it out, but they could not."

Jesus sighed as he looked at the disciples to whom he had given authority to heal. Why had they been unable to do so? Had the cynicism of the world overcome their faith? Did the demons appear mightier to them than God? The lad suffered from a deadly form of evil that could be vanquished only by one whose faith was nourished by continual prayer. As the Master would later explain to them, they had failed because their faith was weak.

"O faithless people!" exclaimed Jesus, turning from his disciples to the father and the crowd. "How long must I be with you before you believe? How long must I endure your lack of faith? Bring the lad to me!" After saying this Jesus took the father and his son and moved a short distance away so that the boy might be healed in private.

Immediately the lad cried out and became convulsed, falling to the ground, writhing, and foaming at the mouth as if the evil spirit possessing him recognized the Master and struggled against him.

"How long has he been like this?" Jesus asked.

"Since childhood," replied the father. "Often the demon throws him into the fire or into water to destroy him. If you can do anything, please help us, please have pity on us."

"If *you* can do anything!" exclaimed Jesus, challenging the father in his own words. No one could question God's power, but faith was necessary to make divine power effective—the father's faith that God could make his son whole. "Everything is possible to him who has faith," declared Jesus.

"I do have faith," the father cried, the tears running down his cheeks, "but help my faltering faith and cure my child in spite of my unbelief."

Noticing that the crowd was coming toward them, Jesus quickly addressed the lad's evil spirit, saying, "I adjure you, come out of this boy and never return!"

The demon screamed and violently convulsed the lad before it departed, leaving him on the ground, limp and unconscious. His pallor was so much like that of a corpse that the bystanders exclaimed, "He is dead!" But Jesus, in his characteristic way, took the boy's hand and lifted him up so that he stood erect.

According to Luke's Gospel, Jesus, in another customary gesture, brought the cured boy to his father while all who were present stood awestruck at the power of God which Jesus had made manifest.

30

Children Whom He Blessed

MK 10.13-16 (MT 19.13-15;   *"Let the children come to me, do*
LK 18.15-17)   *not hinder them; for to such belongs*
                                   the kingdom of God."
                                                    MARK 10.14

"YOU CANNOT ENTER!" Peter's tone was sharp as he barred the doorway of the house where Jesus was staying.

"Your children will disturb the Master," explained another disciple.

In the road stood a group of fathers and mothers surrounded by their children. Some were babies in arms, others were darting about. At Peter's rebuke, lively voices ceased their chattering, dismayed parents exchanged glances, and a high-strung child began to cry. Sensitive to conflict in the adult world, especially conflict they did not understand, the young ones froze in their places, their ebullient spirits deflated. What had begun as an exciting adventure was ending in unhappiness. Peter's forbidding expression and curt words had made everyone feel unwelcome.

The idea of bringing their children to Jesus for his blessing had seemed a good one to the parents. Naturally they wanted their sons and daughters to see a great man. The fathers and mothers also expected that when Jesus laid his hands upon the little heads, as Jacob long ago had laid his hands on Joseph's sons, he would endow the children with some of his own qualities—his joy, his ability to meet every situation triumphantly, his peace, and his oneness with the Lord.

All this was clearly not to be, since Peter and the other disciples were barring the way. These men were like the rabbis who often refused to bother with the young. Religious leaders of the day who took their own spiritual development seriously tried to spend as little time as possible with women and children. Everyone knew that by nature the young were foolish and women a hindrance to lofty pursuits. Children were best dealt with sternly, for it was thought that

> Folly is bound up in the heart of a child,
> but the rod of discipline drives it far from him.
> PROVERBS 22.15

Was Jesus like other rabbis in his response to children? The fathers and mothers had expected him to be different. Once, when his disciples were discussing greatness, he had brought a child into their midst, saying, "Truly, I say to you, unless you turn and become like children, you will never enter the kingdom of heaven. Whoever humbles himself like this child, he is the greatest in the kingdom of heaven" (Matthew 18.3-4).

Surely that was not spoken by a man whom children easily annoyed. There was also his friendly, half-humorous description of boys and girls in the market place playing games of marriages and funerals. And once he had taken a child in his arms, saying, "Whoever receives one such child in my name receives me; and whoever receives me, receives not me but him who sent me" (Mark 9.37).

He had had much experience with younger brothers and sisters. Did not this make him especially cherish those of tender years? His attitude toward the young could have nothing in common with the cynicism of some of the proverbs but must surely reflect Israel's basic delight in her children.

> Lo, sons are a heritage from the Lord,
> the fruit of the womb a reward.
> Like arrows in the hand of a warrior are the sons of one's youth.
> Happy is the man who has
> his quiver full of them!
> PSALM 127.3-5

With these thoughts in their minds, the parents hesitated, reluctant to turn back yet unable to proceed. Mothers shifted their babies to their other arm, while boys and girls who had skipped and pranced on the outward journey looked at the grim-faced disciples and sought the comfort of their fathers' hands.

Suddenly Jesus appeared in the doorway, his face dark with displeasure. It was not with the children that he was indignant, but with his disciples. Would they ever understand him? They were so zealous to protect him from trivial annoyances, but so blind to the real meaning of his mission. When would they cease judging a person's worth by his age or rank and acknowledge the infinite value of every human being? When would they see that receptiveness and lowliness, childhood's most precious qualities, are passports to the kingdom of God?

In a voice of authority Jesus commanded his disciples, "You must let these children come to me, do not prevent them, for," he added, smiling, "the kingdom of God belongs to little ones like these."

Turning to everyone present, disciples and parents alike, he said, "Indeed, I say to you, the person who does not accept the kingdom of God like a child, will never enter it."

Peter, always quick to understand his Master, stood aside, withdrawing his arm that had been barring the doorway. A smile suffused his sunburned young face as he welcomed the parents and lifted one of the toddlers over the sill. From his own family life he knew that these little ones reacted quickly to friendly smiles and kindly words, and they needed a helping hand extended at the right moment.

"The kingdom of God belongs to children like these," the parents repeated, as they watched the charming eagerness of their young ones trooping into the house to surround Jesus. They leaned against him, climbed into his lap, looked up into his face, and fingered his robe. How readily they responded to his outgoing love! None of these children, so freely endowed with God's grace, had yet developed the tough, protective exterior of a self-sufficient adult. Such grown-ups were often ignorant of their own spiritual poverty and were afraid to be outgoing or to accept love, but not so these children. The fathers and mothers saw that this was the way to enter the kingdom of God—

eagerly, receptively, in a spirit of simple dependence like that of a child.

As Jesus took the children in his arms, laying his hand on each small head in the ancient ceremony of blessing, the scene transcended its local aspect in which certain little ones of Galilee received a rabbi's blessing. It became an acted parable revealing God's love and man's appropriate response to that love.

31

The Young Man with Great Possessions

MK 10.17-22 (MT 19.16-30;
LK 18.18-30)

*"Go, sell what you have, and give
to the poor, and you will have treasure
in heaven; and come, follow me."*
MARK 10.21

THE OWNER of the vineyard fingered the gold chain hanging around his neck as he sipped a cooling drink brought him by a servant. From the shade of his house he looked out upon a terraced hillside where laborers filled baskets with bunches of ripe grapes. This sun-drenched vineyard belonged to him, and the sight of his bountiful harvest gratified him. The weather had been favorable and his vines had been carefully pruned and guarded. It was also true that his laborers were loyal to him. He was the sort of man others trusted. Besides his vineyard he owned wheat fields in which the grain had already been harvested.

He was a fortunate man indeed, for, in addition to rich farm lands and vineyards, he possessed many of the good things of life—youth, health, a winning personality, and a high position in the community as one of the rulers of the synagogue.

Yet this day, while watching his laden carts deliver the baskets of grapes to his winepress, he was haunted by a question. Was he somehow missing the best in life? He was looking forward to buying a neighboring olive orchard with this year's profits. It would make him the largest landholder in town. "But will it make me happier?" he asked himself, though he already knew the answer. Jesus had been preaching in the neighborhood and from him the wealthy man had glimpsed a new kind of life. Because it was a life that made great possessions seem trifling by comparison, the young man had become restless and dissatisfied.

To reassure himself that wealth was good, he opened his strongbox and arranged his hoard of shekels and tetradrachmas in piles according to their value, all but caressing the gold and silver coins as he stacked them. Surely these were a sign that God favored him! A tenth of all that his lands produced he owed to God. The young man recalled how his father used to recite the commandments and teach him the obligation of the tithe. Then there were taxes. So much of all this money must be paid to the tax collectors—too much, he thought bitterly, remembering the ruinous demands of the Romans. One of his father's favorite proverbs came to his mind.

> He who trusts in his riches will wither,
> but the righteous will flourish like a green leaf.
> PROVERBS 11.28

The rich man shivered at the thought that his present unhappy mood might be a kind of withering. But that was impossible, he decided, for he had always tried to be righteous and surely his affairs were now flourishing. If prosperity is the reward of righteousness, God certainly looked upon him as a righteous man. He knew his record was clean. He had never killed a man, or committed adultery, or stolen, or borne false witness, or defrauded another, or dishonored his parents. In every way he was a decent man of civilized behavior.

"Then why do I feel cheated of some supreme blessing as if the best in life were passing me by?" he asked himself angrily, banging his fist with such strength upon the table that his gold and silver pieces were scattered and some rolled across the floor.

The blessing he lacked, the blessing of being enfolded by God's love, could not be bought with money, for he knew that it is entirely free. Long ago the great prophet of the Exile had invited those who have no money to come and buy the wine and milk of God's grace "without money and without price" (Isaiah 55.1).

Nevertheless, mused the rich man, there must be some price to pay. It was generally believed that a person had to perform one special act in order to win blessedness and assurance of eternal life. "But who knows what that one act is?" he asked aloud as he stood in the doorway of his house.

At that moment Jesus and his disciples passed by, journeying toward another town. On an impulse the rich man, deciding to ask his question of this popular, itinerant preacher, ran to overtake him. Young as he was, he was panting when he caught up with Jesus and knelt at his feet.

"Good teacher," he began, trying to ingratiate himself with Jesus by flattery, "what must I do to win the fullness and joy of eternal life?"

"Why do you address me as good?" asked Jesus reprovingly. "Perfect goodness belongs only to God. He is the source of human goodness."

The rich young man bowed his head acknowledging Jesus' rebuke. He had often gained what he wanted by playing on the vanity of others. With Jesus that was clearly impossible. One must approach him in complete honesty.

Jesus then began to answer the man's question. "You know the commandments," he said, referring to the ten basic rules involving love of God and love of man. To keep these commandments, Jesus implied, was to possess eternal life and to belong to the kingdom of God. One did not enter the kingdom by doing something spectacular, but by being, day by day, a certain kind of person.

"Teacher," declared the young man earnestly, "I have carefully kept all these commandments since I was a mere boy."

Looking at him and seeing how hard he had tried to live uprightly and how deep was his desire for eternal life, Jesus loved him. Here was a clean and earnest young man, one capable of the high demands of discipleship.

"You lack one thing," Jesus said, perceiving that the rich man's efforts were directed solely toward his own personal happiness. This excellent citizen of unblemished record was basically selfish. He had never lost himself in God. His life did not overflow in loving service to others. He lived strictly within the boundaries of self, untransformed by the grace of God.

At this point in the story, the apocryphal *Gospel according to the Hebrews* adds,

And the Lord said unto him: "How say you: I have kept the law and the prophets? For it is written in the Law: You shall love your neighbor as yourself. But behold, many of your brothers, sons of Abraham, are clad in filth and dying of hunger, yet your house is full of many good things, none of which is given to them."

This apocryphal speech doubtless elaborates Jesus' words, but in essence it points to the young man's need. According to the canonical Gospels, Jesus recommended a drastic program designed to overcome this man's particular enslavement to his possessions and to free him for the life he truly desired. It was a program based on action— go, sell, give, come, follow. It was both a command to cast aside all hindrances and an invitation to discipleship.

"Go, sell what you have, and give to the poor, and you will have treasure in heaven; and come, follow me" (Mark 10.21).

As the young man listened, his face fell and he shifted uneasily on his feet. On both sides of the road stretched his green fields. Nearby stood his barns and winepress. Up the hill climbed his vineyard whose abundant crop would add many silver coins to the hoard already in his strongbox. The rich young ruler stood for a moment reckoning the cost of discipleship, the cost of eternal life, but he found it too high. Momentarily he glimpsed transcendent glory, but without a word he turned sadly away, for he had great possessions.

Jesus and his disciples continued their journey while the young man trudged wearily home, having refused to "take hold of the life which is life indeed" (1 Timothy 6.19).

32

Martha and Mary

LK 10.38-42; JN 11.1-3;
12.1-8 (MK 14.3-9;
MT 26.6-13)

"Martha, Martha, you are anxious and troubled about many things; one thing is needful. Mary has chosen the good portion, which shall not be taken away from her."

LUKE 10.41-42

NOWHERE, PERHAPS, on his frequent journeys did Jesus find a warmer welcome than at Bethany in the home of Martha, Mary, and their brother Lazarus. It was a convenient place for the Master to lodge when he attended the great annual feasts in Jerusalem, for the village was situated on the eastern slope of the Mount of Olives, less than two miles from the Holy City. Travelers approaching Jerusalem from Jericho and the East usually passed through Bethany before climbing the footpath over the ridge of the Mount of Olives. From there they caught their first sight of the walled city of Jerusalem rising in impressive grandeur above the Kedron valley at their feet.

Though Bethany seemed poor beside Jerusalem with its marble palaces and colonnades, its splendid temple and its endless huddle of limestone houses, Martha's large and comfortable house compared favorably with the best in the Holy City. The family's means were sufficient to offer Jesus generous hospitality whenever he visited this suburb of Jerusalem. Their wealth is further indicated by the costliness of the ointment Mary poured from her alabaster jar when she anointed Jesus.

From time immemorial, hospitality to strangers had been a sacred duty among the Hebrews, as stories of the patriarchs show. If hospitality was a necessity of desert life, it became hardly less so when Israel settled in Palestine. Few inns existed there and entertaining strangers was deemed a virtue equal to that of almsgiving. Wayfarers expected kindly treatment and counted on food, shelter, and protection wherever they went. Even an enemy arriving hungry and thirsty was given food and drink. For three or four days after eating his host's bread his safety was guaranteed.

The Law commanded that "The stranger who sojourns with you shall be to you as the native among you, and you shall love him as yourself, for you were strangers in the land of Egypt" (Leviticus 19.34). Because of the fear and desolation experienced by the ancient Hebrews living as aliens in Egypt, their descendants were, in effect, admonished always to imagine themselves in the stranger's place and treat him as they themselves would like to be treated. Was this one of the centuries-old sources of Jesus' Golden Rule?

The ancient custom of hospitality was doubtless one of the factors that made it possible for Jesus and his disciples to travel extensively throughout the length and breadth of Palestine. Later this custom also aided the apostles and their followers to preach the good news of Christ in many parts of the Mediterranean world. "Do not neglect to show hospitality to strangers," wrote a first-century Christian, adding, "for thereby some have entertained angels unawares" (Hebrews 13.2).

When Martha first entertained Jesus at Bethany, she doubtless saw him as just another pilgrim from Galilee in need of food and rest on his way to the Passover in Jerusalem. From a sense of duty she welcomed him and provided him with lodging for the night. Soon, however, when she and her sister Mary perceived that he was more than the usual wayfarer, a warm and intimate friendship developed between the Galilean teacher and the members of Martha's household. Whenever Jesus attended the crowded festivals in the Holy City, he could count on an oasis of rest and friendly understanding in Martha's house.

One day Jesus' arrival here caused unusual commotion. Possibly he came before the rooms had been swept, water fetched from the well, lamps trimmed, and bread baked. Martha was doubtless proud of her housekeeping and did not want it to be judged faulty. A larger group of disciples than usual may have been with Jesus, making her task more difficult. She rushed around distractedly, trying to do everything at once. With frantic haste she began preparing more dishes for her guests than the circumstances warranted, all the while complaining that she had only two hands with which to cope with a thousand and one details. If only someone would bring her another bundle of faggots, or stir the soup simmering over the fire! Where were the spices she used for company meals? Had anyone found her broom or gone to the well to fill the water jars?

Glancing into the courtyard, Martha saw her sister quietly sitting and listening to Jesus. The sight exasperated her. It was good, certainly, to hear what the Master had to say, but should not first things come first, Martha asked herself. Dinner unquestionably came first. "Why should I wear myself out trying to prepare the meal alone, while Mary sits at Jesus' feet idly dreaming the time away?" Martha asked herself bitterly.

Always quick to speak and act, she rushed into the courtyard, fire in her eyes. "Lord, does it make no difference to you that my sister leaves all the work to me?" she demanded, struggling to keep her voice steady. "Tell her to help me!"

"Martha, my friend," spoke Jesus, trying to calm the tempestuous woman before dealing with her difficulty, "you are anxious and fretted because you are preparing too much food for us. We do not need such lavish entertainment. Your graciousness can be expressed in simple hospitality. That will suffice for our needs. We require only a few things" he explained, "—perhaps only one."

"One thing," Martha repeated to herself in surprise. Could it be, she wondered, that he now referred, not to household matters, but to the things of God. Leaving her bread baking in the oven and her pots boiling near the fire, she listened to his words about the one needful thing.

"Your sister Mary has chosen the most important thing," declared the Master. Then he added half-humorously, "—the one best dish, and she must not be dragged away from it."

Martha knew that Jesus often taught, not by giving ironclad rules of behavior, but by making arresting statements or by telling stories in which his listeners could discover truth for themselves. A less skillful teacher confronted with the situation of Martha and Mary might have denounced worry and exasperation as wrong, or have laid down the rule that a simple meal is better than a banquet. But Jesus, by a playful allusion to her sister and "the one best dish," eased the tension and taught Martha the most important thing in life.

She returned thoughtfully to her kitchen with a new viewpoint about her preparations for dinner. Household responsibilities, she knew, were still important, yet not so important that they should be allowed to usurp the center of her life. She had enthroned her duties in the first place in her heart where only God should reign. Her sister Mary, on the other hand, cared supremely for the Lord. Only this mattered. Mary had indeed chosen the "good portion."

Rooms must continually be swept, meals prepared, and guests entertained but, because of her new-found insight, Martha vowed that never again would she allow all this activity to make her petulant and distracted. She was ready now to understand the Lord's teaching when he said,

"And do not seek what you are to eat and what you are to drink, nor be of anxious mind. For all the nations of the world seek these things; and your Father knows that you need them. Instead, seek his kingdom, and these things shall be yours as well." .

LUKE 12.29-31

Martha could at last appreciate the quality of her sister Mary's life, a life that was akin to that of the psalmist who wrote,

> One thing have I asked of the Lord,
>   that will I seek after;
> that I may dwell in the house of the Lord
>   all the days of my life,
> to behold the beauty of the Lord,
>   and to inquire in his temple.

PSALM 27.4

Later, when, according to the story in John's Gospel, Jesus was a
guest in a certain Simon's house in Bethany, Martha was called upon
to serve. On this occasion Mary expressed her devotion to the Master
by anointing him. (As we have already noted, this was apparently
Jesus' second anointing, the first having been by the sinful woman in
the Pharisee's house.)

As soon as Mary opened her alabaster jar of costly ointment the
fragrance of pure nard filled the house, provoking unkind words
about her extravagance. "Why is this ointment wasted," demanded
Judas and other indignant disciples. "It might have been sold for a
large sum and the proceeds given to the poor."

Nard, an aromatic herb imported from the East, was used both to
prepare bodies for burial and to consecrate kings. Mary may already
have used some of the ointment for her brother Lazarus' dead body.
Perhaps her finely attuned nature gave her a premonition of things
to come. Did she anticipate Jesus' kingly triumph upon entering
Jerusalem and did she foresee his death? In view of these her anointing
of him was symbolic both of his kingship and of his death. This
anointing may have had deeper implications if Mary envisioned Jesus
as the Lord's anointed one, the Messiah, the Christ who was to come.

Jesus smiled at Mary, accepting her anointing at its true value as a
sign of her abundant love. "She has done a beautiful thing to me,"
he declared, commending her lack of petty calculation in this act that
issued from her overflowing heart. In his next words, his disciples
heard an implied rebuke of their worldly judgment and the poverty of
their love. "For you always have the poor with you, and whenever you
will, you can do good to them; but you will not always have me. . . .
She has anointed my body beforehand for burying. And truly, I say
to you, wherever the gospel is preached in the whole world, what she
has done will be told in memory of her" (Mark 14.6-9).

33

Lazarus

JN 11.1-44

For as the Father raises the dead and gives them life, so also the Son gives life to whom he will.

JOHN 5.21

ONE DAY Lazarus became ill. News of his sickness spread rapidly through Bethany bringing some of their neighbors to help Martha and Mary with their brother's care. When his condition grew worse, the sisters sent a brief message to Jesus, saying, "Lord, the friend whom you love is very ill."

At this time Jesus was east of the Jordan in the rugged highlands of Perea, several days' journey from Bethany. Sure that the Master would respond quickly to the sisters' message and come at once to Bethany, their friends watched the eastern road for his arrival. Anxious days passed; still he did not come.

At length Lazarus died. His body was washed, anointed with precious nard, wrapped in white linen grave cloths, and carried in a funeral procession to his tomb. The sisters' thirty days of mourning began. For three days Lazarus' spirit was believed to hover near his body, possibly to return to it, but by the fourth day everyone knew that his spirit had departed and that Lazarus' death was final.

On the fourth day the villagers of Bethany saw, among a group of travelers approaching on the Jericho road, the well-known figure of Jesus. "Too late!" they sighed as they hurried to tell Martha of his arrival.

Quickly slipping away from the friends who had come to her house to mourn with her, Martha hurried out to a secluded place to meet

Jesus. "Lord," she cried, "if you had only been here, my brother would not have died!"

It was a statement of faith accompanied by a trace of sorrowful accusation, as if she had said, "Why did you not come in time?" Despite all that had happened, she had confidence in the Master and believed that he had unusual access to God. "Even now," she said, "though Lazarus is dead, I am sure that God will give you whatever you ask of him."

"Your brother will rise again," Jesus assured Martha.

"I know he will rise again in the resurrection on the last day," she replied, like a child mechanically repeating a catechism. Martha expressed a pious belief of the orthodox Pharisees, but at best it seemed vague to her. Anyway, this belief was powerless to end the ache in her heart, the catch in her throat. If only Jesus had something better than this remote hope to offer her!

Again Jesus addressed the grieving woman, the very tone of his voice indicating that he spoke, not of an obscure doctrine, but of present reality. "I am the resurrection and the life," he declared; "whoever believes in me, even if he dies, he shall live, and whoever lives and believes in me shall never die."

He spoke so plainly now that Martha knew what he meant. She knew that despite physical death, those who believe in Christ shall enjoy everlasting spiritual life. With this promise the story moves beyond the dust and sunshine of Bethany, beyond a man's death and his sister's grief, to ultimate verities.

"Yes, Lord," cried Martha, voicing the faith of later Christians, "I believe that you are the Christ, the Son of God who was to come into the world."

Martha belonged to the company of those who "believe that Jesus is the Christ, the Son of God, and . . . have life in his name" (John 20.31). It is this "life" that the story of Lazarus celebrates.

Quietly the narrative resumes its account of actual people living at a particular time, in a certain place. Martha was clearly a real woman, the same person as the one Luke portrayed. She was practical, outgoing, quick to express herself, the busy mistress of a household, a leader rather than a follower, a vivid personality.

Her sister Mary, on the other hand, was quieter and less confident. As we have seen, her interior life, though deep and rich, was largely silent, her nature being more reserved than that of her sister.

During Martha's encounter with Jesus, Mary had remained at home with the mourners until her sister returned to whisper to her, "The Master is here and is asking for you." Then Mary rose quickly and went to the place where Jesus was. She fell at his feet, expressing in this act a devotion for which she had no words.

"Lord," she said, repeating Martha's cry, "if you had only been here, my brother would not have died."

Mary was soon surrounded by her mourning friends, who, seeing her leave the house and thinking that she was going to her brother's tomb, followed her. They wept as she spoke sorrowfully to Jesus. Seeing the grief of all these people, Jesus was himself deeply moved and wept the tears of his true human nature.

Moving to the place where Lazarus' body had been laid, the mourners, following Jesus and Mary, saw that the cave tomb was closed with a boulder.

"Remove the stone," commanded Jesus.

Martha, who had joined her sister, was troubled by Jesus' command and spoke to him of the decay that would surely be disclosed within.

"Did I not tell you," Jesus asked, "that if you believe, you shall see the glory of God?"

Raising his eyes to heaven, Jesus prayed aloud so that all who stood near might know the source of his life-giving power. The Father had sent him into the world to bring life to men, to quicken the spiritually dead. The source of his power and authority was God.

"Truly, truly, I say to you, the hour is coming, and now is, when the dead will hear the voice of the Son of God, and those who hear will live. For as the Father has life in himself, so he has granted the Son also to have life in himself."

JOHN 5.25-26

This truth Jesus was about to demonstrate.

With a loud voice he cried, "Lazarus, come forth." The dead man appeared, his hands and feet bound with linen bands and his face still covered with the grave cloth.

"Unbind him," Jesus directed the bystanders, adding with merciful understanding, "and let him go home."

In that hour many of Mary's friends who had followed her to her brother's grave, having seen this great marvel, believed in Jesus. The occasion must have reminded them of Ezekiel's valley of dry bones, bringing to their minds the Lord's promise:

"Behold, I will open your graves, and raise you from your graves, O my people; and I will bring you home into the land of Israel. And you shall know that I am the Lord. . . . And I will put my Spirit within you, and you shall live. . . . then you shall know that I, the Lord, have spoken, and I have done it, says the Lord."

EZEKIEL 37.12-14

This miracle is the last and most impressive of the Fourth Gospel's series of seven—the water changed into wine at Cana, the official's son healed of fever, the cripple cured at the Pool of Bethzatha, the five thousand people fed, Jesus seen walking on the water, and the blind man given his sight. All these richly symbolic "signs" point to Christ's creative power. As nothing else can, they show forth his glory. The three Synoptic Gospels omit Lazarus' story, but its teaching concerning Christ's authority over life and over death permeates all the Gospels and is basic to the entire New Testament. Lazarus' restoration to life dramatically symbolizes the Christian experience of passing from death to abundant life.

But God, who is rich in mercy, out of the great love with which he loved us, even when we were dead through our trespasses, made us alive together with Christ . . . and raised us up with him, and made us sit with him in the heavenly places in Christ Jesus. . . .

EPHESIANS 2.4-6

Viewed in its context, the story of Lazarus is not hard to understand. It is one of several narratives illuminating Jesus' claim that "the blind receive their sight and the lame walk, lepers are cleansed and the deaf hear, and the dead are raised up, and the poor have good news preached to them" (Matthew 11.5). When these things happened men had been taught to believe that God's reign had begun. The story also anticipates Christ's own resurrection. Finally, this "sign" stands as one of the New Testament's sublime witnesses to faith. Christ came to give men life, a life transcending physical death, for "in him was life" (John 1.4), life so glorious that it triumphed over the darkness of sin and death. He is indeed the resurrection and the life. All who believe in him shall not perish but shall have eternal life.

34

Zacchaeus

LK 19.1-10   *Christ Jesus came into the world to
                                    save sinners.*

                                            I TIMOTHY 1.15

ZACCHAEUS, the tax collector, was a rich man living in one of Jericho's large, comfortable houses. In his day the city was a thriving center of government and commerce, adorned with public buildings and palaces, parks and fountains. A circus, gymnasium, and circular theater had been built here for the amusement of the wealthy people living in comfortable villas. Herod the Great had made the city his winter capital. When December's damp, bone-chilling winds forced Jerusalem's inhabitants indoors, the royal court moved down from the Judean highlands to the Jordan valley to spend the winter months basking in Jericho's semitropical climate.

Herod the Great's palace here had colonnaded courts, loggias, terraces, a promenade, and a sunken garden, all in the style of architecture he had admired on his visits to Rome. Though sacked and burned in the disorders following the King's death, this palace was rebuilt and made even more sumptuous by his son Archelaus, who added to it wine cellars, baths, statuary, and mosaic floors.

Because of Jericho's strategic location on the frontier between Judea and the lands east of the Jordan, the city controlled the commerce of a large, productive region. At Jericho import duties on goods brought from the east by caravan as well as export taxes on balm and other products of the locality were collected.

Zacchaeus presided over a tax office always filled with sharp-eyed officials. They opened bales, inspected baskets and jars of produce, and made out tax bills to the muttered curses of traders who usually felt themselves overcharged. The jingle of coins punctuated loud complaints and low-voiced threats. Here, as we have already observed at Capernaum and other Roman tax offices, justice and service to the public were unknown. The tax collector added as much as he could to the amount of the tax due and pocketed the additional sum. Much of Zacchaeus' wealth came from this source.

Despite all that his money could purchase for him, he was unhappy. The comfort of his villa, the food and expensive wines served at his table, his elegant attire, even the prestige of his official position—all these failed to compensate him for the fact that he was hated for his dishonesty and feared for his power. As with Matthew-Levi at Capernaum, Zacchaeus' fellow Jews despised him as a traitor in the pay of Rome. They regarded his extortions as robbery.

No self-respecting Jew, careful of his ritual purity, would accept an invitation to dine at the tax collector's house, for he was regarded as an outcast of Jewish society, a disinherited son of Abraham. As we have seen, to eat with such a man made a good Jew ceremonially "unclean." "If only my fellow countrymen would treat me as a human being!" sighed Zacchaeus. But all his money, he knew, could never buy respect from them nor peace in his own heart.

When Jericho buzzed with the rumor that Jesus and his followers were approaching the city, the chief tax collector decided to go out to see what the excitement was all about. Such a dense crowd jammed the eastern highway that, being a short man, he knew he would not be able to see over the people's heads. His small stature humiliated him. It was one more shame added to the others he endured. But his years in government service had taught him persistence and resourcefulness. Somehow he would find a way to see Jesus, even if he had to shed some of his dignity to do so.

Running ahead of the crowd along the route Jesus must take into the city, Zacchaeus found a sycamore and quickly climbed it. This tree, with figlike fruit and leaves similar to those of a mulberry, is of a different species from the European or American tree of the same name. Because its dense shade afforded weary travelers relief from the sun, it was frequently planted along roadsides. The sycamore's short trunk was easy to climb and Zacchaeus soon found a perch among its wide lateral branches from which to see Jesus as he passed below.

The Master paused in the tree's shade and looked up. Never before had the tax collector felt so acutely his shame in being a disinherited son of Abraham, a sinner estranged from God. He feared that his undignified perch only emphasized his own lack of self-respect. It was too late to hide among the thick foliage, for Jesus had already seen him.

"Zacchaeus," came the commanding voice from below.

Suddenly the little tax collector felt how inappropriate was a name meaning "pure" and "righteous" for such a soiled and wicked person as himself.

"Zacchaeus," insisted Jesus, "hurry and come down, for I want to be a guest in your house today."

Amazement swept Zacchaeus with almost gale force down from the tree. As he scrambled to the ground he trembled with happiness. At last a member of his own race, and a man of God at that, had treated him with respect and given him a chance to be of service. Perhaps he would no longer be an outcast. He felt forgiven and inwardly cleansed. A sense of new life welled up within him like a spring of water in a dry land.

Hurrying to keep up with Jesus' resolute stride, he walked side by side with the Master through the streets of Jericho to his own house. Along the way the Master listened as the little man poured out the pain and frustrated longings of his heart. So intent was he on his own words that he failed to hear the bystanders murmur their disapproval of Jesus. "Is he really going to eat with a sinner?" some of them asked in shocked surprise. In Jericho as in other Jewish cities, the Pharisees were horrified that Jesus should visit the house of one living outside the Law.

Entering his spacious courtyard and greeting his family who crowded around him, Zacchaeus paused and looked at Jesus. "Here and now, Lord," declared the tax collector, "I give half my property to the poor. And if I have defrauded anyone, I hereby promise to pay it back to him four times over."

The crowd that had gathered at the entrance to the house gasped when they heard this solemn declaration. Roman judges exacted a fourfold restitution for theft as did the Law in the case of a stolen sheep (Exodus 22.1), but what man had ever before voluntarily offered to pay such a heavy penalty for his wrongdoing?

Zacchaeus was determined to make a clean break with his past so that he could begin his new life as the Master's follower unencumbered with old shames. Much of the harm he had done could not be erased—children cheated of childhood happiness, defrauded men dying in bitterness, families spending years in penury—but some restitution could still be made.

Jesus raised his hand in blessing, declaring, "Today salvation has come to this house." By giving away most of the family fortune to right old wrongs, Zacchaeus and his household attained the joyful sense of standing in the presence of God—they indeed experienced salvation.

There is no record of what the Master may have said about the poor of Jericho who were to receive a large part of the tax collector's wealth. Jesus must surely have been glad that their wretchedness would be relieved, but perhaps it was on this occasion that he made the statement long remembered by his followers, "It is more blessed to give than to receive" (Acts 20.35).

Turning to the crowd, which included some who had accused Zacchaeus of disloyalty to Israel, Jesus defended his new follower, saying, "This man is as truly a son of Abraham as any one of you."

"Why so?" heckled one of the bystanders.

"Prove it to us," challenged another.

But to most of those in the crowd at Zacchaeus' door the case was clear. Love of God was basic in the hearts of Abraham's true sons and had always been the distinctive characteristic that separated the people of Israel from other peoples. Zacchaeus, having proved his love of God by his generosity and his restitution, was now worthy to be acknowledged as a true son of Abraham. This tax collector exemplified a truth expressed by one of the Master's later followers. "We love because he first loved us. If anyone says, 'I love God,' and hates his brother, he is a liar; for he who does not love his brother whom he has seen, cannot love God whom he has not seen" (1 John 4.19-20).

The Master's meeting with Zacchaeus epitomized his ministry. Like many of his other encounters with people, this one demonstrated, on a small scale, that Jesus came to give new life to those who turn to him. At Zacchaeus' door, he spoke a final word to his critics and expressed the meaning of the event, saying, "The Son of Man came to seek and to save the lost."

35

Bartimaeus

MK 10.46-52 (MT 20.29-34; LK 18.35-43)

The Father . . . has delivered us from the dominion of darkness and transferred us to the kingdom of his beloved Son, in whom we have redemption, the forgiveness of sins.
COLOSSIANS 1.12-14

JERICHO WAS FULL of beggars attracted to the city's wealth as bees to honey. These ragged unfortunates lived off the charity of prosperous Jews who piously obeyed the Law's command: "as the Lord your God has blessed you, you shall give to him [the poor man]" (Deuteronomy 15.14).

Bartimaeus was one of these beggars. Unlike some who were lazy, shiftless fellows taking advantage of Jewish generosity, Bartimaeus deserved help because he was blind. Begging was virtually the only way he could make his living in a society that accepted poverty and hardship as the inevitable lot of those who could not see. There were many sightless beggars in the land, for blindness was common in a region like Palestine where the sun's intense glare strained men's eyes and dust storms and swarms of flies caused irritations and spread contagious eye diseases.

Day after day Bartimaeus sat by the roadside listening for the approach of someone from whom he could beg. Matthew's and Luke's Gospels give two slightly different versions of this story from the one recorded in Mark. Matthew tells of two blind beggars at Jericho. Luke mentions only one, but he is nameless and stationed on the highway by which travelers entered Jericho from the east. Mark's version, which we shall follow here, not only gives the beggar a name showing him to be the son of Timaeus, but places him on the opposite side of the city from Luke's beggar, on the west road leading from Jericho to Jerusalem.

This road was the famous highway on which the good Samaritan of Jesus' story found and rescued the man who had fallen among thieves. It was a fifteen-mile route, one of the dreariest and most dangerous in Palestine, passing through the awesomely deep and rugged canyon of the Wadi Qelt where robbers had their dens and lay in wait for unwary travelers. Due to the perils of this road, Jesus and his disciples, after bidding goodby to Zacchaeus, joined a company of Passover pilgrims that had assembled in Jericho to make the final stage of their journey to Jerusalem together because they believed that the larger their caravan the safer it would be from attacks by brigands infesting the ravines and desolate gullies of the Wadi Qelt. Undoubtedly many of this crowd of pilgrims were followers of Jesus.

Bartimaeus had surely heard stories of blind men whose sight was restored by Jesus. There was the man born blind in Jerusalem, a blind beggar like himself (John 9.1-41). Taking clay made with spittle, then believed to have healing properties, Jesus had anointed this beggar's eyes and told him to wash in the pool of Siloam. When he had done so, the man returned, seeing, and he declared, "Never since the world began has it been heard that any one opened the eyes of a man born blind. If this man were not from God, he could do nothing" (John 9.32-33). Then he glorified Jesus, saying, "Lord, I believe."

Another story told of two blind men who cried out to Jesus for mercy (Matthew 9.27-31). They felt the Master's touch and heard him say, "According to your faith be it done to you." At this their eyes were opened to behold the wonders of the world.

Still another story concerned a man, outside the village of Bethsaida, whose friends brought him to Jesus. After laying his hands on the blind man and touching his eyes with spittle, Jesus asked him, "Do you see anything?" At first the blind man saw people indistinctly, like trees, walking about, but after Jesus laid his hands on his eyes, his sight was gradually restored and he saw everything clearly (Mark 8.22-26).

Because of these and other reports, for Jesus had opened the eyes of many (Matthew 11.5; 15.30; Luke 7.21), the blind beggar of Jericho hoped that he too might be healed.

Under a brilliant morning sky, Bartimaeus sat in darkness. He was at his customary station beside the road, huddled in his cloak, listening for the babble of approaching voices. Someone had told him that Jesus would be passing this way. When the blind beggar felt the roadway beneath him vibrate with the tramping footsteps of a crowd and heard the sound of voices come nearer, he began to tremble in expectation. This was his chance. It was now or never, because Jesus might not pass this way again. At the top of his lungs the beggar shouted, "Jesus, Son of David, have pity on me!"

"Hush," admonished the leaders of the caravan. The beggar's cry was perilous because "Son of David" was one of the names of the Messiah, the hero who would deliver the Jews from foreign rule. In this unquiet land, seething with plots and revolts, the cry might well be interpreted by the Roman authorities as the signal for an uprising. They might fear that this peaceful crowd of Passover pilgrims was a revolutionary band advancing upon the Holy City to enthrone Jesus as the Messiah. Bartimaeus' cry endangered not only himself but the pilgrims and Jesus as well.

The blind man, unaware of the need for political caution, only knew that the louder he cried, the better his chance of being helped, so he continued to call out, "Have pity on me! Son of David, have mercy on me!"

"Be quiet!" repeated the pilgrims, but the more they rebuked him, the more persistently he shouted. The travelers became irritated by the troublesome fellow, knowing that even if the Romans failed to notice him, his healing would require precious time that would delay the caravan and possibly prevent it from reaching safe camping grounds by nightfall.

Jesus, noticing the beggar's persistence in the face of discouragement, said to his followers, "Call him here."

"Come along," urged those who had been rebuking the blind man, their voices suddenly friendly, "have courage, for the Master is calling for you."

All this time Bartimaeus had been sitting with his cloak around his shoulders, but now he cast it aside as an impediment and jumped to his feet to grope his way through the crowd to Jesus.

The Master asked him his usual question, "What do you want me to do for you?"

"O Teacher," he cried, "let me see!" All his needs, both physical and spiritual, were focused in his one plea.

"Go your way," said Jesus; "your faith has healed you."

For Bartimaeus that day on the Jericho road, Isaiah's prophecy was fulfilled by him who was the Light of the world.

> The people who walked in darkness
>   have seen a great light;
> those who dwelt in a land of deep darkness,
>   on them has light shined.

ISAIAH 9.2

"Go your way," the Master commanded Bartimaeus. Having received his sight, he followed the Master, his way having become the way of Jesus. According to Luke, the once blind man glorified God, and the crowd praised the Lord, seeing in this event more than a kindly deed by which a blind beggar was freed from misery and hardship. To Jesus' followers this act became a sign that their Master was able to deliver them from blindness of heart and poverty of spirit and lead them out of darkness into his glorious light.

VI

DURING HIS LAST DAYS

IN JERUSALEM

36

The Crowds

MK 1.33,37; 2.2,13; 3.7,20,
32; 4.1; 5.21; 6.31-34, 53-
56; 7.24; 8.1; 11.1-10
(MT 21.1-17; LK 19.28-40;
JN 12.12-43); LK 23.27-31,
48; etc.

*When he saw the crowds, he had
compassion for them, because they
were harassed and helpless, like sheep
without a shepherd. . . . and he began
to teach them many things.*
MATTHEW 9.36 and MARK 6.34

THE MULTITUDE that accompanied Jesus on his last journey from Jericho to Jerusalem was not unique. He had been surrounded by great numbers of people since his first preaching tour through Galilee when he had announced, "The time is fulfilled, and the kingdom of God is at hand; repent, and believe in the gospel" (Mark 1.15).

To people well acquainted with misery and despair, Jesus' message brought hope. It gave them a vision of glory. It called them to action. His program began, not with violence such as the Zealots advocated, but with repentance and a quiet cleansing of each man's heart. Then came a summons to faith. Hot-headed individuals, eager to overthrow tyranny, listened in vain for some signal from him to rise up against the wrongdoing of their rulers, but Jesus gave no such signal. On the contrary, he clearly showed himself to be a man of peace. "Blessed are the peacemakers," he said. "Love your enemies and pray for those who persecute you" (Matthew 5.9, 44) and "Be at peace with one another" (Mark 9.50).

Palestine had been bathed in blood time and again by those who used force in their attempts to seize power. Jesus taught men that to change the world and prepare for the reign of God they must begin with themselves. They must first recognize their own sin so that they might then truly turn to God.

Though such teaching alienated a few headstrong individuals, it appealed to the great mass of the people. They could understand it. Jesus' message was simple, and marked with the clarity and directness that are the hallmarks of truth. It accorded with their experience of reality. Its freshness and distinctiveness compelled attention. People heard an authoritative note in all Jesus said and they marveled at the inner assurance of this onetime carpenter from Nazareth. The learned scribes with all their painfully acquired knowledge never spoke with his lucidity and certitude. "He must be a prophet," some men said, remembering the glorious company of Hebrews who once spoke for God. The power of the prophets was his. The words he spoke glowed with divine fire. They were "like a hammer which breaks the rock in pieces" (Jeremiah 23.29).

Surprisingly, Jesus talked like one of themselves rather than in the tiresomely learned manner of the scribes and Pharisees. He knew how humble people lived from day to day and how they thought about the world. Effortlessly he could enter into the ways of thinking of the great mass of his countrymen. His sermons abounded in homely expressions and were often spiced with humor and enlivened with stories.

Despite the popularity of his appeal, he could more than hold his own when arguing with learned religious authorities. His quick mind seized the essential point of every issue and he seemed to understand the meaning of the Scriptures better even than the scribes did. The crowds enjoyed his controversies with his critics and were pleased when the pompous scribes and Pharisees were effectively silenced by Jesus.

The miracles he performed attracted the people more than any other aspect of his ministry. If a few, perceptive individuals saw that his healing acts pointed beneath the surface of life to the reality of God's love, the multitudes in general were carried away by the miracles themselves. Relief from pain and wretchedness was their chief concern. In a land like theirs, controlled by a foreign oppressor and filled with poverty and ignorance, people spent their lives in fear and bitterness hardly daring to hope for an end to their misery. Under these conditions ills of body and mind flourished. So great was the Master's sympathy for all who suffered and so relentlessly, as we have seen, did he combat evil, that the crowds saw him as their physician and friend. They brought him their sick in such endless processions of misery that often Jesus could not preach the message he was sent to proclaim.

One unforgettable picture shows the extent of suffering Jesus encountered in Galilee.

And great crowds came to him, bringing with them the lame, the maimed, the blind, the dumb, and many others, and they put them at his feet, and he healed them, so that the throng wondered, when they saw the dumb speaking, the maimed whole, the lame walking, and the blind seeing; and they glorified the God of Israel.

MATTHEW 15.30-31

It is small wonder that the crowds loved him and some people began to see him as the one by whom God's purposes were to be accomplished, the person of whom it was written, "surely he has borne our griefs and carried our sorrows" (Isaiah 53.4).

Galilee, the scene of much of Jesus' ministry, was a populous province, said by the contemporary historian Josephus to contain 240 cities and villages, the smallest of which numbered fifteen thousand inhabitants. Though this is obviously an exaggeration, in Jesus' day Galilee's teeming fishing ground, its productive farms, and its busy trade routes were, in fact, capable of supporting a large population. The Gospels convey the pressure and clamor of the province's multitudes. This is especially true of Mark's Gospel which mentions the throngs around Jesus some twenty or more times.

In Capernaum, as we have read, so many people came to Peter's house to see Jesus that it seemed as though "the whole city was gathered together about the door" (Mark 1.33). Throngs like these prevented the man on the stretcher from being brought directly to the Master and also made it necessary on another occasion for Jesus' family to relay a message through the crowd to him. With so many people clamoring for him, it was often impossible for Jesus and his disciples to eat.

At one period he "could no longer openly enter a town, but was out in the country." Even here "people came to him from every quarter" (Mark 1.45). Matthew describes him preaching a great sermon on a mountain. Mark's settings for the great crowds are on the shores of the Sea of Galilee.

When his immense popularity threatened to interfere with his real mission, he embarked on a boat and pushed out into the lake. Often this was of no avail. He and the disciples "went away in the boat to a lonely place by themselves. Now many saw them going, and knew them, and they ran there on foot from all the towns and got there ahead of them. As he landed he saw a great throng, and he had compassion on them, because they were like sheep without a shepherd" (Mark 6.32-34).

Once when he visited the northwestern shore of the Sea of Galilee in the fruitful area known as the Plain of Gennesaret,

. . . the people recognized him, and ran about the whole neighborhood and began to bring sick people on their pallets to any place where they heard he was. And wherever he came, in villages, cities, or country, they laid the sick in the market places, and besought him that they might touch even the fringe of his garment; and as many as touched it were made well.

MARK 6.54-56

Wherever he went, whether into Galilee, Samaria, Judea, beyond the Jordan, or north into Syria, "he could not be hid" (Mark 7.24). Everywhere people "sought to touch him, for power came forth from him and healed them all" (Luke 6.19). The crowds clamored for miracles, but faith could not be securely founded on these. Knowing that he could not build his mission upon people who were merely astonished by miracles, Jesus "did not trust himself to them, . . . for he himself knew what was in man" (John 2.24-25).

He also did not trust himself to men's messianic dreams, for he knew that only disappointment awaited those who wanted to make him a political messiah. His mission was not to set men free from Rome, but to liberate them from the enemies of the spirit, from sin and evil so that they might become the sons of God. The five thousand people

who ate the loaves and fishes, believing that the messianic age of divine
abundance was at hand, planned to make Jesus their king, but he,
perceiving their intent, "withdrew again to the hills by himself"
(John 6.15).

Messianic hopes, however, continued to excite the crowds until the
day in Jericho when blind Bartimaeus cried, "Jesus, Son of David,
Jesus, Messiah." Thereafter the air was tense with expectation. People
asked, "Is the Master at last going to Jerusalem to establish his kingdom?"

On reaching Bethany, Jesus' caravan was joined by other Galilean
pilgrims already camping on the hills surrounding the Holy City and
the very air vibrated with excitement. Some kind of demonstration
became inevitable. Would Jesus accept the title many of his followers
desired to give him and enter Jerusalem as its king? False hopes would
be raised if such an entry were forced upon him. How could he show
what manner of king he really was?

The Mount of Olives was the place where, according to the rabbis,
the Messiah would one day appear. This mountain was also the scene
of a vision of the glory of the Lord (Ezekiel 11.23). From this place
around which expectation hovered, Jesus' procession into the Holy
City began. He sent for an ass' colt never before ridden and thus considered in some sense sacred. On this lowly beast, rather than on a war
horse or in a chariot, he rode down the hillside toward Jerusalem,
demonstrating that he was not a conquering Messiah but a man of
peace. His followers, remembering Zechariah's prophecy, understood
why Jesus had chosen an ass and those who had brought swords
sheathed them.

> Rejoice greatly, O daughter of Zion!
> Shout aloud, O daughter of Jerusalem!
> Lo, your king comes to you;
> triumphant and victorious is he,
> humble and riding on an ass,
> on a colt the foal of an ass.
> I will cut off the chariot from Ephraim
> and the war horse from Jerusalem;
> and the battle bow shall be cut off,

and he shall command peace to the nations;
his dominion shall be from sea to sea,
and from the River to the ends of the earth.
ZECHARIAH 9.9-10

The demonstration that might have resulted in a bloody rebellion proceeded peacefully. In honor of the Master some of his followers put their garments on the colt or spread them before him in the road while others cut palm leaves or leafy boughs of myrtle and willow. These they waved as they were accustomed to do in the procession of the Feast of Tabernacles. They remembered its ritual as Jerusalem, the city of memories, rose before them. The morning sun touched with splendor its walls, palaces, and holy temple where for numberless years Israel believed that the Lord had dwelt with his people. In exultation the multitude began to improvise upon the words sung at the great feasts.

Save us, we beseech thee, O Lord! . . .
Blessed be he who enters in the name of the Lord! . . .
Bind the festal procession with branches. . . .
O give thanks to the Lord, for he is good;
for his steadfast love endures for ever!
PSALM 118.25-27,29

So ran the ancient prayer which the people modified on this occasion. "Hosanna!" they cried, meaning "God save him!" It was a cry of joyful homage that was also a prayer.

The glorious kingdom of God seemed near that morning, but the people's cry stopped short of a messianic pronouncement, for their excitement had been checked by the delicate gait of a lowly young ass. Thus we interpret Mark's account, despite the fact that the later Gospels record specifically messianic cries.

Even if the crowd's homage to Jesus was only that accorded to a great teacher, the watching Pharisees feared the ovation.

"Master," they sharply ordered Jesus when he entered the city, "rebuke your followers."

"If they remained silent," replied Jesus, "the very stones of the road would cry aloud."

According to Matthew, the crowds in Jerusalem caught fire from the marchers and asked excitedly, "Who is this man?"

"He is Jesus, the prophet from Nazareth in Galilee," came the reply of those in the procession. Clearly their dangerous messianic fervor of the morning had been channeled into a true expression of love and respect for their beloved teacher.

Even so the chief priests and scribes were troubled. They had long tolerated the profanation of the holy place by buyers and sellers, but when they heard children in the temple repeating the shouts of Jesus' followers, these religious authorities were shocked.

"Hosanna! Glory and salvation to the Son of David!" came the high-pitched cries of the boys who may have been the temple choristers. As Jesus entered his Father's house, these innocent singers perceived what their elders were too blind to see. Like the "sons of Zion" in Psalm 149, the boys rejoiced "in their King." To the men in power, however, the children's praise was blasphemy and therefore a desecration of the temple.

"Do you hear what these children are saying?" the authorities asked Jesus.

"Yes," he replied, "but have you never read, 'Out of the mouth of babes and infants thou hast brought perfect praise'?" Silenced by this quotation from one of the versions of Psalm 8.2, the chief priests and scribes withdrew, leaving Jesus to inspect the temple and its courts before returning to Bethany for the night.

Despite their fear of him, the religious authorities for several days hesitated to attack Jesus because of his popularity with the people. Many of them he healed of blindness and other infirmities. If crowds had impeded him during his ministry, in his final four days they protected him. "All the people hung upon his words" (Luke 19.48) and "the great throng heard him gladly" (Mark 12.37). There is also an intriguing record that "many even of the authorities believed in him" (John 12.41). The majority of the scribes and Pharisees, however, enclosed in their own rigid opinions and prejudices and fearful of any threat to their self-interest, failed to hear the note of reality in Jesus' words. In chagrin touched with envy the religious leaders cried, "Look, the world has gone after him" (John 12.19).

This situation could not last long. Finally the chief priests and elders of the people acted. They found some malcontents and ruffians and, after playing upon their ignorance, succeeded in stirring them up so that they became a hostile crowd that would shout whatever it was told. When Pilate, the Roman governor, asked this rabble what he should do with his prisoner, Jesus, they shouted as they had been instructed, "Let him be crucified!"

This mob, however, was not representative of the Passover throngs to whom Jesus had preached in Jerusalem. Luke describes a grieving multitude of men and women who watched Jesus on his way to Golgotha. Despite the action of their rulers and the shame that had been heaped on Jesus, these people did not conceal their sympathy for one whose words and deeds had opened their eyes to glory. Women wailed and wrung their hands in an outpouring of pity for a good man being led to his death. Jesus accepted their expression of human kindness, but said to them, "Daughters of Jerusalem, you might far better weep for yourselves and your children."

When Jesus died the crowd, moved by awe and terror, beat their breasts and, according to a tradition preserved in Syrian documents, cried, "Woe to us! What a thing has come to pass! Woe to us for our sins!"

The story of the crowds surrounding Jesus does not end on this note. When Pentecost dawned in Jerusalem, forty days after the crucifixion, multitudes who vividly remembered Jesus came to hear his disciple Peter preach. His words stirred them and they believed his witness and "were baptized, and there were added that day about three thousand souls. And they devoted themselves to the apostles' teaching and fellowship, to the breaking of bread and the prayers" (Acts 2.41-42). Thus thousands who had beheld Christ's glory began to live in a new dimension of joy and faith as members of the young Christian Church.

37

The Scribe Who Questioned Jesus

MK 12.28-34 (MT 22.34-40);
cf. LK 10.25-29

*And when Jesus saw that he
answered wisely, he said to him,
"You are not far from the kingdom
of God."*

MARK 12.34

THE SCRIBE walked at a dignified pace through the temple courts in
Jerusalem, his long robe billowing behind him. He moved proudly as
befitted a member of the highly respected group of scribes who formed
an aristocracy of piety and learning. Their members had interpreted
and taught God's Law for the past four hundred years and were justly
proud of their long history, dating, they believed, from the time of
Ezra, their founder. During the past stormy centuries, these zealous
scholars, who were often called lawyers, had defended and strengthened the Law, thus preserving Israel's identity and preventing her,
unlike other defeated peoples of antiquity, from disappearing from
the pages of history.

On his way, perhaps, to meet with his disciples, the lawyer looked
and acted like a typical member of his learned group. He had always
been faithful to their motto found in the preface to the *Sayings of the
Fathers,* "Be deliberate in giving judgment, and raise up many disciples, and make a barrier about the Law." Often he found himself
governing his behavior by the description of an ideal scribe in the
thirty-ninth chapter of the book entitled *Ecclesiasticus,* sometimes
known as *Sirach.*

The scribe walking in the temple courts this morning was different from his fellows in subtle ways. Where they were self-assured to the point of arrogance, his pride was tempered with modesty and friendliness. For all his vast accumulation of knowledge, he still preserved the attitude of a learner. There was a basic humbleness about him appropriate to a man of God. His face bore the marks of long hours spent deciphering the faded writing of old manuscripts. His brow was lined by thought and his keen eyes indicated an active mind. He had escaped the fate of many of his fellows who, in their zeal to preserve ancient wisdom, had grown deaf to the living voice of God.

A group of men talking animatedly in one of the courts caused him to pause. Some Sadducees were asking Jesus a tricky question concerning the hope of resurrection. They denied such a hope because the Law did not mention it. The scribe became fascinated by the interplay of personalities in this controversy. On the one hand was the uneducated prophet from Galilee whom the lawyer suspected of being somewhat naïve, while opposed to him were six or eight sophisticated and very learned Sadducees belonging to the most powerful party in Jerusalem. There could be little question about the outcome of the unequal contest, thought the onlooker, for a country preacher could hardly stand his ground before such formidable opponents.

To the scribe's amazement, however, Jesus showed profound understanding of the Scriptures and answered the Sadducees so wisely that for once they became speechless. This unusual occurrence made the scribe look with new eyes at the Galilean prophet, seeing him as a teacher to be reckoned with. What answer, he wondered, would the man of Nazareth give if he were asked which is the greatest commandment. Yet he hesitated to approach Jesus.

Enmity of the scribes toward Jesus had developed fast. By eating with sinners and breaking the Sabbath laws, the Master, as we have already seen, appeared to be destroying the precious "barrier about the Law." But this was not all. Jesus warned people, "Beware of the scribes, who like to walk about in long robes, and to be greeted with respect in the market places and to have the chief seats in the synagogues and the positions of honor at feasts, who live on the property of widows and make long prayers for the sake of appearances." Such words struck home because they were true, but the defenders of the Law could not forgive Jesus for saying them. He found these official religious teachers so preoccupied with trifling legal details that they had become blind to actual human needs. Behind their great show of learning some of them were hypocritical and dishonest.

Knowing the official opposition of his party to Jesus, the scribe decided to act as an individual. He gathered his robes about him and walked across the stone pavement to the place where the Master stood. He was not the first scribe to show independent judgment. One of his fellows had actually asked to be a disciple (Matthew 8.19). The lawyer in the temple this day did not strut as he approached Jesus, for he did not intend to parade his own learning, nor was he planning to humiliate the Master with a wily question. He was a sincere questioner whose desire for enlightenment was genuine.

"Master," he asked, courteously addressing Jesus with his usual title, "which commandment is the greatest?"

This was no idle question, but one affecting everyone's daily life. Some rabbis insisted that all the commandments of the Lord were equally important. There were, however, 365 prohibitions and 248 positive commands. Did the Lord require his people to know and obey all these? Ordinary men, confused and burdened by the Law's excessive demands, longed to know what one thing God demanded of them.

A generation earlier, a convert to Judaism challenged the great scholar Hillel to teach him the entire Law while he stood on one foot. According to the famous anecdote, Hillel replied, "What is hateful to you, do not do to your neighbor. This is the whole Law; the rest is commentary. Go and learn it!"

The scribe knew Hillel's clever Law-in-a-nutshell, his summary of the ethical commandments, but needed a more positive guide than this one, a commandment that embraced man's relations to God as well as to men. Jesus, he was sure, would throw light on this problem.

"The first and most important commandment is this," Jesus

answered him, " 'Hear, O Israel: The Lord our God, the Lord is one; and you shall love the Lord your God with all your heart, and with all your soul, and with all your mind, and with all your strength' " (Mark 12.29-30).

This was the bedrock of Jewish faith. It was the Shema, the great "Hear thou!" of Deuteronomy 6.4. As Jesus pronounced it the man nodded his head to show his approval. Faithful Jews repeated the Shema twice a day, not only to dedicate themselves continually to the Lord, but to confess their faith in the oneness of God.

To the scribe, the only surprising part of Jesus' words was his addition of a fourth aspect of man's personality to the traditional three. Heart, soul, and strength were well known, but the Master added man's mind or intelligence. The scholar approved this amendment, for in his experience a man's loving response to God was only complete when it involved his understanding.

Out of man's love of God, as Zacchaeus' story demonstrated, is born man's love for his neighbor. It was concerning human relationships that Jesus now spoke, quoting from Leviticus 19.18 and saying, " 'You shall love your neighbor as yourself.' There is no other commandment greater than these" (Mark 12.31).

"Teacher, you are completely right!" The man's voice rose to a high pitch as his lined face glowed with approval. To give one's entire self to God and to practice active good will to one's neighbor—this, he now saw, was rightly the first commandment, the simple yet profound heart of the Law as it was of Jesus' Gospel.

At the Master's pronouncement, the miscellaneous details of the scribe's wide learning suddenly arranged themselves in a significant pattern, as iron filings are formed into a unified design by a magnet. At last he could distinguish basic values from trivial concerns. "This commandment," he said, beginning to see religious matters on a true scale of values, "this commandment is far more important than burnt-offerings, sacrifices, and all the rites and observances that loom so large in our system of worship."

The prophets had taught this truth long ago. One of them had said, "Bring no more vain offerings" (Isaiah 1.13), while another had agreed when he made his famous answer to the question, "What does the Lord require of you?" (Micah 6.8).

The scribe was wise enough to know that he who understands the truth does not always follow it. When he saw the Master smiling at him, he dared to hope that, with Jesus as his guide, he might become obedient to divine command. Then Jesus' words came to him like an accolade, "You are not far from the kingdom of heaven."

38

Nameless Friends in Jerusalem

MK 11.2-6 (MT 21.1-3;
LK 19.28-34) ; MK 14.13-16
(MT 26.18; LK 22.9-12) ;
MK 14.51-52; MT 27.19

*"Rejoice that your names are writ-
ten in heaven."*

LUKE 10.20

THE GOSPEL stories of Jesus' last days in Jerusalem casually mention
four men and one woman, all of them nameless, who gave or attempted to give help to the Master when hostile forces closed in
around him. Are these five people to be numbered among his friends?
Their actions seem to put them in that category. Their stories suggest,
as did our study of the crowds, that Jesus made a profound impression upon the inhabitants of the Holy City and that scores of them,
including the individuals identified in this chapter, became his followers.

The first, the owner of the ass and her colt, was a person whose
existence is implied in Mark's Gospel, though the man himself never
actually appears. He lived in Bethphage, a village on the western slope
of the Mount of Olives and he performed an important service for
Jesus. It had all been arranged beforehand—the precise requirements
and the password. Did Jesus himself make the arrangements? Was
secrecy necessary in view of threatened danger?

Early on the morning of Jesus' entry into the Holy City, the man of
Bethphage looked across the valley toward Jerusalem where Passover
crowds were already astir. It was time for him to be up and about his

task. He took his colt, dancing with high spirits in the morning sun, and led this young beast through village lanes to the doorway of a certain house where he tethered it. Bystanders asked why he did this. The owner's reply was strange. "If anyone tries to take this colt away, you must ask, 'Why are you untying the colt?' "

The bystanders nodded.

"If this person answers, 'The Lord has need of it and will send it back here immediately,' you are to let the animal go," explained the owner.

Again the bystanders nodded, never questioning who the Lord was or the owner's reason for lending his colt.

All proceeded according to plan. Two disciples appeared, gave the password, and were allowed to lead the colt away. The bystanders dispersed, not realizing, perhaps, that they had played a part in the drama being enacted that day in Jerusalem.

What of the colt's owner? Was his animal returned to him after fulfilling its symbolic mission? Undoubtedly it was, for that was the arrangement with this man of Bethphage whom we see as one of Jesus' reliable and helpful friends.

On Thursday of his last week Jesus did not go into Jerusalem, as had been his custom on the previous days, but remained outside the city limits until evening in the comparative safety of Bethany. He planned, however, to eat the Passover at nightfall with his disciples in the Holy City, the place where the great feast was always celebrated. The chief priests and scribes were openly plotting his death, so that his plans had to be kept secret. This need for secrecy was undoubtedly the reason for the wordless action that took place on Thursday morning at the city gate.

A man bearing an earthenware water jar on his shoulder waited near the gate, watching all who entered the city. Women usually carried these water vessels to supply their household needs, while men bore the larger containers made from animal skins, hence a man with a jar was unusual enough to be noticed. Two strangers entered the gate and, seeing the man carrying the water vessel, immediately knew he was the person they had been instructed to follow. Without a word the strangers quickened their pace, covertly trailing the water-carrier while he led them by narrow byways and crowded streets to a certain house.

There the two strangers, whom Luke identifies as Peter and John, knocked on the door to which they had been so mysteriously led. The householder was expecting them and waited for them to give the password.

Peter and John gave it. "The Teacher says, 'Where is the guest room in which I am to eat the Passover with my disciples?' "

Satisfied that these two strangers were really Jesus' emissaries, the householder led them up his outside staircase to a large upper room on the roof where everything was ready: the floor swept and clean, rugs laid, cushions arranged, and a table set up for the meal. These careful preparations and the friendliness of the householder must have brought smiles of pleasure to the tense faces of Peter and John and convinced them that their Master would be safe in Jerusalem that evening.

Who was the householder? Possibly he was either John Mark, author and compiler of the oldest Gospel, or Mark's father. According to Acts 12.12, John Mark's mother was the mistress of a large house in Jerusalem where Christ's followers gathered. This house may well have been the one used earlier by the disciples as their headquarters after the resurrection (Acts 1.12-14), as well as the one where Jesus ate the Last Supper. If the same house was the scene of these three different meetings, then Mark or his father could have been the householder who sent out his watercarrier as a secret scout and pre-pared the room for Jesus.

When the supper was over that Thursday evening, the Master descended from the upper room with eleven disciples (Judas having already departed) and made his way through dark streets past the city gate, and out to the Garden of Gethsemane. There, after his arrest by soldiers of the sanhedrin, "a young man followed him, with nothing but a linen cloth about his body; and they seized him, but he left the linen cloth and ran away naked" (Mark 14.51-52).

Who was this young man? Why was he not wearing a warm robe on that chilly night? The situation in which he figures can be reconstructed in this way. Friends of Jesus, learning late that evening of the sanhedrin's plot to arrest him, may have hurried to the house where he had eaten the Last Supper only to find him gone. One can imagine them whispering their urgent message: "Soldiers have been dispatched to arrest the Master! We must warn him. Where is he?"

The householder, or some young man at the house, awakened by this alarm, without pausing to dress, snatched up a linen cloth and wrapping it around himself as he ran, sped to Gethsemane. His warning came too late, for when he arrived Jesus had already been taken into custody.

If, as we surmised earlier, the householder was John Mark or his father, then the young man of this story may also have been John Mark. This episode, puzzling because it is entirely irrelevant and found only in Mark's Gospel, may be John Mark's portrait of himself, his only personal record in the Gospel bearing his name.

The fifth shadowy and, in this case, somewhat legendary figure was that of a woman, Pilate's wife. Roman wives sometimes accompanied their husbands to the more peaceful provinces of the empire. According to Matthew's account, Pilate was weighing the issues of the case against Jesus when his wife sent him a message.

"Have nothing to do with that innocent and righteous man," she begged, "for my dream about him last night troubled me greatly."

Pilate was as deaf to his wife's warning as was Caesar on the day of his murder. Caesar's wife had urged him not to go to the Forum because a dream had revealed to her what would befall him there.

Was Pilate's wife merely trying to protect her husband from a rash act, or did she know Jesus as an innocent and righteous man whom she wanted to save? We do not know. Perhaps she was a woman true of heart and blessed with spiritual insight like that of other Roman women who in the years to come would acknowledge Jesus as Lord. If so, Pilate's wife may, like others in Jerusalem, have glimpsed the Master's transcendent glory.

39

Judas Iscariot

MK 3.19; JN 6.70-71; 12.4-6;
MK 14.10-11, 18-20; 43-46
(MT 26.14-16, 21-25, 47-50;
LK 22.3-6, 21-23, 47-48;
JN 13.2, 21-30; 18.2-5);
MT 27.3-10; cf. ACTS 1.16-20

"Would you betray the Son of man with a kiss?"

LUKE 22.48

SUPPER BEING OVER in the upper room, Judas Iscariot rose from the table and strode to the door. The Master had already told his disciples of his plan to spend the night outside Jerusalem's walls beneath the olive trees of Gethsemane. This was the information for which Judas had waited—the information he had agreed to sell. Now he must be on his way. The hour was growing late and armed men would be assembling at the high priest's palace. For thirty pieces of silver Judas had bargained to betray his Master.

Outside it was dark, the darkest night Judas had ever known. Blinded by the sudden absence of light, he stumbled on the stairs, but recovered himself and descended with a heavy tread to the street. Looking back over his shoulder, he made sure that no one followed him. He found it strange that his departure had not been challenged, for Jesus had distinctly said to them all at the table, "One of you— one now eating supper with me—will betray me."

Judas shivered in the chilly night air as he recalled the shock this statement had produced. Had each man been too horrified at the possibilities he saw in his own heart to accuse his fellow?

"Is it I?" one after another had asked.

"It is one of you Twelve," replied Jesus, declining to name the traitor but emphasizing the shamefulness of the deed by adding, "It is one who is dipping bread into the dish with me."

Nothing was considered more despicable than betraying a person with whom one had eaten. By ancient custom, table companions respected one another's personal safety. The sort of treachery of which Jesus spoke seemed unthinkable to the disciples and while they struggled to understand the coming betrayal, Judas slipped away unnoticed.

Matthew's Gospel adds that at the table Judas himself asked the same question as did the others, "Am I the man, Master?" He received the answer, "You have said so." John's Gospel enlarges upon the scene and adds that the Master whispered to Judas, "What you are about to do, do quickly."

Once in the dark street, Judas looked to right and left but saw no one. Jerusalem's inhabitants were indoors by now and the Passover visitors had departed for their camps on the surrounding hills. So far so good, thought Judas though his breath still came in short gasps. The conspirators had stipulated secrecy, fearing a popular outcry if Jesus were openly arrested. They planned to take him stealthily and at night.

With difficulty, for his feet seemed clumsy, Judas blundered through deserted streets, cursing when he tripped on the rough pavement or lost his way amid unfamiliar, twisting alleys. Jerusalem was not his city and he hated it. He hated its crowds, its deluded crowds shouting, "Hosanna! Blessed is he who comes in the name of the Lord." He hated the eleven men who had been his companions, month after month, on a misguided mission of preparing for a kingdom that would never come. Judas hated himself for having been taken in by a foolish dream.

During those first sunlit weeks with the Master in Galilee he had been enthusiastic for the kingdom Jesus proclaimed. No sacrifice for it seemed too great to Judas. For once in his life he experienced good will toward everyone, even the stupid and the hostile. After Jesus called him to be a disciple, and he found himself in a close-knit fellowship, he felt liberated from his usual cramped self. He seemed to be living in a new dimension, a realm of light and freedom where everything seemed possible.

When Jesus entrusted him with the money of their little group, he was proud to have his astuteness recognized. If only his advice had been taken and more authority given him! It was here that everything began to go wrong. He was convinced that Jesus had blundered in not choosing him but making Peter leader of the Twelve. No wonder he was soon out of step with the entire group. Only last week Jesus had rebuked him for his criticism of Mary of Bethany, though he knew his criticism was justified. Anyone could see that she was foolishly extravagant with her ointment.

At the heart of his black misery that night as he made his way through Jerusalem was one man, Jesus, the misguided visionary who had once been his dearest friend. Judas saw it all clearly now. The Master lacked what every ruler must have—ruthlessness. He preached love in a world clearly governed by hate and he was therefore unfit to rule.

While these thoughts raced through the disciple's mind, an inner voice kept repeating, "Betraying a friend—betraying one whom you loved."

"No!" shouted Judas into the darkness, "not betraying! I am defending Israel, protecting her from error, exposing a false messiah."

If Jesus were indeed the Lord's anointed, Judas argued with himself, no man could harm him. The Scriptures proved that.

> For he will give his angels charge of you
> to guard you in all your ways.
> On their hands they will bear you up,
> lest you dash your foot against a stone.
> PSALM 91.11-12

Every way he looked at it, Judas knew his act would come out all right. If Jesus really were the Messiah, legions of angels would rescue him, thereby proving to all men who he was. But if he were not the Messiah, he deserved to die. Satan won the argument in Judas' mind or, as one of the Gospels interprets it, "Satan entered into Judas called Iscariot" (Luke 22.3).

Reaching the high priest's palace, Judas knocked on the gate and was immediately admitted into the courtyard that already swarmed with men armed with swords and clubs. An officer brought Judas a bag of coins which he opened in the light of a bonfire. He counted thirty pieces of silver, the agreed price, the price of a slave.

What did the authorities buy with their bag of silver coins? Probably they bought only Judas' services as a guide to a place where Jesus could be secretly arrested. Some interpreters think that Judas also sold the high priest information concerning his Master's claim to be the Messiah, information on which a charge of blasphemy could be based.

The armed rabble and a few officers left the courtyard following the torchbearers and Judas. The sign that was to identify Jesus to these men had been hastily agreed upon. It would be a kiss. Judas led the way, his inner voice now silent and the torturing indecision of the past months ended. He held his bag of silver coins tightly, knowing that they guaranteed a new life for him. He had other coins safely hidden away, coins taken now and again from the common purse. There were enough now to buy a field outside Jerusalem. Jesus had warned against avariciously piling up riches. "But what other security or happiness is there than riches?" Judas asked himself.

Torchlight probed the darkness under Gethsemane's olive trees, illuminating the calm face of a man standing there alone. With the rabble shouting at his heels, the traitor approached the well-known figure. "Master!" exclaimed Judas, giving Jesus the kiss with which disciples customarily saluted their rabbi.

"My friend," said Jesus, trying at this ultimate moment to bring Judas back to his best self, "Why have you come?"

It was over in a moment. The disciples vanished into the darkness. Jesus was bound and led away. The sight brought Judas to himself. Alone under the olive trees, his anger spent, he trembled in revulsion at what he had done. Where were the legions of protecting angels? He told himself that this was not the way he wanted it to end. He wanted to force the Master's hand and compel him to use for himself the power he had often exercised for others. "Why does he not seize his kingdom?" cried Judas in bewilderment and despair.

He ran back through the empty streets of Jerusalem to the chief priests and elders. They had provoked him to this evil deed. The blame be upon them!

"I have sinned in betraying an innocent man," he cried, throwing down at their feet the thirty pieces of silver.

The authorities turned their backs on him, refusing his money. This traitor was becoming a nuisance now that his usefulness to them was over. "What has your sin to do with us?" asked the self-righteous chief priests and elders, disdainfully glancing at the abject figure of Judas. "It is your own affair."

According to Matthew, whose account differs from the legend in Acts, Judas flung his thirty silver pieces into the temple and, in an agony of despair, went out and hanged himself. Being blood money it could not be added to the temple funds, so the priests used it to purchase from the potters a field where strangers and poor people might be buried.

The depth of Judas' remorse measured his character, one that, as the Master had seen, was capable of greatness. If he had been a shallow person, he might have shrugged off his self-reproach. To Judas it became unbearable. Ordained for an outstanding role, he fell a prey to his own sordid impulses. Had he been loyal to the glory he witnessed, he might, with Peter and the others, have helped to change the world.

40

Simon of Cyrene

MK 15.21 (MT 27.32;
LK 23.26) ; ROM 16.13

*Bear one another's burdens, and so
fulfil the law of Christ.*

GALATIANS 6.2

WITH EACH STEP Simon felt his burden dig deeper into his shoulder.
He feared that the scar made by this heavy crossbeam would be with
him always. His flesh was bruised and abraded and his muscles ached
as he strained forward toward Golgotha. Resentment boiled within
him. Criminals always carried their own crossbeams, which were
fastened to uprights at the place of execution. One of the three men
being led away to death had fallen beneath his cross and was unable
to proceed farther with his load. Simon was carrying it.

He was angry with the Roman soldiers in charge of this execution
who, disdaining to carry the shameful thing themselves, had thrust it
upon him. Though he had explained to them that he was an innocent
passerby coming in from the country, merely a Jew visiting Jerusalem
for the Passover and therefore ignorant of the whole affair, the soldiers
had laughed at him and shoved him along. Simon knew that they
had taken advantage of him, a stranger. Back home in his own city of
Cyrene such an indignity as this would hardly befall one as well
known and respected as he. He hoped his wife and two sons, Alexander and Rufus, safe now in their North African home, would never
learn of his humiliating task today.

By narrow streets echoing with jeers and insults, through one of
the city gates, and on to the skull-like mound called Golgotha, Simon
doggedly trudged, often jostled by people trying to get a better

view of the condemned men. Amid shouted taunts Simon heard wailing. "Woe to us!" lamented many along the way. "What a thing is this that has come to pass!"

The man from North Africa looked up sharply. What *had* come to pass? For whom were these people crying and beating their breasts? Could it be that their wailing was for the third man whose cross he carried? Listening closely, he began to pick up words and scraps of conversation—"Jesus." "Master." "Prophet from Nazareth." "Never did man speak as he did." "He went around doing good." "He healed our infirmities." "Son of God." "The Messiah." "The Christ."

"So that is it," exclaimed Simon, "a miracle-worker and another self-deluded messiah. No wonder the governor wants him out of the way!" In far-off Cyrenaica, Simon had learned in the synagogue he attended that the true Messiah would one day come. But this tortured man about to suffer an ignominious death surely could not be he.

Yet Simon was glad it was this man's cross he carried. The other two men were obviously criminals, but there was a quality about Jesus that attracted him. The burden of the cross now seemed lighter. They had almost reached Golgotha. When Jesus turned toward a group of weeping women, Simon saw his face for the first time and heard the accents of his voice.

"Weep not for me, daughters of Jerusalem," he heard the condemned man say. "Weep, rather, for yourselves and your children."

"How can one so near exhaustion spare a thought for others, when only torture and death lie ahead of him!" Simon exclaimed to those standing near.

Jesus may have heard him, for the two men were close. Out of eyes dark with pain yet amazingly filled with love and gratitude, the Master looked at Simon. Here, the stranger from North Africa knew, was a prince among men, a man whose source of strength lay too deep to be overwhelmed by defeat, pain, sorrow, or even death.

"What is his secret?" wondered Simon, as hammers drove nails into flesh and three crosses were set up against the morning sky.

"If only I had know him before all this," sighed the man whose shoulder still ached from the weight of the wooden crossbar. "I wish I had been his friend. Such a man I would have followed to the ends of the earth!"

As he watched during the long hours of the crucifixion, Simon was visited by a strange exaltation, for it was slowly borne in upon him that this was no ordinary execution. Though the man upon the central cross was dying, there was a splendor about him not of this world, for, with arms outstretched, Jesus appeared to Simon to be reigning in divine glory.

The fact that Simon's sons, Alexander and Rufus, are mentioned without comment in Mark's Gospel suggests that they were so well known to the first readers of this Gospel that their names needed no explanation. These readers were probably the early Christians living in Rome to whom the apostle Paul sent greetings. Some of these people he mentioned by name, among them a certain Rufus and his mother. "Greet Rufus, eminent in the Lord," wrote the apostle, graciously adding, "also his mother and mine" (Romans 16.13).

Were this Rufus and his mother the son and the widow respectively of Simon of Cyrene who on the Friday of the crucifixion became a follower of the Lord?

41

The Penitent Thief

LK 23.39-43   *For godly grief produces a repent-*
                               ance that leads to salvation.
                                              2 CORINTHIANS 7.10

DESPITE BLINDING PAIN, the crucified man's inner vision became
clear. In the final agonizing hours of his life, the fog of his self-
deception lifted, showing him the world as it is. He saw the folly
of his misspent years during which every choice he had made was
evil. Some perverse impulse always urged him to take the wrong fork
in the road, the turning that he knew he should avoid. In his devil-
may-care way he had never doubted that all roads would finally meet
or that, when he had had enough of waywardness, he could return
to the beginning and start afresh. He had never expected his life to
end like this in torture and humiliation, hung on a cross beside two
other men. After seeing other malefactors like himself caught and
executed, he had proudly boasted that, even if the wages of sin be
death, he would never pay such a price.

The best life could give him was his goal. What was wrong with
that? He pursued pleasure and power with singleminded zeal, always
goaded to more daring adventures to attain them, never entertaining
a thought for the people he encountered. Once he was a thief stealthily
stealing whatever he could. Next he joined a robber band in the hills,
plundering the helpless and laughing at their ruin. He finally became
a member of a revolutionary group, smashing and destroying for the
sake of power, a headier stake than a caravan's wealth. Trampling

upon everything and everyone representing law and order and imposing his will on terrified villages gave him a wild sense of authority.

But the law had closed in on him, trapped him, hastily tried and convicted him as a criminal, and sent him out to Golgotha. Last week he rode high as an outlaw. This morning he hung upon a cross.

Through the screaming and cursing of his fellow criminal dying near him, he heard the man on the center cross speaking, the man above whose head was the strange, scornful inscription: THIS IS THE KING OF THE JEWS.

The first malefactor wondered what this Jesus was saying in his extremity of pain. Then a mocking thought entered his mind. "As a king, this man must be giving orders to us his chief ministers, to me on his right, and to that other fellow on his left. Does he know that he is only a king of shame, a king of death?" The thief was about to taunt Jesus with this when he stopped, suddenly ashamed to ridicule one dying with him.

What is Jesus really saying, the thief asked himself. From the center cross the words came to him distinctly, "Father, forgive those who have placed me here, for they know not what they do."

So that was it—a prayer for his tormentors! Instead of cursing them, this mysterious man prayed for them. The malefactor had never known anything like this before—had never met such a man. This so-called King of the Jews was supremely unselfish and able to forgive the greatest wrong against himself. From a life of total selfishness the malefactor looked across at Jesus and was amazed at the vast gulf separating them. "Who is he really?" the dying man asked himself.

At this time his fellow criminal, the one who had been caught and condemned with him, maddened by suffering and still fighting his fate, took up the jeers of the watching crowd and cried out to Jesus, "Are you not the Christ? Why then do you not save yourself and us?"

The first thief, feeling this mockery to be unjust, responded quickly. "You should be afraid of God," he called out. "You and I are being punished in the same manner as this good man. It is merited punishment for us, for we are getting only what we deserve, but this man never did anything wrong."

A verse from the Scriptures learned in the far-off days of his childhood came to the thief's mind. The words described one who, like this man,

> . . . was numbered with the transgressors;
> yet he bore the sin of many,
> and made intercession for the transgressors.
>
> ISAIAH 53.12

"If only he would intercede for me, one of the greatest of transgressors," murmured the dying man. "If only I had known him earlier and followed him!"

He reproached himself for the many wrongs he had committed and as he did so he felt a strange peace possess his heart as if he no longer bore the heavy burden of his sins. Painfully turning his head toward Jesus before it was too late, the onetime thief saw Jesus no longer as someone dying a shameful death, but as a man transfigured. He must indeed be a king, thought the criminal, a king who will finally reign in triumph over his glorious kingdom.

With a strangled cry the dying man pleaded, "Jesus, remember me, be gracious to me when you come into your kingdom." He could face death unafraid in the company of Jesus.

Immediately, from the center cross came the promise, "I tell you truly, today you will be with me in Paradise."

42

The Centurion at the Cross

MK 15.39 (MT 27.54;
LK 23.47)

*"Every one who acknowledges me
before men, I also will acknowledge
before my Father who is in heaven.*
MATTHEW 10.32

FOR HOURS the centurion had been engaged in a hateful task. Though he was accustomed to the sight of death, executions sickened him. No matter how deserving of punishment criminals might be, he found it repugnant to be in charge of their crucifixions as he was this morning on Golgotha. He had steeled himself to perform this duty, but he looked forward to the time when he could no longer be ordered to carry out these brutal tasks. When his twenty years in the Roman army were completed, he would take his pension and retire to his farm in far-off Italy.

Most of his years in the army had been spent in various parts of the empire, from the Rhine to Syria, among many different kinds of people with a wide variety of beliefs and customs. He was the sort of man who greeted new experiences with an open mind, for he was neither intolerant nor bigoted. By virtue of his dependability and his skill in overcoming difficulties, he had risen through the army ranks to his present command. In it he enjoyed considerable prestige and high pay. He was a good officer, watching over his hundred soldiers, checking their weapons, keeping them well supplied with food, drilling and disciplining them until they were an efficient fighting unit, one of the best among the sixty companies of the legion.

The three condemned men whose execution he was responsible for had been dying on their crosses for hours. At last the crowd was thinning out, leaving fewer people to jeer at the man upon the center cross. The centurion noticed that his soldiers were whiling away the tedious hours with one of their games of chance. The dying men were quiet. No serious disturbance was likely to be made by the handful of Jesus' friends waiting nearby because most of them were women. Checking the situation, the centurion found it satisfactory, yet he felt strangely restless, unable to shake off an overwhelming sense of depression. Was it due to the strange darkness beginning to envelop Jerusalem and its surrounding hills?

Words spoken by Jesus from the cross haunted him, the prayer for his executioners, and his promise to the dying criminal. Ignorant as this Roman officer was of the psalms, he doubtless heard the terrible cry, "My God, my God, why hast thou forsaken me?" as words of despair and abandonment, not knowing that they were the opening verse of the Twenty-second Psalm. Had the centurion read this psalm he would have been struck by its many prophetic references to the scene before him—the scorning and mocking, the cry "Let the Lord rescue him," the physical suffering, the thirst, the piercing of hands and feet, the casting of lots for the condemned man's raiment. But the psalms were unknown poetry to the centurion, so it did not occur to him that Jesus was perhaps reciting the entire psalm to himself and deriving strength for his ordeal from its glorious affirmation of faith.

> Yet thou art holy,
>   enthroned on the praises of Israel.
> In thee our fathers trusted;
>   they trusted, and thou didst deliver them.
> To thee they cried, and were saved;
>   in thee they trusted, and were not disappointed.
>   PSALM 22.3-5

When Jesus was crucified, someone offered him wine mixed with myrrh, a drug prepared by a group of kindly women of Jerusalem to help deaden the pain of criminals undergoing execution. The centurion was impressed by his refusal to drink the proffered wine.

"Such courage as Jesus has! He prefers to meet death with a clear mind. All his words show him to be a good man, even a great one. Surely such a man is innocent!"

While the darkness grew so intense as almost to obscure the crosses, the centurion trembled. Then he heard the voice of Jesus praying, "Father, into thy hands I commit my spirit." Death is not triumphing over this man, thought the centurion, he is laying down his life. With a loud cry of victory, "It is finished," Jesus bowed his head and died.

The centurion leaned for support upon his spear. He had never witnessed a death like this one. Here was no usual criminal, no ordinary man even, but surely a person of godlike quality. The soldiers were awestruck too, ceasing their game to stand beside their captain. Slowly raising his arm toward the lifeless body on the center cross, he saluted the greatness he had witnessed there and said, "Truly this man was a Son of God."

43

Joseph of Arimathea

MK 15.42-46 (MT 27.57-61;
LK 23.50-56; JN 19.38-42)

> *He was a member of the council,
> a good and righteous man, who had
> not consented to their purpose and
> deed, and he was looking for the
> kingdom of God.*
>
> LUKE 23.50-51

JOSEPH WAS THANKFUL that his robe concealed his knees, for, as he
waited in the Roman governor's audience chamber, they were shaking
violently. He had come to ask a favor of Pilate, one that might
cause the Roman authorities to suspect him. It would certainly make
him a marked man among his own countrymen in the sanhedrin.
As Joseph fingered his gold chain and tried to take his mind off
his anxieties by thinking of his broad fields and sunny vineyards
in Arimathea, fear gripped him. What if Pilate refused his request?
Joseph steadied himself with the knowledge that friends or relatives
could, if they asked for it, usually obtain the body of an executed
criminal for burial. But Joseph's petition would align him with the
friends of Jesus. That was its danger.

Always before this Joseph had managed to avoid trouble. Rich and
comfortable, he asked only to be allowed to enjoy himself. Though
he was a man of ideals and lived uprightly, looking for God's speedy
intervention in the world, he clung tenaciously to his ease and safety.
Jesus' mission had moved him greatly, centered as it was in the kingdom of God, but Joseph had hesitated to give public support to the
prophet from Nazareth and was content to be a secret disciple like his

colleague Nicodemus. Joseph had absented himself from the last tumultuous meeting of the sanhedrin, having been unwilling to consent to Jesus' death.

Impatient with waiting, he questioned the guard at the door, "When will Pilate come?" Joseph observed that the sun, which had been hidden when Jesus died, had now come out again and slanted low through the palace windows. It was late afternoon of the day of Preparation. Before the Sabbath lamps were lit that evening Jesus' body must be buried. Joseph recalled the Law.

And if a man has committed a crime punishable by death and he is put to death, and you hang him on a tree, his body shall not remain all night upon the tree, but you shall bury him the same day, for a hanged man is accursed by God; you shall not defile your land which the Lord your God gives you for an inheritance.

DEUTERONOMY 21.22-23

To carry out the Law as a loyal Jew and to preserve the fair land of Israel from defilement—these, Joseph told himself, were sufficient reasons for his request. Moreover it was an act of piety to bury a dead stranger. Jesus, however, was no stranger to Joseph of Arimathea and all these reasons for making his request of Pilate were merely excuses to conceal his unavowed devotion to the Master.

"Why should a man of God who went about preaching and doing good be thrown into a common grave with criminals?" Joseph asked himself. He shuddered at the thought of Jesus' body being desecrated. Joseph felt powerfully drawn to the dead prophet whose movement was now crushed and whose claims to messiahship were discredited. "If only I had helped him earlier!" the councilor kept saying to himself, ashamed of his belated support. "Long ago I heard in his teachings an authentic word from the Lord."

In a flurry of guards and functionaries Pilate strode into his audience chamber and sat down. Joseph of Arimathea immediately came forward to ask his favor.

"Dead already!" exclaimed Pilate, knowing that crucified men seldom died in the few hours this man had been on the cross.

The governor had had too much experience in these matters not to require proof, so he sent for the centurion in charge of the execution. Joseph meanwhile waited in a fever of apprehension. He had already ordered his men to obtain ropes and to open his new tomb, but would his wife be able to procure a linen shroud at such short notice?

Suddenly, to the sound of a sword clanking against armor, the centurion entered the chamber, saluted Pilate, and reported tersely, "He is dead."

Without hesitation Pilate gestured with his hand toward Joseph and said, "You may take the body." Then he turned to other business.

The sun was already setting when the councilor and his men reached Golgotha. There Nicodemus joined them, bringing a large quantity of spices, myrrh and aloes, to place within the folds of the shroud. Hastily they lowered Jesus' body from the cross, wrapped it in the scented winding sheet, and carried it to Joseph's tomb in a nearby garden. The Law forbade the burial of a criminal in a family sepulcher, but Joseph's was new, having been recently purchased when he moved with his family to Jerusalem.

The tomb in which they placed the body was a vault cut into a rocky hillside and closed by a heavy, circular stone shaped like a grindstone. This could be rolled along a groove cut in the rock. By the time the men had placed the body within the tomb and rolled the ponderous stone into place at the entrance, three stars had appeared in the sky and the Sabbath trumpet had sounded its final blast. Throughout the Holy City and on its surrounding hills, little flames of yellow light appeared as the Sabbath lamps were lit in every home. Looking up and seeing them a strange joy filled Joseph's heart.

> Arise, shine; for your light has come,
>   and the glory of the Lord has risen upon you.
> For behold, darkness shall cover the earth,
>   and thick darkness the peoples;
> but the Lord will arise upon you,
>   and his glory will be seen upon you.
>   ISAIAH 60.1-2

44

The Faithful Women

MK 15.40-41, 47; 16.1-8
(MT 27.55-56,61; 28.1-10;
LK 8.1-3; 23.49,55; 24.1-12;
JN 19.25); JN 20.1-10

*There were also many women there,
looking on from afar, who had followed Jesus from Galilee, ministering
to him.*

MATTHEW 27.55

TOO NUMB with grief and fatigue even to weep, a little group of
women huddled together, wrapped in their cloaks against the evening's
cold. They gazed into the dusk, straining to see what was taking place
in a certain garden not far away, but afraid to approach it closer. The
voices of strangers came to them, though their words were muted.
Soon they heard a rumbling, grating sound as of a heavy stone being
moved. The tomb, they knew, had now been closed. This was the end
—the end of a life of surpassing goodness and the end of all their
expectations. These women realized that much more than a good man
was buried in the sepulcher—it entombed their dreams of an Israel
reborn, and their hope that their children might live, not in misery
and despair, but fearless and free under the glorious banner of Christ.
Presently they saw the burial party's torches flicker and disappear.
Darkness shrouded the garden. The women shivered in the growing
cold. A Sabbath silence reigned over the Holy City.

On the nearby hill of Golgotha and starkly silhouetted against the
evening sky stood three crosses. The scene reminded the mourning
women of an ancient lament, David's funeral dirge for Israel's first
king.

"Thy glory, O Israel, is slain upon thy high places!
How are the mighty fallen!"

2 SAMUEL I.19

Kingly though Jesus was, these women honored him for more than his regal personality. It was the little things they remembered about him that made their tears flow. His mighty acts and triumphant words might be fit subjects for an elegy, but tonight the women's lips trembled too much for such a tribute. In the darkness each one of them remembered Jesus' friendly words and deeds that gave him, in their eyes, a nobility above that of kings. Did ever a man show greater courtesy than his to the daughters of Israel? Did ever a man comprehend them so fully? No wonder so many of them became his followers. What other prophet before him had made women proud to be women? Jesus never showed them the subtle condescension of most men, for he treated women as human beings in their own right, not as inferior creatures ordained to be men's helpers. The rabbis' daily prayer, "Oh God, I thank thee that I was not born a woman," was unthinkable on Jesus' lips.

Tonight the stars shone brightly over the Judean hills as on a night not so many years before when shepherds heard the herald angel sing. Birth and death—what did they signify? Beneath the cold stare of distant stars, it seemed to the women at that desolate moment that life had no meaning. Had God, they wondered, withdrawn beyond the ramparts of the stars? Or perhaps he did not exist at all. If there were a God why did he allow one who served him well to die in shame upon a cross?

Yet the women recalled the words Jesus uttered in the midst of agony, "This day . . . with me in paradise" and "Father, into thy hands. . . ." With these words ringing in their ears, and with all their memories of the Master's life, the sorrowing group looked again at the stars and saw them twinkling with a more friendly light, beautiful, remote, mysterious, the handiwork of God. The memory of Jesus' final cry rekindled the women's faith in the nearness of the Lord and Jesus' oneness with him. These mourners knew that men will die and even the stars will change, but the Lord endures and his love prevails. Shall not all who partake of his spirit also endure, they asked, and shall not the years of him who was one with the Father have no end?

Shrouded in their cloaks, the grief-stricken women made their way through the starlit darkness, each one guarding the ember of her faith and finding comfort in the ancient wisdom of a psalm.

> Of old thou didst lay the foundation of the earth,
>   and the heavens are the work of thy hands.
> They will perish, but thou dost endure;
>   they will all wear out like a garment.
> Thou changest them like raiment, and they pass away;
>   but thou art the same, and thy years have no end.
>   PSALM 102.25-27

Spirited women though they were, and able to meet crises and cope with life's many difficulties, the past day had seemed well-nigh unbearable to them. They had been roused at daybreak with news of Jesus' arrest. Following their Master wherever he was led, to the high priest's palace, to Pilate's judgment hall, and outside Jerusalem's walls to Golgotha, they were always kept at a distance from him whom they loved by a cordon of Roman soldiers. Even so they followed him. Except for the beloved disciple who supported Jesus' mother during the long ordeal, the women saw none of the other disciples during the nightmare hours of the crucifixion. Despite personal danger and mental anguish, the women stood near enough to his cross for Jesus to see them and perhaps take comfort from their presence. They grieved that they had been able to do so little for him who had done so much for them.

The final horror had been spared them. When Jesus laid down his life and they realized that they were powerless to prevent desecration of his body, a group of strangers had arrived to give it seemly burial, the burial they had just now witnessed from afar. The women no longer feared that Jesus' body would be thrown into a common grave or exposed in the Roman way to deter would-be criminals.

Unable to see whether the strangers, in their haste, had completed the burial rites, the women resolved that, as soon as the Sabbath ended, they would go to the sepulcher to pay their last respects to the lifeless body. They would anoint it with nard and wrap it in a linen cloth perfumed with fragrant myrrh and aloes.

Wearily returning to their lodgings to prepare ointments and spices, the women glanced toward the tomb, trying to fix its exact location in their minds. They rehearsed each detail of the death and burial, knowing that one day they would be questioned about these events which they alone of all Jesus' followers had witnessed.

Who were these courageous women whose loyalty and love sustained them through the long day as they looked on from afar? All the Gospels mention Mary Magdalene who seems to have been in some sense the leader among the women as Peter was among the twelve disciples. Her story will be told in the next chapter. Only the Fourth Gospel describes Jesus' mother with the beloved disciple at the foot of the cross. A third Mary was also present, described by both Mark and Matthew as the mother of James and Joses (called Joseph in Matthew's Gospel). As we have already noted, this James may have been the disciple James the Less. The Gospel of John identifies this Mary as the wife of Clopas.

Besides the Marys there were other women, some of whom we have already mentioned in connection with the identity of Zebedee's wife. Mark names Salome but gives no clue to her identity. Luke adds Susanna and Joanna, the latter described as the wife of Chuza, Herod's steward, and hence a person af wealth and social position. Matthew adds Zebedee's wife who was, of course, the mother of the disciples James and John. To this list the Fourth Gospel adds Jesus' mother's sister.

The Synoptic Gospels agree that at the cross the six women whose names are given were accompanied by "many other women who came up with him to Jerusalem" (Mark 15.41). Most of them were Galileans who had responded to Jesus' proclamation of the kingdom of God and had devoted themselves to its fulfillment. A few of these women may have been wealthy, all served Jesus and ministered to his needs as they traveled with him on his missions, finally going with him up to Jerusalem for the Passover.

Not a few of the women had seen their loved ones cured, or had themselves been "healed of evil spirits and infirmities" (Luke 8.2). As we noted earlier, Joanna, the wife of Chuza, may have been the Capernaum official's wife and mother of the son cured by Jesus. Perhaps some of the other grateful women who figure in the Gospels were among those watching at the cross and sepulcher. Was the widow of Nain there, and Peter's mother-in-law? Had Jairus' wife and daughter come? Were the Samaritan woman and the Canaanite woman there, far from home and in foreign surroundings? Martha and Mary, who lived just over the Mount of Olives, were undoubtedly present.

Though we do not know the names of all in the weary group that returned through Jerusalem's gates on the star-filled Sabbath evening, we know that they were witnesses of Jesus' death and burial and would soon be witnesses of his glory.

VII

AFTER HIS RESURRECTION

45

Mary Magdalene

LK 8.1; MK 15.40,47; 16.1-
18; JN 20.1-18; also references of the preceding chapter

"I have seen the Lord!"
JOHN 20.18

MARY MAGDALENE caught her breath and stopped short in astonishment, the jar of ointment she carried falling from her hand. Beside
her the other women trembled. It was very early in the morning of
the first day of the week, the third day after they had watched Jesus'
body placed within Joseph of Arimathea's tomb. In the dim light
of dawn all was peaceful and still in the garden. There were no foot-
prints in the dew, yet the frightened women knew that someone
had been here earlier, for in front of them the entrance to Jesus'
tomb gaped open. During the night something had happened. Who
had rolled away the huge boulder that closed the tomb? Was Jesus'
body still within?

Assuming that the worst had happened, Mary Magdalene was
sure Jesus' enemies had moved the great stone and stolen the body to
wreak their vengeance on it. Shuddering in horror, she groped absent-
mindedly for her jar of ointment for which she now had no use.

A woman of action, not one to give way to prolonged lamenta-
tions, Mary exclaimed, "Someone must find his body!" Dry-eyed, she
turned abruptly and ran out of the garden while the other women
stood gazing in stupefaction at the empty tomb.

Since the day long ago when Jesus had freed Mary from her "seven
devils," she had been one of his most able and loyal followers, happy
to minister to one who had introduced her to a new order of being.

The faith he had imparted to her did not weigh her down; it was not a burden she had to carry; instead, it carried her, lending zest to her days and a song to her heart. But this morning everything was changed and her buoyancy had vanished. With Jesus not only dead but discredited as a prophet, his disciples in hiding, a few sorrowing women trying to bring the whole catastrophic event to a dignified close, now this must be faced—the bitter reality of an empty tomb. Mary's heart sagged under the weight of a faith that had become only a burden.

Skirting the ugly outcrop of rock called Golgotha, Mary averted her eyes from the three crosses and thought longingly of her own beautiful town of Magdala far away beside the blue Sea of Galilee. An impulse to return there assailed her, to run away from all the heartbreak and despair of Jerusalem, but she kept on going toward the Holy City, past guards at the gate, through devious lanes and narrow streets of the still-sleeping city to the house where Peter lodged. Mary hoped that he and the disciple whom Jesus loved would know what to do in this crisis.

Her sharp rap brought Peter to the door. "Mary! What is it?" he asked, alarm sharpening his expression and bringing out the weary lines in his face.

"They have taken the Lord out of his tomb," sobbed Mary, "and we do not know where they have laid him."

Squaring his drooping shoulders, Peter reached for his cloak and sped toward the empty tomb, followed by the beloved disciple.

Bodily fatigue deepened Mary's acute despair. Not knowing what to do she slowly retraced her steps to the grave, still carrying her jar of ointment. It reminded her of happier days. On one of them a penitent woman had poured fragrant oil from an alabaster flask on Jesus' feet. On another, Mary of Bethany had used costly nard to anoint the Master. Remembering these two acts of loving gratitude, Mary Magdalene grieved that, in a final act of devotion, she could not anoint his body for burial.

Reaching Joseph's garden, she found it quiet and deserted. The women who had accompanied her here earlier had already departed, as had Peter and his companion. No breeze stirred the leaves. Even the birds were silent. It was as though nature were hushed, waiting for something to happen. There was no evidence that, a short time before, Mary's companions had seen here a vision of angels and had departed, some trembling and afraid, but others eager to report what they had seen and heard.

"We heard the angels say," they later testified to the disciples, " 'Why seek the living among the dead? He is not here. He is risen and goes into Galilee where you shall see him'."

The disciples shrugged their shoulders when the women reported this message. "An idle tale," they all agreed, wrapping themselves in gloom, though Peter and the disciple Jesus loved wondered at the angel's words, having themselves returned from the empty tomb where they had seen the strange sight of the undisturbed grave cloths.

Knowing nothing of these events, Mary Magdalene lingered beside the sepulcher, alone and weeping. Finally, peering within, as Peter and his companion had done, she saw two angels, like the cherubim of God's Mercy Seat, one at the head and one at the foot, where Jesus' body had lain. Though he had died between two criminals, two angels guarded his burial place. Long ago God had spoken, "I will meet with you, and from above the mercy seat, from between the two cherubim that are upon the ark of the testimony, I will speak to you . . ." (Exodus 25.22). Was this the new Ark of a new Covenant? Was Christ henceforth to be the meeting place of God and man?

Mary was so overcome by grief that she did not understand the meaning of her vision and her tears continued to flow. "Why do you weep?" asked the angels.

"Because they have taken away my Lord and I do not know where they have laid him."

Turning around, she became aware of someone near her. She lowered her head to hide her tears, but the stranger repeated the angels' question, "Why are you weeping?"

He evidently knew that she grieved for someone she had lost, for his second question was specific, "Who are you looking for?"

He is the gardener, thought Mary, the man who cultivates this plot of ground. He may have removed the body. "Sir," she implored him, "if you have removed my Lord from his tomb, please tell me where he is, and I will take him away."

"Mary!"

At the sound of the familiar voice speaking her name, Mary turned to look at the stranger.

"O my Master!" she cried, beholding in an ecstasy of joy this mystery beyond human comprehension. Here was Jesus who had died upon the cross, now radiantly alive in a new mode of being, yet still himself. Mary knew him at once, even recognizing his voice which had often seemed to her "like the sound of many waters" (Revelation 1.15). Swiftly she knelt, stretching out her hands to clasp his feet and hold him lest she lose him again.

Jesus stepped away from her. "Do not cling to me," he said gently, indicating that she must not hold him back. "I have not yet ascended to my Father," he continued. "But go to my brethren and tell them that I am ascending to my Father and yours, to my God and your God."

Mary withdrew her outstretched hands and folded them in the attitude of prayer. Her old friendship with Jesus amid the green hills of Galilee and along the dusty roads of Judea was changed into a new, spiritual relationship transcending time and space. She knew that his transitory life as Jesus of Nazareth had not ended, as she had feared, in shame; it was now raised into the eternal presence of God.

After Jesus spoke, he passed from Mary's sight. Her weeping had endured for the night, but joy came to her on this morning; the new morning of the world. She must be up and about the task Jesus had given her.

Leaving her jar of ointment beside the tomb, she ran, light-footed, back into the city, having beheld in the stillness of Joseph's garden the supreme miracle, the sign of God's final triumph. Finding the disciples, she made known to them all that had happened, witnessing to them the almost incredible fact, "I have seen the Lord!"

46

Cleopas and His Companion

LK 24.13-35

*"God raised him on the third
day and made him manifest; not to
all the people but to us who were
chosen by God as witnesses."*

ACTS 10.40

SEVEN MILES can be a long distance for despairing men. To Cleopas
and his companion, plodding wearily along the road connecting
Jerusalem with Emmaus, their feet seemed leaden and the journey endless. Relieved though they were to be leaving the Holy City and
returning to their homes, they were haunted by the recent events
they had witnessed. Everything had happened so quickly, so unexpectedly. Only last week they had cheered and waved leafy branches
as Jesus rode triumphantly into Jerusalem. Now he had been dead
for three days and something in their hearts had died with him. Today
the fresh mountain air they breathed along the upland reaches of the
road gave no lift to their spirits, nor did they delight in the valleys
now green and in places ablaze with almond blossoms. All their
thoughts turned inward as they discussed in mournful tones the heartbreak of the past days.

"What are you talking about that makes you so sad?" asked a
stranger who suddenly appeared and fell into step beside them.

Cleopas and his companion looked up, their faces masks of sorrow.
They did not resent so kindly a question, but they were astonished
that anyone could ask it. "You must be the only visitor to Jerusalem

who does not know what things have happened here!" exclaimed Cleopas.

"What things?" asked the stranger.

Cleopas needed no further encouragement to open his heart to the unknown wayfarer. Talk came tumbling from him as he described Jesus of Nazareth, a prophet who performed wonderful deeds, and spoke true and powerful words. "He was favored by God and honored by many people," declared Cleopas, "but our chief priests and rulers condemned him to death and handed him over to the Romans to be crucified."

"We, his followers," he continued, indicating his companion in a sweeping gesture wide enough to include many people, "we hoped that he was the Messiah who would liberate Israel. But he is dead now, crucified, and today is the third day since he died. How can he be the Messiah, since it is written that whoever is hanged upon a tree is accursed?"

Without waiting for a reply Cleopas continued, "This morning some of the women belonging to the company of his followers brought disturbing news. They said that at dawn, when they went to prepare his body for burial, they discovered that his tomb was empty. They also told a story of angels who declared that Jesus is alive. But this cannot be, for two of his disciples who later went to the tomb also found it empty, but saw no sign of Jesus."

Throughout this long recital, the stranger listened patiently. Then, to the traveler's surprise, he chided them, saying, "O foolish men! How dull your minds! How long it takes you to understand what the prophets have said! Was it not ordained that Christ should suffer before entering into his glory?"

The two men stopped in the middle of the road to look at each other in surprise. Why had they not thought of that before? Long ago Jesus himself had said, "The Son of man must suffer many things, and be rejected by the elders and the chief priests and the scribes, and be killed" (Mark 8.31). He had clearly indicated that his kingdom would come, not miraculously or through the use of force, but through suffering like that endured by the enigmatic figure of the

Servant described in the scroll of Isaiah's prophecies. The terrible fate that had just overtaken the Master was, then, no accident, nor did it disprove his Messiahship. On the contrary, his death at the hands of evil men seemed to be in accordance with the inscrutable design of God.

As the three travelers walked on toward Emmaus, the stranger quoted passages from the Scriptures. Beginning with Moses and the prophets, he showed how words they spoke long ago pointed to Christ. Thus in terms familiar to Cleopas and his companion, in the very words of the Scriptures, the stranger interpreted the meaning of recent events, and in so doing created possibly the first version of the passion story.

At the place where the side road to Emmaus branched off the main highway, the stranger indicated that he was traveling farther, but the two men of Emmaus stood uncertainly at the crossroad, reluctant to say goodby to their new friend. His unique insight into the written words of God had encouraged them. He had lightened their burden of sorrow and had made their way seem short.

"Come and stay with us," they pleaded. "These roads are dangerous after nightfall. Evening now approaches and the day is almost over."

The wayfarer accepted their invitation and rested with them at Cleopas' home while the sun set behind the Judean hills and evening spread its hush over fields and meadows. A simple meal was soon placed on the table before them. As honored guest, the stranger took the loaf and, after pronouncing the ancient words of blessing, "Blessed art thou, O Lord our God, King of the world, who dost bring forth bread from the earth," he broke the bread and gave it to them.

In just this way Jesus used to bless bread, thought Cleopas. The stranger's voice had the same strong resonance that Jesus' friends had often noted in his voice. The mysterious traveler's hands made gestures like those Jesus used to make.

Suddenly the men's eyes were opened to the reality before them. This wayfarer was Jesus. He was their Lord in all the ineffable glory of his risen body. Awestruck, the two men stretched out their arms to touch him but as they did so he vanished, leaving only his empty place at the table. The men looked at each other in wonder. "Why did we not know him sooner?" one of them asked. "Did not our hearts glow within us while he talked with us on the road and while he explained the Scriptures to us?"

Late as it was, Cleopas and his companion put on their cloaks and, taking their staffs in hand, returned to the disciples in Jerusalem to report their astonishing news. When they entered the dark room where faces glowed in the lamplight, the two men from Emmaus felt excitement in the air. Their arrival was greeted with the joyful cry, "The Lord has risen!" Other voices joined in the exultant chorus, "He has risen indeed and has appeared to Peter!"

Cleopas and his companion then recounted their story of the stranger on the road, telling how they, too, had seen Jesus, recognizing him in the breaking of bread.

Suddenly, without warning, though the doors were shut, Jesus himself stood in the midst of this company of disciples and followers. Some of them, still unable to believe the astonishing news that he had risen from the dead, were frightened, believing him to be a spirit. Even those who disbelieved soon became convinced that it was really he when they saw his wounded hands and feet and when they watched him eating some of their broiled fish.

Finally, the risen Lord led the little company of his witnesses out to Bethany where he blessed them as he departed. They would now know him, not at a particular time or in a particular place, whether Nazareth, or Bethany, or Jerusalem, but he would be with them always and everywhere as the living center of their faith.

47

Thomas

MK 3.18; JN 11.16; 14.5;
20.24-29; 21.2

*That which was from the begin-
ning, which we have heard, which we
have seen with our eyes, which we
have looked upon and touched with
our hands, concerning the word of
life—the life was made manifest, and
we saw it, and testify to it, and proclaim to you the eternal life which
was with the Father and was made
manifest to us—that which we have
seen and heard we proclaim also to
you, so that you may have fellowship
with us; and our fellowship is with
the Father and with his Son Jesus
Christ.*

I JOHN 1.1-3

THOMAS WAS not among Jesus' followers when they first beheld their
risen Lord. Doubtless this disciple had fled from Jerusalem on the day
of the crucifixion, but when strange rumors of his Master's resurrection reached him in his place of hiding, he hurried back to the Holy
City. There he listened sometimes wistfully, sometimes disdainfully
while Mary Magdalene, Peter, Cleopas, and the others gave their
witness concerning the risen Lord. At the end he always shook his
head in disbelief. Such stories, he thought, were compounded of
dreams and longing. They were the hallucinations of overwrought
minds. Jesus had not really returned; it was a phantom. Thomas
noted that the narratives were confused and somewhat contradictory,

lacking what he understood to be the true substance of reality. Tales like these were not for him. His mind was made up. With all the obstinacy of one who wanted to believe the stupendous news yet found it incredible, he declared that Jesus could not be alive after his death on the cross.

Thomas prided himself on his common sense and his intellectual honesty. He was indeed a sincere man of great integrity, if somewhat stubborn. His feet were doggedly planted on the solid ground of fact. Slow to perceive and understand and little given to flights of imagination, he had to be absolutely sure before committing himself.

Some of these characteristics of Thomas had come to light earlier when Jesus spoke with his disciples of his approaching death. "When I leave you," the Master had said, "I go to prepare a place for you, but I will come again to welcome you to my home, that where I am you may be also. You all know the road to the place where I am going."

Literal-minded Thomas interrupted at this point, confused by the figurative language. He wanted Jesus to spell out this teaching. "Lord," objected Thomas, "because we do not know where you are going, how can we know the road there?"

"I myself am the road," Jesus explained. "No one comes to the Father except through me."

Now that Jesus was no longer with them to explain difficult points to Thomas, he clung to his own theory of the resurrection stories. He was convinced that whatever it was that Mary Magdalene had seen through her tears at the tomb it could not be a real person. Cleopas' tale of a mysterious traveler encountered in the uncertain light of dusk could also be explained away. As for Peter's story, who could credit the evidence of a broken, distraught man?

Still mourning his Master, and bowed down with the weariness of his grief, Thomas was amazed at the extraordinary vitality of Jesus' other followers. They had become changed men and women. Their eyes were clear and bright, their voices strong and buoyant. Only a week after the sorrow of the crucifixion had overwhelmed them, they seemed to be living under a spell of joy. "It is, however, a spell,"

Thomas told himself, "and it certainly cannot last, based as it is upon self-deception. Sooner or later truth will puncture the shining bubble of their rapture, leaving them the most miserable of people." Thomas added to himself his firm conviction, "Nothing lasting was ever built on falsehood."

From a sense of loyalty to his dead Master, Thomas still came to the upper room to talk and pray with his fellow disciples and the faithful women. These meetings were always secret and held behind closed doors for fear of the rulers of Jerusalem who had so recently put Jesus to death. During these days his followers began to exchange memories of him, memories which, as they were repeated from person to person, became some of the exquisitely wrought anecdotes that were later incorporated into the Gospels.

One day Thomas, irked by stories of the resurrection, made his own position clear by stating, "No, I cannot believe that our Master is alive."

The shocked glances produced by his outburst caused him to qualify his statement somewhat by adding, "—unless I see the nail prints in his hands and put my finger in them and thrust my hand into his wounded side." For Thomas an apparition would not suffice; he wanted to be sure that the risen Christ was identical with his beloved Master.

Dismayed by so uncompromising a statement, the disciples knew that it would be difficult for them to convince an unbelieving world of the resurrection if they could not overcome the doubts of one of the most loyal disciples.

That Thomas was loyal they all admitted. They remembered that once, when the Master's cause seemed doomed and his life in danger if he returned to Judea, he decided nevertheless to go to Bethany on behalf of Martha, Mary, and their brother Lazarus. On that occasion Thomas, immediately supporting the Master's perilous decision, rallied the other disciples with his cry, "Come, let us go into Judea with him, even if it means dying with him there." Surely this was unqualified loyalty, thought the disciples, ruefully remembering their own recent behavior in Gethsemane.

As memories like this one occurred to the disciples, they suddenly noticed a strange brightness filling the room. Hearts beat faster as everyone glanced up, looking first at one and then at another of those present. All at once they saw Jesus standing in their midst, transfigured yet still the Master they had known so intimately.

"Peace be with you!" he said in his well-remembered voice, stretching out his arms to bless them all.

Turning to Thomas, he held up his wounded hands. "Thomas, my friend," he said, "see my hands and touch them and the wound in my side. Do not doubt, but believe."

The Lord knows me as of old, thought Thomas; he knows that I am prone to doubt. He remembers how hard it is for me to understand.

Though only moments before, Thomas had demanded tangible proof, now he made no move to touch Jesus. Doubt was swept away by a tidal wave of joy flooding his being. At last he knew that Christ, having overcome death, as the others had testified, was radiantly alive in a glory not of earth. In an illuminating flash of insight, Thomas, for once not slow of understanding, perceived that this event explained the miracles. It was the climax of them all, the final great sign proclaiming who Christ was. In the resurrection, Thomas recognized the living heart of faith, a faith not yet fully grasped by the other disciples.

Thomas now understood that Jesus who had dwelt among them in all his humanity was more than a man of surpassing goodness, more than a supremely gifted Galilean teacher, more than a prophet who spoke in the Lord's name. Jesus was himself one with the goodness, the truth, the wisdom, the love of God. Jesus gave abundant life to many, for in him was life. He enlightened those groping in darkness, for he was the light of men. The estranged and the abandoned who came to him he transformed into the children of God, for he was the Son of God.

The richness of Christ's love had, from the beginning been freely poured out upon his followers. The heart of his message, the source of his power was the ultimate reality of love, God's love, which Jesus demonstrated at every moment of his life. From the shepherds of Bethlehem to doubting Thomas, many who came to him had beheld his glory, which was his manifestation of the divine love.

At last Thomas understood Jesus' words, "He who sees me sees him who sent me" (John 12.45). As the Fourth Gospel states, "No one has ever seen God; the only Son, who is in the bosom of the Father, he has made him known" (John 1.18.) Through the mystery of Christ's sufferings and in the glory of his resurrection, his once doubting disciple saw who the Master was. From a full heart Thomas made the first confession of full Christian faith, exclaiming to the risen Christ, "My Lord and my God."

Those in the upper room listened to Thomas in amazement, but one day his confession would become theirs. Paul was to phrase their faith explicitly, "For in him [Christ] all the fulness of God was pleased to dwell . . . and you have come to fulness of life in him" (Colossians 1.19; 2.9).

To his disciples gathered in the upper room and especially to Thomas, the risen Lord spoke, commending their faith and saying, "You believe because you have seen me."

Then, mindful of the multitudes who in the years to come would believe in him through the witness of these disciples, Christ gave them all his blessing, saying, "Blessed are those who have not seen and yet believe."

Index

Format by Lydia Link
Set in Intertype Garamond
Composed, printed and bound by The Haddon Craftsmen, Inc.
HARPER & ROW, PUBLISHERS, INCORPORATED